WINNIPEG CYCLING

30 Great Routes to Explore Winnipeg and Beyond

MARGARET LARSON

Prairie Heart Press
Winnipeg, MB

Cycling is potentially dangerous: accidents causing harm can and do happen. Riders are responsible for their own personal safety and use of the information contained in this book is at their own risk. Routes are suggested only and may not be appropriate for all skill levels. Publisher and author have made every effort to ensure routes and descriptions are accurate and on public property as of the publication of this book; however, no person shall rely on any of the contents of this publication and the publisher and the author expressly exclude all liability for direct and indirect loss suffered by any person, arising from injury, fines, or property damage, resulting in any way from the use or reliance on this publication or any part of it. New cycling paths are constructed regularly in Winnipeg and road and other construction/repair work may alter routes/directions; always adhere to local laws, safety regulations, and local signage.

Published April 2021 by Prairie Heart Press, an imprint of Story Perfect Inc.

Prairie Heart Press
PO Box 51053 Tyndall Park
Winnipeg, Manitoba R2X 3B0
Canada

Visit http://www.prairieheartpress.com for more Canadian prairie books.

To Sanford, the love of my life
To Craig and Emily, the joys of my life

Contents

Introduction

You might be wondering who is writing this book and what credentials I bring to this project. Am I part of a cycling club? Am I a sports trainer of some sort?

The truth of the matter is I am simply someone who enjoys cycling longer distances, who likes to cycle mostly on trails, and who thinks Winnipeg is a great place to explore. So, in essence, it is my combined love of cycling and Winnipeg, that are my credentials.

You might also be wondering if I have been an avid cyclist my whole life and the answer to that is no. I always did enjoy cycling but, to be honest, found it a real pain to get the bike out of the garage and, when I did, never really knew where I wanted to ride. Cycling was just a lot of work. So, decades went by without me touching my bike. However, that all changed when, in my late 40's, I met Sanford, the man who would become my second husband.

Sanford is, what I consider, an avid cyclist. He never gets on his bike thinking he has to get in some exercise. No, he just enjoys it. He prefers cycling as his mode of transportation over taking the car. He cycles to work, to the store, to friends, and for pure pleasure. Cycling is just something he fits in at all times, because he wants to.

Through him, I really learned to appreciate cycling. When we first met, he lived in Portage la Prairie and one of the things we often did was go out on our bikes for a ride. He made cycling an adventure as we explored trails around Portage or headed to various spots for a picnic. In those early days, I was quite out of shape and had no stamina for cyling. However, he was always patient with me, stopping for me to catch up or if I needed a break, and he never criticized once. I remember those early days and the excitement I felt at having cycled 10 km, I felt like it was such a huge achievement! I found it exhilarating and I became totally hooked on the sport.

Over time, we did more and more cycling and I become more fit and could go longer distances. I started to cycle to work in the summers and we often cycled if going to Cinematheque, or to the Fringe Festival, or just for groceries. My bike went from being a seldom used contraption sitting in the garage gathering dust to a much-cherished way of getting around. I found the more I rode my bike, the more I wanted to ride it and the less an issue it became to drag it out of the garage.

My husband and I live on two different continents, he lives in Australia and me here in Winnipeg, so we are not always together. I used to find I did most of my cycling when he was around but, with time, I wanted to keep up the cycling even if he wasn't in Winnipeg. I have a wonderful friend, Erica, who also enjoys cycling as much as I do. In the beginning, we would cycle from our homes to places in the neighbourhood or take our bikes to other spots and go on some trails in that area. But they were usually short rides and although enjoyable, it always seemed like a lot of work to pack up the bike, go for a short ride and then go home. I loved it, but was also frustrated by it.

Eventually, I got into cycling longer distances. Initially, I would just get on my bike and cycle around the city without any kind of plan. By doing this a few times, I discovered distances in the 30 km range were my "sweet spot". This distance felt like I had a work-out without totally exhausting myself and I often felt the cyclist's version of a runner's high.

A few years ago, I started to map out a few 30 km routes in my end of town, trying to stay on trails as much as possible. I never saved those first plotted rides and each summer would have to rewrite them. Then, two years ago, since I was cycling fairly regularly, I thought I would make an effort to design routes taking in all parts of the city and make a permanent record.

Plotting out those rides became the seed that germinated into this book you are now holding. Writing it became a passion. I loved sitting with my maps plotting out routes, looking for bike trails in all parts of the city, and even beyond the perimeter, and then trying to figure out how to connect as many trails as I could in a single ride. The routes made me explore parts of the city I had never been to before and I was often taken by the beauty of Winnipeg. Cycling along riverbeds, over bridges, through parks, past sculptures and murals, and past tourist sites, it is hard not to appreciate all that Winnipeg has to offer.

Because of all the wonderful things to see and do in Winnipeg, I decided to make this book a bit more than just cycling routes. You can, of course, just cycle the routes for exercise only, and there is nothing wrong with that, but you might also, at times, enjoy trying one of the coffee stop suggestions or exploring Winnipeg further and taking in one of the points of interests I have included. No matter how you use this book you will see a lot of Winnipeg by bike.

I have designed 30 rides. If you go for one ride a week, starting in the middle of April and ride to the end of October, you would do each ride once, with no repeats. You would have covered at least 900 km and have explored much of the city and some areas beyond its perimeter, stopped for lots of cups of coffee and probably discovered some things about Winnipeg you didn't know.

Writing this book has been fun, an adventure and a learning experience. The only downside to writing this type of book is that, at this point in Winnipeg's developing cycling culture, I know the minute it is published there will be all kinds of new cycling paths popping up not included here. However, perhaps this book will spark your passion for cycling and adventure and you will design some of your own favourite routes incorporating the newer trails.

In closing, I hope this book inspires you to get out and cycle and to explore. I hope this book brings a lot of fun into your life as you reap the health benefits of cycling. So, time to get off the couch, get the bike out of the garage, take this book, and go explore!

Enjoy!

Why Cycle?

There are many reasons to take up cycling.

First and foremost, cycling is pleasurable. There is nothing that feels as exhilarating as really kicking it on the bike when the wind is at your back or as rewarding as having completed a stretch with what seemed like gale force winds blowing against you. The ability of cycling to elicit such positive emotions is a powerful draw.

Cycling slows down the world and, if you cycle through the seasons, allows you to take more notice of the life cycles of nature. Springtime is marked by the arrival of Canada geese, in summer families of goose, gander and goslings can be seen around the ponds and at times, walking across trails in single file, and in the fall, the distinctive V formation in the sky as they take flight for warmer climates. With the trees, you observe the budding in the spring, enjoy the shade from the green canopy in the heat of summer, the changing canvas of colours in the fall, and finally, as the leaves drop and the trees return to their bareness, the crunch of crisp leaves under your tires. You become aware of the changing climate: the wet, warming spring, the sometimes horribly hot and humid summer days, and in the fall, the coolness of the breeze and the picking up of winds. That's just three examples but there are many other nature cycles to notice.

Cycling stimulates your senses. In quiet stretches along trails, you hear the birds chirp and the breeze rustle through leaves. When in full bloom, you can smell the fragrance of the flowers. You feel the climate on your body: the wind, sun or rain. You notice aromas from restaurants and you become acutely aware of the traffic sounds around you.

Cycling gives you the opportunity to become more familiar with Winnipeg. You become aware of new neighbourhoods, streets, and parks. You notice various pieces of art work placed around the city, interesting looking buildings and businesses you didn't know existed. All of a sudden you become aware of bike repair stations, available public toilets and water fountains. If you don't already feel this way, you will come to appreciate all the beauty and diversity that is Winnipeg.

Cycling is for everyone. You are never too old and you don't have to be at a certain fitness level to begin to cycle. As a matter of fact, cycling is one of the gentler sports. You also don't need a lot of skill to cycle. As with most sports though, the more you cycle, the more experience you get and the more you know how to handle yourself on the bike when it comes to corners, how fast you can go, and how you like to gear your bike up or down.

Cycling can be a solo experience or enjoyed with family and friends. Cycling solo can be a meditative experience. As you pedal through the kilometers, you feel your daily stressors melt away and you can feel your mind begin to switch off and experience the calm and well-being from being active outdoors. Or, you can cycle with a loved one, family, friends, or an organized group. It is a great activity to be shared. It's a fun date activity with your partner, as it gives you a chance to enjoy each other's company, while doing something beneficial for your health. Whole families can also get out and cycle together. It's a fun way to be active with the family. The very youngest can be put in one of a variety of carriers. It is a good social activity with friends or groups as you can chat while cycling or include a coffee break for socialization.

Cycling is cheap. Once you have the basic equipment you need to enjoy this sport, there are no more fees involved. No clubs to join, no facility fees. The only money you might want to spend is for a coffee stop to break up the ride.

Cycling can be as relaxed or intense as you want. You can cycle to whatever energy level you wish. You can go flat out and really get your heart pumping and the endorphins flowing or you can go at a more leisurely pace, taking lots of stops along the way, enjoying the scenery and nature as it unfolds before you.

Cycling is a flexible sport. There are no rules to enjoy this sport. You don't have to cycle for any longer than you want and you don't have to go any specific distance for it to be fun or beneficial for you.

Cycling makes you feel good. When you work your body, it releases endorphins into your system, and this gives you feelings of euphoria. It is a natural high that is healthy and doesn't cost you money or harm you in any way.

Cycling can be so much more than just getting out and doing exercise. You can turn the ride into a mini site seeing adventure, taking in one or more of the many tourist attractions Winnipeg has to offer. Or you could turn it into a dining experience, either having a picnic somewhere, or stopping at a restaurant for a meal. Or you could use it to gather your own food and pick saskatoons in mid-July to mid-August. Or you could use your imagination and add other elements to the bike ride and make a day of it. The options are endless!

Cycling is practical. Once you are used to cycling, and particularly because Winnipeg is not so big, most destinations are within easy cycling range which allows you to jump on the bike to commute, shop, run errands, or visit friends. Cycling frees you from the worries of parking and saves you the expense of running the car, plus you get the added benefit of exercise.

Cycling is environmentally friendly. Cycling does not burn off fossil fuels so does not contribute to air pollution. Bikes do not require motor oil which is considered a hazardous waste when it comes to disposal. Bicycles take a lot less energy to make than a car. Cycling does less damage to road surfaces.

Cycling is a good workout for your body. It is an aerobic exercise, making it good for your heart and lungs. It strengthens the muscles in your body. The downstroke of pedaling uses muscles in your buttocks, thighs, and calves, the upstroke uses the hamstrings and flexor muscles in your hips. Keeping balanced and upright uses abdominal muscles and holding the handlebars and steering uses muscles in your arms and shoulders. It is gentle on your joints and preserves cartilage because it is not a weight bearing activity like walking or running. So, if you suffer from muscle strain, foot problems, knee troubles, back pain or impact-related injuries, cycling may just be the sport for you.

Cycling can give you more stamina for your everyday activities. As you become more fit, the benefits of cycling spill over into the rest of your life. You will have more stamina and more energy to live your life and do the things you want to do.

Cycling is a great calorie burner. Cycling at 15 km hour burns 260 calories each hour of cycling.

There is lots of literature stating cycling can help to improve sleep, control weight, reduce risks of cardiovascular diseases such as stroke, high blood pressure and heart attack, reduce risk of bowel and breast cancers, decrease the risk of diabetes, may help to prevent falls and fractures, reduce mental health conditions such as depression, stress and anxiety. I am not a doctor and it is not the intent of this book to make health claims. Should you be interested in more information of the impact of cycling on the above, I would suggest you discuss this with your doctor or do some research on your own for more information.

Cycling can be a real game changer to your life. Being healthy throughout your lifetime is such a wonderful gift you can give to yourself. Exercise is always part of a healthy lifestyle. For many people, finding a sport they can enjoy, to the point of actually wanting to do it, can be difficult. Many other types of exercise require memberships, expenses, scheduling, and perhaps a skill level or fitness level that may be beyond you. Cycling doesn't have any of that. So why not give it a go and start to enjoy the pleasures and benefits of cycling.

What You Need

Actually, this chapter is not only about what you need, but also about what I call "nice to have".

A good bike

You don't have to have a super expensive bike to enjoy cycling, but you do need a bike that is in good working condition.

If you have a bike that's been sitting in your garage or basement for years, or if you do use your bike regularly but never do any maintenance and/or you do not know anything about bikes, take it into a bike shop for a tune-up. Bikes are like cars in that way. They need to be maintained. Generally, in a tune-up, the technician will do a safety check, ensure the brakes and gears are working properly, lubricate the chain and cables, and inflate the tires to the correct pressure, plus miscellaneous other things. An annual tune-up is a good idea to stay on top of the wearable parts of the bike and catch issues with the brakes, spokes or gears before they become a problem while cycling.

A proper fit

Along with a good bike, you have to have a proper fit of your bike to you. Cycling is a great exercise for your body, but if your bike does not fit you properly it may cause harm. A poor fitting bike, depending on the issue, can lead to neck and back problems or knee issues. If your bike is not a good fit, your first thought should not be "I need a new bike", instead, you just need to have your present bike fitted to your body properly. There are quite a number of adjustments that can be made. There are different kinds of bike seats that can be chosen for comfort and fit, the seat and handle bars height can be adjusted, and there are several configurations of bike handle bars that can be used which alter the way you sit on the bike. Some adjustments you might be able to do yourself, but you can also go to a bike shop for help. If you are plagued with issues, it may take several adjustments before you hit on the correct configuration for your bike and your body. The main thing is not to give up! It will be worth the hassle.

Safety Equipment

This is covered in the next chapter *How to Stay Safe*. I have provided a short list here but for more information on these items consult the next chapter. Please note that some of these things are not options but mandatory.

- Bicycle Helmet (mandatory for children under 18)
- Front and Rear Bike Lights (mandatory)
- High Visibility Clothing (optional)
- Mirror (optional)

Bike bell

I have travelled in many countries where cycling is a major form of transport and in those countries, you constantly hear bells go before cyclists pass you. Here, it seems we are afraid to use our bells, not wanting to bother the person we are about to pass, so we either pass without letting them know, or we hang around on our bikes going really slow, waiting for people to notice and move out of the way. Nonsense! Use a bike bell, or if you don't want to get a bell, say something, e.g. "bike passing" or "excuse me", as approaching people, particularly if they have children, a dog, or wander from side to side on the path. It is a courtesy to let people know you are passing and it may avoid an accident should they suddenly move into your path.

Repair gear, cell phone, or CAA membership

A flat tire or other issues can happen at any time while cycling and you should be prepared to handle these situations. If you're handy and know how to fix flat tires and do other maintenance on your bike, you should carry the necessary gear to do these repairs. If you're not handy, it's a good idea to carry your cell phone so you can call someone to come and rescue you and take you and your bike to a repair shop. If you have a CAA membership, they now offer a new service called CAA Bike Assist. If your bike breaks down or has a flat, you can access their emergency road service for your bike. If possible, they will fix your issue on the spot, but if that can't be done, they will take you and your bike either home or to a repair shop. More information about CAA Bike Assist can be found on their website. www.caamanitoba.com/auto/roadside/bike-assist

Cell phone

I know I mentioned above that you should carry a cell phone for accessing help when trouble arises, but here are four other reasons to take your phone with you.

- A map app such as Google Maps or Open Street – Although I have done my very best to make the directions clear, sometimes it still might be

  difficult to figure out where you are, so a map app can be a great help in making sure you are on track.
- Cycling app – It can be fun to use a cycling app and it should be noted that most can be used for walking as well. These apps map your route, calculate your speed, note change in elevation, track your cycling time, allow you to share your rides, etc. There are many cycling apps available and it is a matter of personal choice for what you like. Look on the Internet or in the App Store on your phone for features of various apps and reviews before deciding on one.
- Taking photos – There are many photo opportunities – wildlife, flowers, sculptures, sites, etc.
- Scanning QR codes – Whenever a web address is listed in this book, a QR code is included for easy scanning to visit the website.

Bicycle carrier for the car

In terms of using this book, you need to be able to transport your bike to various starting points throughout the city. If you can put the back seats down in your car, you can take the front wheel off your bike and put it in the trunk. I used to do that and for the most part, that worked fine. But I have had two or three occasions where I couldn't get the wheel back on quite right or the brakes seemed to have shifted and this just led to problems. So, for me, I personally prefer a bike carrier so I don't have to take apart my bike. There are many different kinds of carriers at many different price levels. The one I have, clips onto my trunk. It is easy to put on and take off. Another advantage to bike carriers is that they hold more than one bike, a must if there is more than just your bike to transport. Bike carriers are sold in a variety of places: bike shops, Canadian Tire, on Amazon, etc.

Bike pannier

What's a pannier? Panniers are named after the French word used for baskets and are the bags carried on your bike. They require a frame to be mounted and then the panniers can be attached to the frame on either side of the wheel.

Having a pannier on your bike allows you to carry things with you; a tool kit, a tire pump, water bottle, maps, snacks, etc. Some are waterproof, protecting your belongings from getting wet. It is much more convenient and more comfortable than carrying a backpack, particularly in hot weather.

Besides carrying the necessities for rides, panniers also allow you to do some shopping when out because now you have a place to carry your items safely. So, if you are out for coffee and want to buy some extra donuts for later, you can. Perhaps you will do the ride intended for picking saskatoon berries and with a pannier, you have a way to transport them home.

The nice thing about panniers is they can easily be detached from your bike, and some convert into backpacks. There are many styles of panniers, depending on what your intended use is. They can be a little pricey but well worth the investment.

Bicycle lock

This is not the item to skimp on! You need a good lock to, unfortunately, protect your bike from being stolen. There are several different kinds that offer good protection so it is worthwhile to determine which one you would like to use. Besides a good lock, some cyclists go to additional measures to protect their bikes, such as using more than one lock or removing the seat or a wheel.

The length to which you want to go is up to you. I, personally, only use a strong cable lock and I'm glad I didn't skimp on the quality. One time, my husband and I took our bikes to a play during the Fringe Festival, and we locked them up together, outside the venue, with my cable. When we returned after the play, someone had tried to steal our bikes. They had worked away at the cable with some sort of cutters and got through the covering and a few strands, but eventually they gave up because, I guess, it was just too difficult to cut through. At that moment, I was very happy for my investment.

Water bottle carrier

I don't think I really have to say anything about the need for a water bottle carrier. You need to have water on your rides and this item is a convenient way to carry the bottle. You could actually skip the bottle carrier if you have a pannier.

The list provided above is essentially a basic list and a good place to start. As you cycle more and more, you may feel you need some additional items for either safety or enjoyment. If this is the case, buy what you need/wish so you continue to enjoy cycling.

How to Stay Safe

As with anything in life, you need to be aware of potential hazards and do what you can to prevent them, as accidents do happen. Do not fool yourself into thinking if you just cycle on bike trails, these safety rules do not apply. Accidents happen anywhere; on trails, sidewalks, streets, etc. As a matter of fact, in Manitoba, on average, 158 cyclists are hospitalized for cycling related injuries yearly, and of those, several result in serious injury or death.

Here is a list of some tips for cycling safe and some safety equipment required/recommended.

Be aware of how you feel
- Cycle healthy. I think this goes without saying, but don't cycle if you are not well or feeling fatigued. You need to be alert to what is happening around you and being sick or tired will dull your senses.
- Stay hydrated. Drink water before, during and after a ride. Water serves to regulate body temperature, lubricate joints, and transport nutrients required for energy. If you become dehydrated, it can lead to mental and physical fatigue and your body can't perform as it should.
- Stay fueled. Have you ever heard the word "bonking", in relation to endurance sports such as cycling or running? I hadn't, at least not until I experienced it. Another phrase to describe bonking is "hitting the wall" and it refers to the depletion of your glycogen stores which provide the energy you require while performing endurance exercises. When this happens, you experience sudden fatigue and a total loss of energy.

This happened to me once when I did a bike ride to Lockport and back. When I was halfway home I "bonked out", I couldn't pedal another rotation, the effort required for the downstroke of the pedal was just too much exertion. So, I got off my bike and walked, and even that felt difficult. After walking for a bit, I thought it would be easier to get back on the bike, but I was wrong, I just couldn't continue and decided to walk again. I managed to get home by alternating between walking and cycling, but mostly walking. It's a horrible feeling that I don't want to experience again.

To avoid bonking you need to ensure you are properly fueled. For myself, I make sure I eat a more substantial meal before heading out on long bike rides, and if I start to feel "off" while cycling, I will eat something. That works for me, but may not necessarily be how you like to handle this. There is a lot of information on the internet on this topic to give you ideas.

- Stay cool. It's important to prevent heat stroke which occurs when the body's cooling mechanisms aren't able to stop the body's core temperature from increasing. Although more prevalent on a very hot day with the sun beating down, it can happen at any time. The most common symptoms include confusion, dizziness, fatigue, headache, muscle cramps, nausea, and/or vomiting. Heat stroke can be dangerous and even lead to death. If symptoms become worse over time, you need to seek medical attention immediately.

One of the best ways to avoid heat stroke is to drink plenty of water, before, during and after cycling, to keep hydrated. The reason for this is because one of the ways the body cools itself is by sweating. You should also wear breathable clothing to allow the sweat to evaporate from the body.

- Protect yourself. Wear sunscreen. No explanation needed, just do it.

Maintain your bike

You would think this is a no-brainer, but you might be surprised. Keep your bike roadworthy. If you don't know much about bikes, you should take it to a bike shop to have it regularly serviced. Before you start a ride, you should test your brakes to ensure they are okay and check your tires to see if they need more air. If you notice any differences in your bike's handling, don't delay, take it in to be looked over by a bike technician.

A bicycle helmet

In 2013, Manitoba passed a law that made helmets mandatory for children under 18 whether cycling on their own or if a passenger on the bike or being towed. Unfortunately, it is not mandatory for adults to wear helmets. I say this because the number one cause of death in cycling accidents is head injuries.

I consider helmets the number one priority for safety when cycling. Your head needs to be protected...period. Even if it is a really short ride. Even if you are only cycling on a bike trail. Even if you don't want to. You cannot predict when, and if, you will fall or go flying from your bike, but if you do, you will never again question the need for a helmet. My partner once had an unexpected fall and his helmet quite possibly saved his life.

Fit is important when it comes to helmets, so take some time adjusting yours.

YouTube has videos explaining how to get a good fit or you can talk to the knowledgeable sales staff in bike shops.

High visibility clothing

You need to be seen by drivers, other cyclists and pedestrians. Obviously, they should be looking for you, too, but high visibility clothing makes it easier for them to notice you. This is particularly true if you are cycling in the early morning, as the sun is setting, or in the dark. During the day, try to wear bright fluorescent colours, and during the night, wear reflective clothing. Consider getting one of those bright yellow or orange reflective safety vests. They are lightweight, easy to slip on over your clothes and suitable for both day and night.

Front and rear bike lights

In Manitoba, it is mandatory, by law, to have a white light on the front and a red or amber light on the back of your bike. A blinking LED light can also be put on the back of your bike to make you even more visible at night. If you do cycle in the evening, I also highly recommend investing in a front light that is powerful enough to light your path ahead by several feet. Front lights are generally categorized into "see" and "be seen" classifications and you want a "see" one. This should help prevent unintentionally cycling into a pothole or into some other obstruction on the road because you can't see it. It will be a bit of an investment, but if you're ever caught out at night, you will be glad you have one. In addition, if you do cycle a lot when it is dark, you might also like to put reflectors on your pedals or elsewhere on the bike for even more visibility.

Bicycle mirror

If you find it difficult to check behind you while cycling, or even if you don't, you might like to consider a bicycle mirror. A quick glance in a cycling mirror can tell you if the coast is clear to move into a lane of traffic or you can see if someone is about to cycle past you. It just generally helps to keep you out of harm's way.

Bicycle mirrors come in various forms, they can be helmet mounted, handlebar mounted, or even mounted on your glasses.

Avoid rain

If you are able to control when you cycle, avoid rain. Rain can make visibility less for both you and the drivers around you, cause the roads and trails, particularly crushed limestone, to become slippery and also affect your brakes making them less effective. Although you might think it fun to cycle through puddles, they may be hiding potholes or other hazards that are not visible, so try to go around them.

Obey traffic rules

Being on a bike doesn't allow you to ignore traffic rules. You should always cycle on the same side of the road as you would drive on, use hand signals for all your turns, and obey all traffic light signals and signs. If you are crossing the path of a car or a car will be crossing your path, e.g. a turning vehicle going across a cycling lane, be particularly careful as the driver may not have seen you, so be ready to stop or if possible, make eye contact, so you know they have seen you. While on the road, if with others, cycle in single file, and keep as close as practical to the far right of the lane. Do not weave in and out between parked cars. Always stay alert. Watch for opening car doors, potholes, debris on the road and traffic. When crossing train tracks, maneuver your bike so you cross at a 90-degree angle to avoid your wheel getting caught in the tracks. Always be respectful of motorists, other cyclists and pedestrians.

When in a group and you encounter a potential hazard, it is a good idea to shout hazards out to following cyclists, e.g. "bollard", "car left", "door", or point out ground hazards like broken glass.

Sidewalk cycling

In Manitoba, cycling on the sidewalk is illegal, unless your rear wheel is less than 16 inches, in other words, a kid's bike; the only exception being if the sidewalk is a designated multi-use path. Cycling on the sidewalk isn't as safe as you might think. The main danger is when crossing back lanes, driveways and intersections. Cars approaching the street from a back lane or driveway, may have no warning you are there, particularly if there are fences around the properties on the corners, until you are literally crossing the street in front of them. Another danger occurs when drivers are turning and you are on your bike approaching the intersection. The driver is on the lookout for pedestrians, not cyclists, and may not have noticed you approaching the intersection. Because you would travel faster than a pedestrian you may suddenly be in the intersection unexpectedly from the driver's perspective.

Cycling on sidewalks also creates an unsafe environment for pedestrians.

Types of bike lanes

There are lots of different types of bike lanes in Winnipeg. Here is a list of them and what they mean.

Painted bike lane

These lanes are designated by solid painted white lines with diamond and bike symbols within. The diamond indicates limited use and the bike indicates cyclists, so the two symbols together mean the lane is reserved for cyclists. The bike lane therefore provides a defined space for cyclists and also acts as a visual cue to motorists that cyclists have a right to be there.

It is important to be aware that although you are cycling in a bike lane, cars may also enter that space. Most bike lanes are placed either against the curb or to the left of the parking lane. In both cases, motorists may have to cross or enter the bike lane when turning, and in the latter case, to access or exit a parking space. Of note for passing parked cars, always watch for doors opening.

Although a bike lane has a solid white line on both sides, it does not mean you cannot leave the bike lane. You may have to leave the bike lane to change lanes, make a turn or leave the road. As in all cases, stay alert to the traffic around you when doing these actions.

Protected bike lane

A bike lane that is physically separated from motorists by curbs, planters, vehicle parking, etc.

Buffered bike lane

A bike lane with a painted buffer or posts.

Shared bus / bicycle diamond lane

This lane is reserved for buses, right-turning vehicles and cyclists. It is important to note this lane is only in effect during rush hour times, either in the morning or the afternoon; signage will be posted indicating designated hours in use.

Sharrow

A sharrow is located on the curb side of the road and indicated with a painted bike symbol and two spaced arrows above it. It is different from a bike lane in that it does not include a designated space for cyclists. The purpose of sharrow signage is as a visual reminder to motorists and cyclists that they must share the road. They are generally used on roads with lanes wide enough to accommodate side-by-side car and bicycle traffic.

Green paint

Green paint is used in areas of caution, i.e. some intersections or busy streets, to increase the visibility of a bike lane.

Multi-use path

Multi-use paths are shared by pedestrians and cyclists and are also physically separated from motor vehicles. On these paths, cyclists yield to pedestrians.

Collisions with a car

In Manitoba, four cyclists are killed and 78 are injured in collisions annually. In 90% of the cases where the cyclists were killed, they were not wearing a helmet. A good reason to be sure you are wearing your helmet!

Should the worst happen and you get into a collision with a car, or you witness a collision, these are the steps to follow:

- Attend to any immediate injuries or concerns.
- Move out of the way of traffic.
- Exchange particulars:
  - Cyclists – provide name, phone number, address and type of bike.
  - Motorists – provide name and licence number, registration number, phone number, address, vehicle type, plate number and vehicle owner (if different from driver).
- Note where, when, and how accident occurred and note any damages and injuries.
- If there are any witnesses, get their names and phone numbers.
- Report to Autopac as cyclists are entitled to claims on injuries and damages to their bicycle

Note: Bicycles are not insured through Manitoba Public Insurance so if a cyclist is found responsible for a collision, they could be liable for damages to a vehicle and be responsible for any damage to their own bicycle.

For more information go the Manitoba Public Insurance website. https://www.mpi.mb.ca/

MPI

The above list of safety tips should not be considered definitive. There are some excellent resources on the internet for both safety options and cycling safely. One source I came across that I particularly liked is the MPI booklet entitled Bike Safety. I highly recommend you take a look at it. https://www.mpi.mb.ca/documents/Adults CyclingBooklet.pdf

Bike Safety Booklet

Safety cautions

In each individual ride, I have listed safety cautions specific to that ride. However, because the same caution is listed for multiple rides, an icon has been inserted for easier reference.

Below is a legend of icons and their associated safety caution.

Crushed limestone trails / dirt trails / wood chip trails

- Can have deep ruts which, if your bike wheel gets caught in one, can cause a fall.
- Can be slippery when wet.
- Can be quite bumpy.
- Are more strenuous to cycle than roads.

Street / highway travel

- Stay alert!
- Use hand signals when turning to communicate your intentions to drivers.
- Watch for car doors opening when passing parked vehicles.
- Follow all road rules.
- Wear high visibility clothing.
- Be particularly cautious at intersections.

Floating bus stops

- Some major traffic routes with bike lanes have floating bus stops which allows cyclists to bypass stopped buses. At these stops, the bike lane goes onto the sidewalk before the bus stop and back onto the road after the bus stop.
- Be mindful of pedestrians on the sidewalk.

Flooding

- In the spring and into the summer, some bike paths near the rivers may be flooded and you will have to detour to the nearest roads.

Bears

- Be aware if cycling in areas where you might encounter a bear.
- Attach a bear bell to your bike.
- Carry bear spray.
- For more information check out the Be Bear Smart publication by the province of Manitoba.
- https://gov.mb.ca/fish-wildlife/pubs/fish_wildlife/bear_smart_booklet.pdf

How to Use This Book

Before going on any ride, you should preview it and perhaps look up some suggested websites in order to make each ride an experience you can enjoy. Being prepared for your adventure will make all the difference. Don't be caught without a pannier to carry shopping or berries, exact change for the river taxi, knowledge of operating hours and tour times for attraction, or bug spray!

Each ride follows the following format:

Ride name	• Descriptive name highlighting something about the ride.
Location	• Section of the city the ride covers.
Introductory paragraphs	• General description of the route. • How I chose the name. • Possible coffee stops. • Points of interest. • Websites for more information.

Quick notes	• At a glance view of:
	    ○ Length of ride.
	    ○ Where to park.
	    ○ Options to shorten ride and their length.
	    ○ Bike repair stations.*
	    ○ Coffee stops.
	    ○ Bathroom stops.
	    ○ Points of interest.

Trails	• All trails used in the ride.**

Safety cautions	• Indicated by an icon.***
Detailed directions	• Total km is the cumulative distance traveled from the start of the ride.
	• Interval km is the distance covered within that specific step.
	• Direction is the action required e.g. right, left, straight.
	• Location, notes

- Location, notes
  - o Each step begins with the exact location where the direction occurs. This is written in bold letters.
  - o Following the exact location, in unbolded letters, are detailed directions listing streets or landmarks you pass till the next step.
  - o Bathroom stops, coffee stops, points of interest, instructions to shorten, notes, cautions, and any other relevant information at the appropriate step of the ride.
    - ▪ For a quick reference, an icon for each of the above is located in the Legend Table below.

Map	• Big picture view of the route.
Websites	• QR codes for useful websites which can be checked during the ride.

*Bike Repair Station – These free-standing stations are installed by the City of Winnipeg and include a pump, stands, screwdrivers and wrenches so you can do minor adjustments to you bike, if needed.

**Trails – Some of the trails have official names, but many trails do not, and in those cases I made one up, in order to make the directions clear.

***Icons – See the Legend Table below.

It is surprisingly difficult to write directions. I don't know how many versions I played with before landing on the one I used in this book. There are many obstacles. Streets with no signage. Streets that start out as one name and then change to another name. Trails with no name. Trails with multiple names. Trails that split in the middle of nowhere and then split again. Trails that go on one side of the street and then to the other. Trails that are difficult to find. I think you get the idea. In spite of all these challenges, I hope, that in the end, when you follow these directions, you find them easy to understand. I would advise, however, that you take your cell phone with you and, if some directions leave you scratching your head, you can pull up google maps or some other street view, which should, hopefully, clarify the directions.

If you are familiar with the trails or streets in an area of the city, you might just choose to follow the bolded street/trail names and not bother reading the rest of the box. There is no right or wrong way to get from one trail to the next and if you have a better way of going, feel free to follow your own path.

The map is simply a big picture view of the route. With most rides 30 km or more, it is impossible to make a detailed map showing street names in the space allotted within this book. However, along with the detailed description, the map should help you navigate the course.

If you're wondering how long a ride will take, a good estimate is that you will cycle about 15 km per hour. Of course, you might be faster or slower, but this will give you a starting point. So, for a 30 km ride, it should take about two hours with no stops. Then, add in any stops and you will have a ballpark idea of the length of time you need to schedule for your adventure.

Legend of all symbols used in the book:

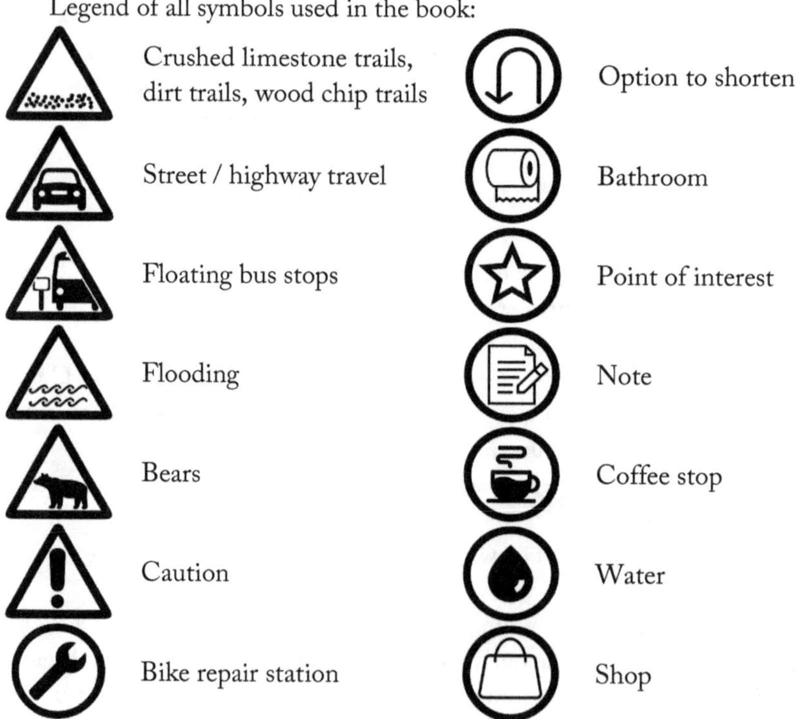

You are now ready to use this book to its full potential! Enjoy!

The Routes

North Coast

North Winnipeg

Although this ride uses a fair number of trails, it is mostly cycled on the road, but on low stress streets. In the first half of the ride, the route along Roch, Poplar and Brazier is a Neighbourhood Greenway, meaning it is a route which has things like speed bumps and traffic circles to slow traffic, thereby attracting a lower volume of vehicles and making it an ideal route for cycling. In the second half of the ride, much of the route is along Scotia Street, which is a Sunday/Holiday Bicycle Route which restricts motor vehicle traffic to one block on those days. The entire ride is mostly long stretches of cycling on single roads in the north end of Winnipeg hence the name, North Coast.

I have offered two unique coffee stops for consideration. You really can't go wrong with either choice. One is Prairie's Edge in Kildonan Park and the second is Mountain Bean Coffee Company on Henderson Highway. Prairie's Edge prides itself in serving creative dishes made from local foods. You can stop here for breakfast, lunch, dinner or just a coffee or an ice cream. There is seating either inside or outside on their patio, which overlooks the duck pond. https://www.opentable.com/r/prairies-edge-winnipeg

Prairie's Edge

The second option, Mountain Bean Coffee Company, at 2001 Henderson Highway, has a cozy log cabin feel with lots of wooden tables and chairs, many big comfy leather chairs and a fireplace. There is also some seating outside. Here you can savour a coffee, a small lunch or a snack. http://www.mountainbeancoffee.com

Mountain Bean

There are three points of interest along this route, two art installations and one park. *Light Through* by Bernie Miller is located along the Disraeli Active Transportation Bridge. *Light Through* consists of sixteen stainless steel structures which have historic photographs of the bridge and its surroundings. What makes the photographs unique is the artist developed software to translate the images into patterns of holes, which when light shines through them, give a unique view of the image. http://winnipegarts.ca/wac/artwork/light-through

Light Through

St. John's Park, located on Main Street, at Mountain Avenue, was purchased from the Anglican Church for $15,000 by the Winnipeg Parks Board in 1893. At the time of its purchase, it was located in the suburbs of Winnipeg. When the city took possession, the land was wild, but soon afterwards was transformed with a formal garden in the shape of a six-pointed star with radiating pathways and a wooden bandstand was built. More information on the park's history, with pictures, is located at the northwest corner of the park on some information boards. St. John's Park is also home to the Healing Forest, a memorial to Indigenous children lost to the residential school system, missing and murdered Indigenous women and girls, and Indigenous children lost in the child welfare system. It is located on the north side of the park just west of the wading pool. It is a circular learning space and there are several huge rocks with Aboriginal artwork surrounding the circle. The Healing Forest is meant to be a place where those who have been affected can come for reflection, meditation, and healing. It is well worth a stop to take a look.

Along Bunn's Creek is a series of signs entitled *The Seven Teachings*. The teachings are Anishinaabe in origin and are the basic virtues necessary for a full and happy life: respect, love, courage, honesty, wisdom, humility and truth. On one side of each sign are wood carvings of an animal, representative of each teaching, done by students at John G. Stewart School. On the other side are digital collages related to each teaching which were put together by artist Becky Thiessen from artwork created by Knowles Centre youth.

Enjoy the coast!

Quick Notes

Distance – 29.1 km

Parking – Park on residential streets near the corner of Rothesay Street and Maxwell King Drive

Option to shorten – yes

Roch Loop – 16.6 km

Suggested coffee stops – Prairie's Edge at Kildonan Park in the Chief Peguis Pavilion, Mountain Bean Coffee Company at 2001 Henderson Highway

Bathrooms – Northdale Shopping Centre at 975 Henderson Highway, St. John's Park by the wading pool, Kildonan Park in the Chief Peguis Pavilion, Bunn's Creek Centennial Park, coffee stops

Points of Interest –

Light Through Art Installation on the Disraeli Active Transport Bridge

St. John's Park on Main Street at Mountain Avenue

The Seven Teachings Art Installation along Bunn's Creek Trail

Trails

Arby Multi-use Path – asphalt

Ernie O'Dowda Park Path – crushed limestone/asphalt
Midwinter Multi-use Path – asphalt
Disraeli Active Transport Bridge – asphalt
North Winnipeg Parkway Trail – crushed limestone
Alfred-Burrow Link Path – crushed limestone
St. John's-Redwood-Aberdeen Park Path – asphalt/crushed limestone
Kildonan Park Trail – asphalt
Kildonan Park Golf Course Trail – crushed limestone
Chief Peguis Greenway Trail – asphalt
Sun Valley Park Path – crushed limestone
Northeast Pioneers Greenway Trail – asphalt
Bunn's Creek Trail – crushed limestone

Safety Cautions

Detailed Directions

Km Total	Km Leg	Direction	Location, notes
0	0	Start	**Corner of Rothesay Street and Maxwell King Drive.**
0	3.01	Straight	**Rothesay Street;** cycle past Saddleridge, Foxgrove, Glenway, Bonner, Bunn's Creek Parkway, McIvor, Gilmore, over Chief Peguis Trail, and past Donwood to Sutton Avenue, located one block before Springfield Road.
3.01	0.39	Right	**Sutton Avenue;** cycle to River East Collegiate and opposite the entrance to the school is a lane called Graduate Path.
3.40	0.29	Left	**Graduate Path/Arby Multi-use Path (asphalt)/Arby Bay;** cycle to the end of Graduate Path and cross Springfield at the cross walk. Directly ahead is the Arby Multi-use Path leading to Arby Bay. Continue straight on Arby and cross McKay at which point Arby becomes Roch Street.

3.69	3.72	Straight	**Roch Street;** cycle past McKay, Edison, McLeod, Rossmere Golf Club, Leighton, Kimberly, Neil, the lights at Munroe and Johnson to Poplar Avenue, where Roch Street ends.
			Northdale Shopping Centre: Because there is no bathroom stop at the beginning of the ride and the next one is a distance away, there is an option close to Roch Street, if needed, which requires only a slight detour.
			When you reach McLeod Avenue, turn right to Brazier Street and turn left. Cycle past Maxwell and the apartment block to the entrance into the back of the Northdale Shopping Centre. There are bathrooms located in the McDonald's or Sobeys.
			When done, return to Brazier and turn right and then left at Dunbeath Avenue. Cycle to Roch and turn right to continue.
7.41	0.32	Right	**Poplar Avenue;** cycle to Brazier Street.
7.73	0.59	Left	**Brazier Street;** cycle past McIntosh, Gordon, Dearborn, Mighton, Riverton and Talbot to Midwinter Avenue.
			Directly across Midwinter is the Ernie O'Dowda Park Path.
			Roch Loop: When you reach Midwinter Avenue, do a U-turn and follow the same route back to the start. Distance – 16.6 km.
8.32	0.28	Straight	**Ernie O'Dowda Park Path (crushed limestone/asphalt);** cycle to the path beside the Red River, turn right.
			The trail exits onto the Midwinter Multi-use Path.
8.60	0.23	Left	**Midwinter Multi-use Path (asphalt);** cycle to the Disraeli Active Transportation Bridge.
8.83	0.21	Left	**Disraeli Active Transport Bridge (asphalt);** cross over the Red River to Rover Street.
			***Light Through* Art Installation:** These stainless-steel pictures showcase historic photographs of the bridge and the surrounding area.
9.04	0.41	Right	**Rover Street;** cycle under the Disraeli Bridge to the end of the street where it meets Hallet Street. At this corner,

			is Michelle Jean Parc and the North Winnipeg Parkway Trail.
9.45	0.55	Straight	**North Winnipeg Parkway Trail (crushed limestone);** cycle through Michelle Jean Parc, past Norquay Community Centre and past Pritchard Point Park as the trail runs beside the Red River. When the trail splits, veer left up the incline to exit onto Burrows Avenue.
10.00	0.09	Left	**Burrows Avenue;** between houses #143 and #149 is a path which takes you to the next street.
10.09	0.09	Right	**Alfred-Burrows Link Path (crushed limestone);** follow the path between the houses, across the back lane and exit onto Alfred Avenue. Across Alfred, is the St. John's-Redwood-Aberdeen Park Path. **Caution:** The opening in the fence by the back lane is quite narrow.
10.18	0.69	Right	**St. John's-Redwood-Aberdeen Park Path (asphalt/crushed limestone);** these trails are still part of the North Winnipeg Parkway. Cycle through Redwood Park and continue straight. The trail splits before the Redwood Bridge, veer right to cycle under the bridge and along the edge of the Red River before the trail climbs up to Saint John's Park. Continue on the trail along the back of the park till it exits onto St. Cross Street. **Note:** If the trail is flooded under the bridge, when the trail splits, continue straight, cross Redwood, go down the ramp to pick up the trail beside the river and continue as the trail climbs up to St. John's Park. Alternatively, once across Redwood, continue to Main Street and turn right. Cycle past Shoppers Drug Mart and the Ukrainian-Orthodox Holy Trinity Church to St. John's Park. Turn right onto the park trail and follow the path to the river and then left along the edge of the park to the exit on St. Cross Street.

		(star / toilet icons)	**St. John's Park:** Take a few minutes to enjoy this historic park and view the Healing Forest. **St. John's Park:** Bathrooms are located by the wading pool but are only open when the pool is open.
10.87	0.47	Straight	**St. Cross Street;** cycle past Mortimer Place and Machray to Cathedral Avenue.
11.34	0.13	Right	**Cathedral Avenue;** cycle one block to Scotia Street.
11.47	2.52	Left	**Scotia Street/Forest Avenue;** stay on Scotia Street for many blocks. At Marymound Inc. Scotia curves left and becomes Forest Avenue. Cycle to the first street, Marymound Way. **Note:** Scotia Street, from Anderson Avenue, at St. Cross Street, to Armstrong Avenue is designated as a Sunday/Holiday Bicycle Route, from 8am to 8pm, by the city of Winnipeg. This means, on those days, motor vehicle traffic is restricted to one block.
13.99	0.12	Right	**Marymound Way;** cycle one block to Leila Avenue.
14.11	0.34	Right	**Leila Avenue;** cycle past the Leila Tot Lot to Scotia Street.
14.45	0.31	Left	**Scotia Street;** cycle past Newton and Armstrong and enter Kildonan Park. Just past the entrance, to your right, is the Kildonan Park Trail which intersects with the road.
14.76	1.35	Right	**Kildonan Park Trail (asphalt)/Kildonan Park Golf Course Trail (crushed limestone);** cycle the Kildonan Park Trail as it follows along the edge of the Red River. At the edge of the golf course the trail changes from asphalt to crushed limestone and becomes the Kildonan Park Golf Course Trail. At the end of the golf course, the Chief Peguis Greenway Trail begins. **Kildonan Park:** Bathrooms are in the basement of the pavilion located in the centre of the park beside the main parking lot. They are open daily from 8am to 9pm.

			To get there, when you enter the park, stay on the road, now called Riverview Drive and just before the Witch's Hut turn left at Lord Selkirk Drive. This road takes you to the Pavilion. Because Lord Selkirk Drive is a one-way street, after using the bathrooms, exit the parking lot at the south end by the children's playground, to McKay Drive. Turn left, cycle past the Kildonan Park Outdoor Pool, and as the road curves left, McKay Drive becomes Riverview Drive. At the curve, the road meets with the Kildonan Park Trail which runs along the river. Continue ride as above. **Prairie's Edge:** Feeling a bit hungry or just feel like getting an ice cream? This restaurant can accommodate either. Prairie's Edge is located in the same pavilion as the bathrooms, so follow directions above to get there.
16.11	5.19	Left	**Chief Peguis Greenway Trail (asphalt);** cycle to the second right turn, just before Main Street, which leads over the Kildonan Settlers Bridge. Just past the top of the bridge, the trail moves off the bridge and veers to the right. The trail splits, but stay to the right and cycle under the bridge to the north side of Chief Peguis and continue straight across Henderson Highway, over Sugar Point and across Gateway. Before Lagimodière, the trail splits, take the trail to the left which exits at Springfield Road.
21.30	0.13	Straight	**Springfield Road;** cycle to the edge of Sun Valley Park South to access the Sun Valley Park Path.
21.43	0.29	Left	**Sun Valley Park Path (crushed limestone);** follow the trail as it goes along the edge of the park and veers left around the water and then exits on Southwell Road.
21.72	1.28	Right	**Southwell Road/St. Moritz Road/Strongberg Drive;** cycle past Manthorne, Wynyard, and Sage Wood and across Sun Valley where Southwell Road becomes St. Moritz Road. Cycle past Rushmore, Tomkins and across McIvor where St. Moritz Road becomes Strongberg Drive.

			Strongberg curves left and the first street is Green Meadows Avenue.
23.00	0.54	Right	**Green Meadows Avenue/John Huyda Drive;** cycle across Ragsdill where Green Meadows becomes John Huyda Drive. John Huyda curves to the left and intersects with Mitchelson Way.
23.54	0.15	Right	**Mitchelson Way;** cycle to Bonner Avenue.
23.69	0.52	Left	**Bonner Avenue;** cycle across Gateway to the Northeast Pioneers Greenway Trail located between Gateway Road and Raleigh Street.
24.21	0.69	Left	**Northeast Pioneers Greenway Trail (asphalt);** cycle past McIvor, to the second exit to the right, which is located after the bench. This exit leads to the Bunn's Creek Trail.
24.90	2.79	Right	**Bunn's Creek Trail (crushed limestone);** cycle across Raleigh to the beginning of the trail. The creek is on your left until you cross McIvor Avenue, then it is on your right. Stay on the path as it travels through Bunn's Creek Centennial Park, across Rothesay and Bonner. Once across Bonner Avenue, the creek is on your left again. The trail exits at Henderson Highway. ***The Seven Teachings* Art Installation:** These are the virtues necessary for a full and happy life: respect, love, courage, honesty, wisdom, humility and truth. **Bunn's Creek Centennial Park:** The public bathroom is open daily 8am – 4pm.
27.69	0.13	Right	**Henderson Highway;** cycle one block to Knowles Avenue. **Mountain Bean Coffee Company:** This coffee shop is located a half block to the left, at Bonner Avenue, from where the trail exits on Henderson Highway. There is both indoor and outdoor seating. After your stop here, return to where you left off.

27.82	0.60	Right	**Knowles Avenue;** cycle past Daman to Rothesay Street.
28.42	0.68	Left	**Rothesay Street;** cycle past Emerson, Glenway, Foxgrove and Saddleridge to Maxwell King Drive.
29.10	0	End	**Corner of Rothesay Street and Maxwell King Drive.**

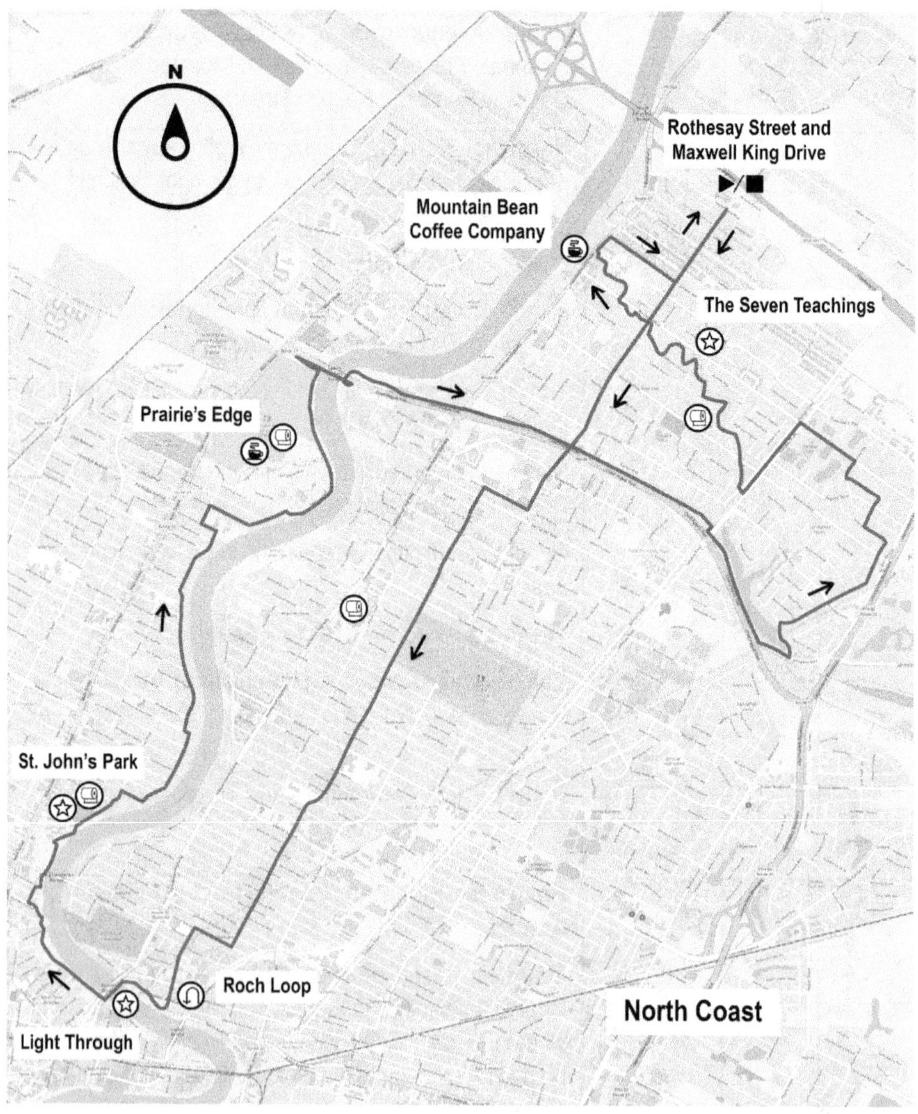

Creek to Creek

Northeast Winnipeg

Whenever I do this ride, I feel like it's over before I know it. I think it's because this route is in only one area of the city so it doesn't seem as if I travel all that far. However, it still is a 30 km ride.

Perhaps another reason it seems short is because it's so scenic. Much of the ride is done along various bodies of water and with that you get the beauty and sounds of nature with wildflowers, birds, frogs, squirrels, and rustling leaves. It's all somewhat mesmerizing.

There is really only one coffee spot along the way and that is the Tim Hortons on Gateway Road. If you decide to shorten the route, Tim's is just past the turnoff. I have included a detour in the detailed directions below if you want to get your coffee in before taking the short loop.

A point of interest, located along Bunn's Creek, is an art installation called *The Seven Teachings*. The teachings are Anishinaabe in origin and are the basic virtues necessary for a full and happy life: respect, love, courage, honesty, wisdom, humility and truth. On one side of each sign are wood carvings of an animal, representative of each teaching, done by students at John G. Stewart School. On the other side are digital collages related to each teaching which were put together by artist Becky Thiessen from artwork created by Knowles Centre youth.

Because the ride goes from Bunn's Creek to Eagle Creek Drive, I chose the name Creek to Creek, but a close second was Bike Your Bunn's Off.

Enjoy!

Quick Notes
Distance – 30.0 km
Parking – Kildonan Park at 2015 Main Street, park in lot by the Chief Peguis Pavilion
Option to shorten –
    Creek Loop – 23.4 km
Suggested coffee stop – Tim Hortons at 1139 Gateway Road
Bathrooms – Kildonan Park in Chief Peguis Pavilion, Public Bathroom in Bunn's
    Creek Centennial Park, coffee stop
Point of Interest –
    The Seven Teachings Art Installation along Bunn's Creek Trail

Trails
Kildonan Park Trail – asphalt
Kildonan Park Golf Course Trail – crushed limestone

Chief Peguis Greenway Trail – asphalt
Northeast Pioneers Greenway Trail – asphalt
Bunn's Creek Trail – crushed limestone
Countryside Crossing Trail – crushed limestone
Red River North Trail – asphalt
Eagle Creek Trail – crushed limestone
Raleigh Trail – crushed limestone
Kildonan Parkway Trail – asphalt/crushed limestone/dirt

Safety Cautions

Detailed Directions

Km Total	Km Leg	Direction	Location, notes
0	0	Start	**McKay Drive;** ride starts on McKay Drive by the children's playground at the southeast corner of Kildonan Park parking lot. **Kildonan Park:** Bathrooms are in the lower level of the Chief Peguis Pavilion located just off the parking lot. They are open daily from 8am to 9pm.
0	0.29	Left	**McKay Drive/Riverview Drive;** as the road curves left, McKay Drive becomes Riverview Drive. Shortly after the curve, the road meets with the Kildonan Park Trail which runs beside the river.
0.29	1.23	Right	**Kildonan Park Trail (asphalt)/Kildonan Park Golf Course Trail (crushed limestone);** cycle the Kildonan Park Trail as it follows beside the Red River. At the edge of the golf course, the trail changes from asphalt to crushed limestone and becomes the Kildonan Park Golf Course Trail. At the end of the golf course, the Chief Peguis Greenway Trail begins.

1.52	4.03	Left	**Chief Peguis Greenway Trail (asphalt);** cycle to the second right turn, just before Main Street, which leads over the Kildonan Settlers Bridge. Just past the top of the bridge, the trail moves off the bridge and veers to the right. The trail splits, but stay to the right and cycle under the bridge to the north side of Chief Peguis and continue straight across Henderson Highway. Just before Gateway the trail climbs up to Sugar Point and as you go down, this trail intersects with the Northeast Pioneers Greenway Trail.
5.55	0.35	Left	**Northeast Pioneers Greenway Trail (asphalt);** cycle to the second exit trail to the left which leads to the beginning of Bunn's Creek Trail.
5.90	1.87	Left	**Bunn's Creek Trail (crushed limestone);** cycle across Raleigh Street to the beginning of Bunn's Creek Trail. The creek is on your left until you cross McIvor, then it is on your right. There are many exit paths from this trail, stay on the path which runs beside the creek and do not turn off or go over any bridges. Cycle the trail as it travels through Bunn's Creek Centennial Park, to Rothesay Avenue, which is the next street you come to after McIvor. Before you get to Rothesay, is the sign for "Honesty", one of the *Seven Teachings* art installation. **The Seven Teachings Art Installation:** These are the virtues necessary for a full and happy life: respect, love, courage, honesty, wisdom, humility and truth. **Bunn's Creek Centennial Park:** The public bathroom is open daily 8am – 4pm.
7.77	1.00	Right	**Rothesay Avenue;** cycle past the stop signs at Bonner, Glenway, Foxgrove and Saddleridge. Before the next street is Countryside Crossing Trail.
8.77	0.57	Left	**Countryside Crossing Trail (crushed limestone);** follow this trail which runs alongside ponds and cross Willowside Bend.

			The trail exits on Maxwell King Drive.
9.34	0.16	Left	**Maxwell King Drive;** cycle to Henderson Highway and the Red River North Trail.
9.50	1.67	Right	**Henderson Highway/Red River North Trail (asphalt);** cycle on the path along the east side of Henderson Highway. Pass the perimeter and go several blocks to Eagle Creek Drive, which is one block past Pritchard Farm Road. There is a light at this corner. **Note:** The path is separate from the highway for only a few blocks. You then cycle on the shoulder of Henderson Highway for a short distance.
11.17	0.14	Right	**Eagle Creek Drive;** shortly after turning the corner, is a crushed limestone path to your left.
11.31	3.42	Left	**Eagle Creek Trail (crushed limestone);** follow the trail along the edge of the pond, cross Old Orchard Road and cycle along the second pond. Cross Eagle Creek Drive and there is a trail on both sides of the pond. Take either one, as the trail on the left crosses the pond to join the trail on the right. Cross Mowat, continue cycling with the pond to your left, when the trail splits, keep left along the edge of the pond, cross Eagle Creek and the trail goes along another pond which is to your right. Cross Woodstone, past one last pond on your left, and the trail curves right at Raleigh Street. **Caution:** There are many dips and curves on this path and the trail is close to the water. Be careful you do not lose control of your bike and land in the pond!
14.73	6.62	Straight	**Raleigh Street/Raleigh Trail (crushed limestone)/Northeast Pioneers Greenway Trail (asphalt);** there is a crushed limestone trail along the west side of Raleigh from the Eagle Creek Trail to East St. Paul Sports Complex. Across Raleigh is another crushed limestone trail which continues past the Sports Complex, under the Perimeter Highway and joins with the Northeast Pioneers Greenway Trail.

			Continue straight across Knowles, Headmaster, Bonner, McIvor, Chief Peguis, Springfield and McLeod to Kimberley Avenue. **Tim Hortons:** Would coffee hit the spot right about now? Tim's is located on Gateway between Springfield and McLeod and there is an exit trail from the Northeast Pioneers Greenway Trail leading to Tim's. **Creek Loop:** Just before Chief Peguis, turn right onto Chief Peguis Greenway Trail as it goes up Sugar Point and continues straight. Return to Kildonan Park Golf Course Trail and continue, where indicated below, to return to start. Distance – 23.4 km. **Note:** The Creek Loop turns off before you reach Tim Hortons. If you want to get in a coffee first, continue straight on the Northeast Pioneers Greenway Trail a short distance past the turnoff. Tim's is located on Gateway between Springfield and McLeod and there is an exit trail from the Northeast Pioneers Greenway Trail leading to Tim's. When done, return to the spot where turn off onto Chief Peguis Trail and continue as indicated.
21.35	2.07	Right	**Kimberley Avenue;** cycle across Raleigh, Golspie, Watt, Roch, Brazier and Henderson to Kildonan Drive.
23.42	4.14	Right	**Kildonan Parkway Trail (asphalt)/Kildonan Drive;** this section of the Kildonan Parkway Trail is made up mostly of Kildonan Drive and paths through two parks. Kildonan Drive ends at a stop sign at Helmsdale, turn left and when the road curves right, Helmsdale becomes Kildonan Drive. When you reach Fraser's Grove Park and Kildonan Drive turns right, continue straight on the path which runs through the park and exits back onto Kildonan Drive at Larchdale. Cycle to the end of Kildonan Drive and take the crushed limestone trail straight ahead which leads up an embankment and into Bergen Cutoff Park. The trail splits, turn left towards the river. The trail curves right and exits back onto Kildonan Drive.

			Turn left at the multi-use path just past Essar. This path intersects with Chief Peguis Greenway Trail just before the underpass at Kildonan Settlers Bridge.
27.56	1.01	Right	**Chief Peguis Greenway Trail (asphalt);** cycle to where the path splits and turn left and left again to cycle up and over the Kildonan Settlers Bridge. Just before Main Street the trail splits, turn left and continue to Kildonan Park Golf Course Trail.
28.57	0.83	Right	**Kildonan Park Golf Course Trail (crushed limestone)/Kildonan Park Trail (asphalt);** cycle behind the golf course and into Kildonan Park. The Kildonan Golf Course Trail is made of crushed limestone and when you pass the Golf Course, the trail is asphalt. This is the beginning of the Kildonan Park Trail. Take the second right exit from the trail, just after Lord Selkirk Creek, to Peguis Drive, by the Witch's Hut. **Caution:** There is a steep dip at the end of the trail as it exits to the road. **Creek Loop continued:** Continue from this step to return to Kildonan Park parking lot.
29.40	0.05	Left	**Peguis Drive;** the first street to your right is Lord Selkirk Drive.
29.45	0.41	Right	**Lord Selkirk Drive;** follow this road back to the parking lot.
29.86	0.17	Left	**Kildonan Park parking lot;** cycle through the lot to the southeast corner by the children's playground and to McKay Drive.
30.03	0	End	**McKay Drive.**

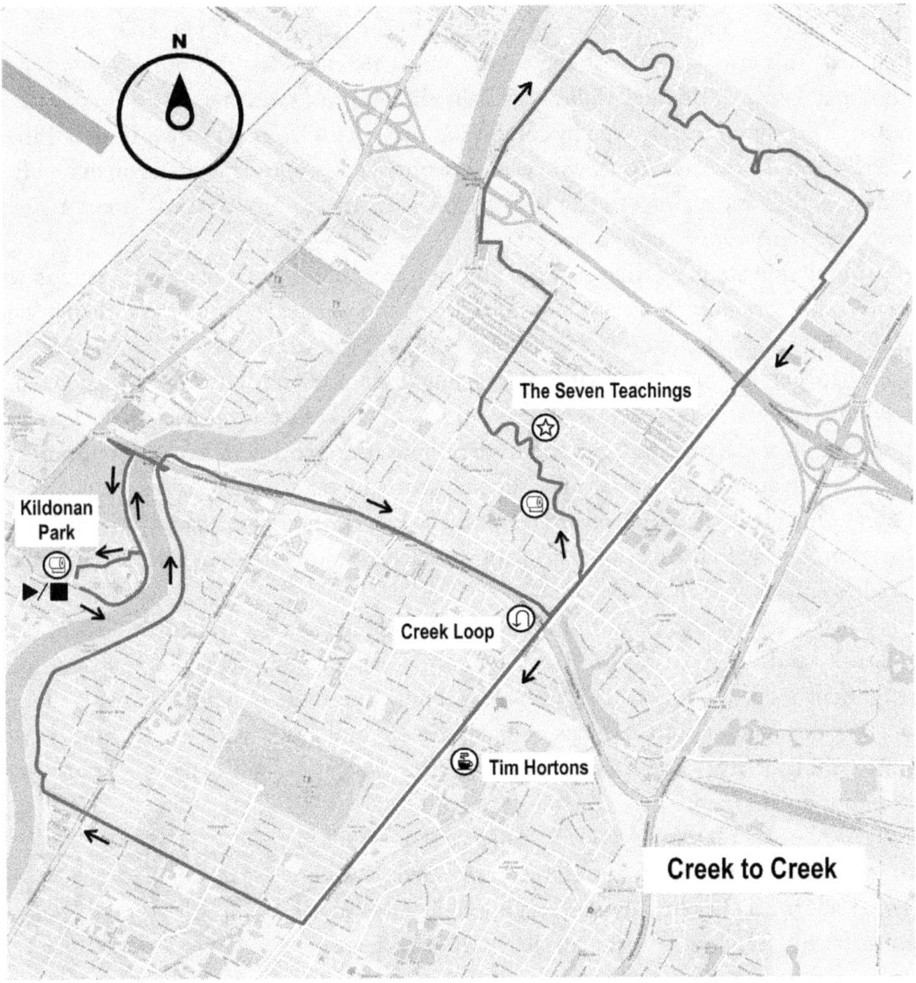

N
The Seven Teachings
Kildonan
Park
Creek Loop
Tim Hortons
Creek to Creek

Transcona Bound

Northeast Winnipeg

Transcona and the railways have a tied history. In 1909, when Transcona was founded, this was the site of the repair shops for the Grand Trunk Pacific and National Transcontinental Railways. Even the name, Transcona, has a link to the railway! The name was derived by combining the "Trans" from Transcontinental, and "cona", from Lord Strathcona, who was instrumental in building the Canadian Pacific Railway. Still today, more than 100 years later, these railway yards are a major employer in this community.

This ride starts at Kilcona Park and has a bit of an awkward beginning, as to head south, we must first cross Lagimodière to the west side of the road, then cross Chief Peguis and again cross Lagimodière to get back to the east side. There is no access to get to this point without crossing Lagimodière. The route then heads towards Kildonan Place, across Regent and to St. Boniface Industrial Park. After a spin around the Industrial Park the route follows the South Transcona Community Path, which runs along the edge of the railyards and ends at the Malteurop Malting Plant. This plant is a point of interest, as it is one of the largest barley and malting barley producers in the world. This plant produces 90,000 tonnes of Pilsen malt, used as a base malt for mostly lagers.

From here, the route turns around skirting along the west and north sides of the railyards and then passes downtown Transcona and through the surrounding neighbourhood, heading to the Transcona Trail. The route only follows the trail for a short distance and then turns on Day Street and leads back to Kilcona Park approaching it from the east. The ride covers much of Transcona, so Transcona Bound is an apt name.

While in Transcona, you might like to spend a bit of time here. One of the coffee stops recommended, L'Arche Tova Café is a Transcona favourite. It is a café with a social conscience, serving great meals while providing meaningful employment to individuals with developmental disabilities. Their menu can be found at this site https://www.larchetovacafe.com. If a sit-down meal doesn't appeal to you, the option of ice cream from Dairy Queen is available. It is located just past Regent on Day Street.

L'Arche Tova Café

To learn more about Transcona, step into the second point of interest, the Transcona Museum, located a few doors down from the L'Arche Tova Café. This museum was founded in 1967 and has as its mission to maintain and promote the history, stories and community of Transcona. If you decide to not take in the museum, it is worth it to at least go and look at the building, as it is the only designated heritage building in Transcona. This building was originally built in 1925 by the Bank of Toronto and later served as the Transcona Municipal Office before being used as a museum. https://www.transcona museum.mb.ca

Transcona Museum

As you can see, there is lots to explore here. Enjoy!

Quick Notes
Distance – 32.0 km
Parking – Kilcona Park parking lot located off Lagimodière Boulevard at McIver Avenue
Option to shorten – yes
        Kilcona Loop – 16.7 km
Suggested coffee stops – Food Court in Kildonan Place at 1555 Regent Avenue W, L'Arche Tova Café at 119 Regent Avenue W, Dairy Queen at 100 Victoria Avenue E
Bathrooms – Kilcona Park, Kildonan Place at 1555 Regent Avenue W, coffee stop
Points of Interest –
        Malteurop Malting Plant at 3001 Dugald Road
        Transcona Museum at 141 Regent Avenue W

Trails
Kilcona Trail – asphalt
Chief Peguis Greenway Trail – asphalt
Archambault-Inderjit-De Graaf Trail – crushed limestone
Peguis Multi-use Path – asphalt
Reenders Multi-use Path – asphalt
South Transcona Community Path – asphalt
Plessis Multi-use Path – asphalt
Pandora Path – asphalt
Park Circle Trail – crushed limestone
Windsong Trail – crushed limestone
Transcona Trail – asphalt
Harbourview-Kilcona Trail – asphalt/gravel

Safety Cautions

Detailed Directions

Km Total	Km Leg	Direction	Location, notes
0	0	Start	**Kilcona Trail;** the trail starts in the middle of the southwest edge of the parking lot. **Kilcona Park:** Bathrooms are located just south of the parking lot, up the hill. They are open daily from 6am to10pm.
0	1.14	Right	**Kilcona Trail (asphalt);** follow the trail as it skirts around the hill where the bathrooms are located and heads towards the water. When the trail splits, veer left, and when the trail splits again at the edge of the body of water, go right. Cycle over the bridge between the two ponds. Take the trail which curves right. Cycle over a second bridge and continue straight to the edge of the park where the trail turns left. The trail exits at the corner of Norris and Springfield Roads.
1.14	0.14	Right	**Springfield Road;** cross Lagimodière Boulevard to the next street Molson Street/De Vries Avenue.
1.28	0.27	Left	**Molson Street;** cycle to the end of the street and the beginning of the Chief Peguis Greenway.
1.55	0.88	Straight	**Chief Peguis Greenway Trail (asphalt);** follow the trail across Chief Peguis, and then turn left to cross Lagimodière. The trail continues straight and then curves to the right along the edge of Sunrise park and exits to Shauna Way.

2.43	0.04	Left	**Shauna Way;** cycle to first street, Silver Fields Lane.
2.47	0.45	Right	**Silver Fields Lane/McLellan Drive;** cycle across Jacques and Grassie, at which point the street name changes from Silver Fields Lane to McLellan Drive. Cycle past Williamson and Rutledge Crescents. Archambault Park is immediately to your right and has a path running through it. Note there is no break in the curb to access the trail.
2.92	1.54	Right	**Archambault-Inderjit-De Graaf Trail (crushed limestone);** cycle through Archambault Park, across Grantsmuir and through Inderjit Claire Park. When the trail splits, turn right, cycle across Reg Wyatt, through the greenspace and across Reg Wyatt again, through De Graaf Nature Reserve and exit to Concordia Avenue E.
4.46	0.26	Left	**Concordia Avenue E;** cycle past Reg Wyatt to Peguis Street.
4.72	1.82	Right	**Peguis Multi-use Path (asphalt);** cycle on the multi-use path on the west side of Peguis Street. Cycle past Prairie Crocus, Ravelston, El Tassi and Almey to Reenders Drive. **Caution:** There is a small section, between Prairie Crocus Drive and Ravelston Avenue where the bike path is interrupted and there is also no sidewalk. Use caution till the path resumes. **Kilcona Loop:** At Almey Avenue/Cal Gardner Drive turn left onto the Cal Gardner Multi-use Path. Cycle past the Prairie Landing apartment block and parking lot to the Devonshire Park Path on your right. Cycle through the park keeping the pond to your left. The path exits onto the Transcona Trail. Turn left and cycle past the back of Club Regent and across Transcona Road. The trail then turns to the right, over the railway tracks and turns left. Cross Plessis and Hoka to Day Street. Turn left on Day Street and continue, where indicated below, to return to start. Distance – 16.7 km.

6.54	0.28	Right	**Reenders Multi-use Path (asphalt);** cycle the multi-use path on the north side of Reenders. Once past the back of Canadian Tire, there is an entrance into the Kildonan Place parking lot. **Note:** There is no exit path off the multi-use path to this entrance nor a break in the curb.
6.82	1.92	Left	**Kildonan Place parking lot/Rougeau Avenue;** cycle straight, past the shopping mall and across Regent at the lights. Once across Regent the road is called Rougeau Avenue. Cycle past Rougeau Garden, Trudell, Wendilene and Bernie Wolfe Park and Community School to Bournais Drive. **Kildonan Place:** There are several sets of washrooms located within the shopping centre. **Kildonan Place Food Court:** A food court is located close to the entrance by Dollarama.
8.74	1.48	Right	**Bournais Drive/Beghin Avenue;** stay on Bournais Drive and cross Dugald Road at the lights. The street name changes to Beghin Avenue as you enter St. Boniface Industrial Park. Some of the businesses passed include East Side Ventilation, Ecoline Windows, Mid-West Packaging Limited, Vita Health Products Inc, and Color Ad Packaging as you cycle past Durand, De Baets, Paquin and Mazenod Park Retention Pond to where Beghin ends at Rue Camiel Sys Street.
10.22	1.18	Left	**Rue Camiel Sys Street;** cycle past FedEx Ground Terminal, Broadstreet Properties, Nomandeau Roofing Ltd, and CGC to De Baets Street.
11.40	1.25	Left	**De Baets Street;** cycle past Penner Doors and Hardware, Gateway Bookbinding Systems, Encore Metals, Fastener Warehouse, GS Granite Outlet Ltd, Esdale Printing and Award Marble, as you pass Paquin and Durand to get back to Beghin Avenue.
12.65	0.28	Right	**Beghin Avenue;** cycle back to the entrance of St. Boniface Industrial Park.

			To your right, before Dugald Road, is the South Transcona Community Path.
12.93	3.11	Right	**South Transcona Community Path (asphalt);** this trail runs beside Dugald and crosses to the north side of Dugald at the first corner, Guy Savoie Drive. Cycle across Plessis Road and continue to the end of the trail at Webster Avenue, just before the Malteurop Malting Plant. **Malteurop Malting Plant:** Feast your eyes of one of the largest barley and malting barley production facilities in the world.
16.04	1.83	U-Turn	**South Transcona Community Path (asphalt);** cycle back to Plessis Road and the Plessis Multi-use Path on the east side of the street.
17.87	0.85	Right	**Plessis Multi-use Path (asphalt);** cycle past the west end of the railway yards, across Kernaghan to Pandora Avenue W. Cross to the Pandora Path on the sidewalk on the north side of street.
18.72	1.64	Right	**Pandora Path (asphalt);** cycle past the stop signs at Hoka and Bond to Day Street. There is a Petro-Canada Station just before the corner.
20.36	0.44	Left	**Day Street;** cycle past Melrose, Regent, Victoria and Yale to Ravelston Avenue E. **L'Arche Tova Café:** Located on Regent, just left of Day Street, this café is a Transcona favourite. They feature an all-day breakfast menu plus a lunch menu. Be sure to check their website for hours of operation. **Transcona Museum:** Delve into Transcona's past at this cozy museum. It is located a few doors past L'Arche Tova Café. **Dairy Queen:** If a sit-down restaurant is not of interest, there always is ice cream. A Dairy Queen is located at the corner of Day and Victoria.
20.80	0.98	Right	**Ravelston Avenue E/Park Circle Trail (crushed limestone);** cycle past Kanata and straight into Park Circle along the Park Circle Trail and out the other side, back onto Ravelston.

			Cycle past Roanoke, Leola and Rosseau to Wayoata Street where Ravelston ends.
21.78	0.10	Left	**Wayoata Street;** cycle to the next street, Coldstream Avenue.
21.88	0.39	Right	**Coldstream Avenue;** cycle to the end of the street and across Widlake Street to enter Victoria Jason Park parking lot. At the corner of the lot is the entrance to the Windsong Trail.
22.27	0.26	Straight	**Windsong Trail (crushed limestone);** cycle straight through the park and exit on Redonda Street. There is no break in the curb when you exit to the street.
22.53	1.39	Left	**Redonda Street;** cycle past the stop signs at Kildare, St. Martin, McMeans and Paulley. Past Paulley Drive is access to the Transcona Trail.
23.92	1.66	Left	**Transcona Trail (asphalt);** cycle to the next cross street, Day Street.
25.58	2.77	Right	**Day Street;** cycle across Gunn and stay on Day as it curves right and then left, ending on Springfield Road. **Kilcona Loop continued:** Turn left at Day Street and follow the rest of the directions below to the start.
28.35	1.51	Left	**Springfield Road;** this is a busy road but there are wide shoulders which are good to cycle on. Cycle past Wenzel and Cox to the entrance of Harbourview Park and Recreation Complex and the Harbourview-Kilcona Path.
29.86	1.95	Left	**Harbourview-Kilcona Trail (asphalt/gravel)/Service Road;** the trail starts immediately to your left, once you turn into Harvourview Park and runs along the edge of the park and exits to a service road. Follow the service road as it turns right and then left. This service road ends at the Kilcona Park parking lot.
31.81	0.15	Left	**Kilcona Park parking lot;** cycle to the head of the Kilcona Trail.
31.96	0	End	**Kilcona Trail.**

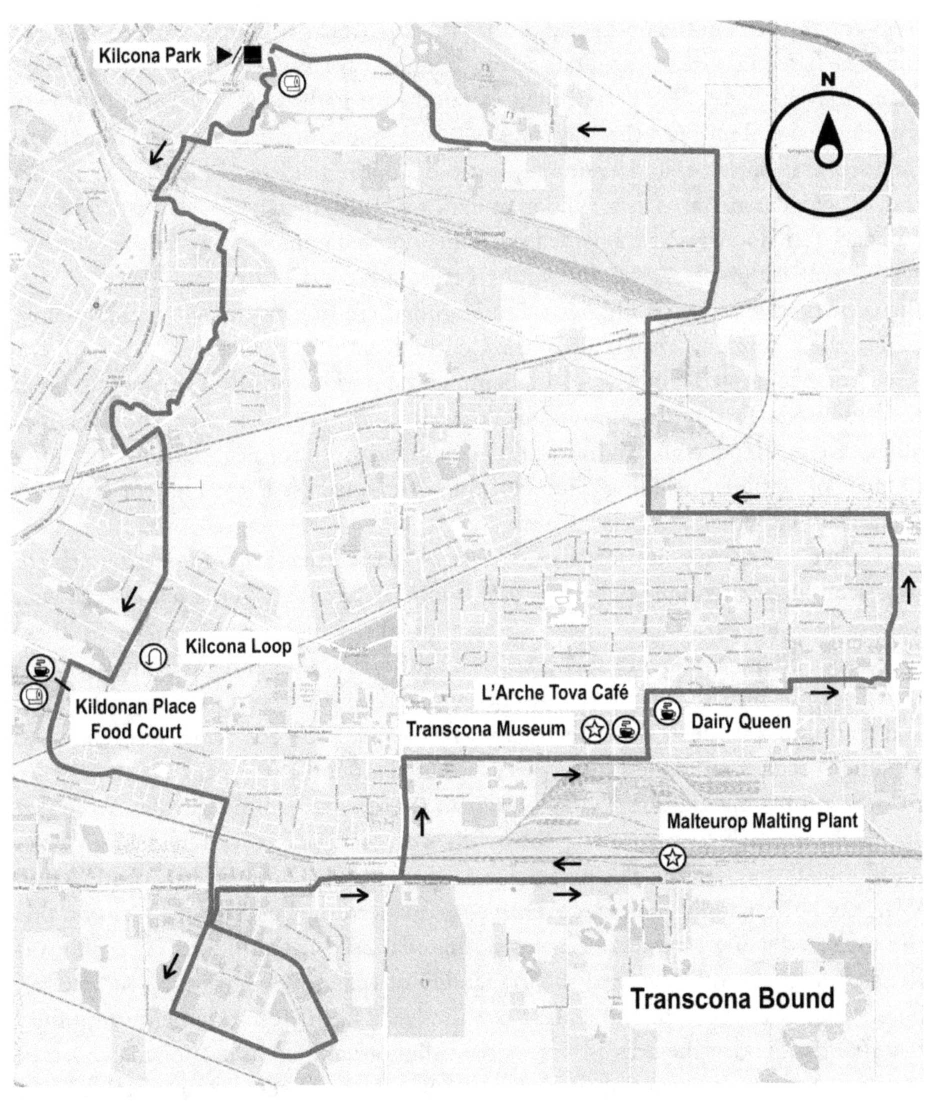

Kilcona Park
Kilcona Loop
Kildonan Place
Food Court
L'Arche Tova Café
Transcona Museum
Dairy Queen
Malteurop Malting Plant
Transcona Bound
N

Wolf Train

Northeast Winnipeg

This entire ride is in the north end of the city. It starts at Kildonan Park and follows the Chief Peguis Greenway Trail across Lagimodière Boulevard to its end. From there, the route leads to a path through a number of parks and then works its way to the Transcona Trail. On the way back, we cycle the Cordite Trail, go through the Transcona Bioreserve, and eventually cycle on Springfield to Henderson. Another trail off Henderson takes us to Kildonan Parkway Trail, then back over the Red River and back to Kildonan Park. I named this route, Wolf Train, Wolf, because of the two sets of wolf sculptures, called *Pursuit*, by Peter Sawatzky, located on Chief Peguis at the corners of Henderson Highway and Lagimodière Boulevard, and Train, because part of the Transcona Trail is along the Central Manitoba rail line.

For a suggested coffee stop, I recommend Tim Hortons near the beginning of the Transcona Trail or if you would like to wait till closer to the end of the ride, once you arrive at Henderson Highway and Springfield, you can head left or right for a number of options including Tim Hortons, McDonald's, Pizza Hut, or Salisbury House, among others.

There are three points of interest. First is *Pursuit*, made up of two groupings of wolf sculptures, mentioned above, located on Chief Peguis. These ten bronze wolf sculptures, each weighing between 700 and 800 pounds, pay homage to these creatures, and are a reference to Chief Peguis' historical signature. Within each pack of wolves, for realism, each one is uniquely posed with its head at a different angle and its running stride at a different stage. The artist, Peter Sawatzky, is a renowned Winnipeg sculptor, who has many pieces situated around Winnipeg.

Second is the Cordite Trail which is in the second half of the ride. It is a dirt and grass trail which runs along the south side of the Cordite Ditch in an open meadow-like field at the northern edge of Transcona. During the Second World War, the British and Canadian governments financed the building of a plant on this site to manufacture cordite, an explosive material used in munitions. This site was perfect for this plant because of the availability of water, fuel, power, labour and rail lines. When the war ended, the plant was used as a Japanese Internment camp for a few months. Today the area is serene, providing a natural habitat for marsh birds, hawks, geese, ducks, coyotes, foxes and other wildlife. There are interesting signs along the way explaining the history and well worth the read.

And third is the Transcona Bioreserve. This site used to be home to the Domtar Wood Preservative Plant until it closed in 1976. Much was done to clean up this land after its closure and today it is a wonderful prairie reserve, filled with frogs croaking in the spring and colourful wild flowers, butterflies, and song birds in the summer.

Having the start/stop in Kildonan Park gives you the opportunity to make a whole day adventure out of your ride, as, after the ride, you can take a swim in their Olympic size outdoor pool, stroll through the gardens or along Lord Selkirk Creek, stop by the duck pond, check out the panels of the Hansel and Gretel fairy tale in the Witch's Hut, have an ice cream or meal at the pavilion, or pack a picnic to enjoy outside. Just a ride or a day adventure, your choice.

Have fun!

Quick Notes

Distance – 34.4 km

Parking – Kildonan Park at 2015 Main Street, park in the lot by the Chief Peguis Pavilion

Options to shorten – yes

    1 – Chief Peguis Loop – 14.4 km

    2 – Transcona Loop – 13.4 km *For this loop, park near the corner of Regent Avenue and Peguis Drive

Suggested coffee stops – Tim Hortons at 1495 Regent Avenue, several choices along Henderson Highway, close to Springfield Road, such as McDonald's, Tim Hortons, Salisbury House, Pizza Hut, etc.

Bathrooms – Kildonan Park at 2015 Main Street, coffee stop

Points of Interest –

    Pursuit Art Installations on Chief Peguis Greenway Trail at Henderson Highway and Lagimodière Boulevard

    Cordite Trail

    Transcona Bioreserve

Trails

Kildonan Park Trail – asphalt

Kildonan Park Golf Course Trail – crushed limestone

Chief Peguis Greenway Trail – asphalt

Archambault-Inderjit-De Graaf Trail – crushed limestone

Peguis Multi-use Path – asphalt

Cal Gardner Multi-use Path – asphalt

Devonshire Park Path – asphalt

Transcona Trail – asphalt

Cordite Trail East – dirt/grass

Transcona Bioreserve Trail – crushed limestone

Cordite Trail West – dirt/grass

Bergen Cutoff Path – crushed limestone/dirt

Kildonan Parkway Trail – asphalt

Safety Cautions

Detailed Directions

Km Total	Km Leg	Direction	Location, notes
0	0	Start	**McKay Drive;** ride starts on McKay Drive by the children's playground at the southeast corner of Kildonan Park parking lot. **Kildonan Park:** Bathrooms are in the lower level of the Chief Peguis Pavilion located just off the parking lot. They are open daily from 8am to 9pm.
0	0.29	Left	**McKay Drive/Riverview Drive;** as the road curves left, McKay Drive becomes Riverview Drive. Shortly after the curve, the road meets with the Kildonan Park Trail which runs beside the river.
0.29	1.23	Right	**Kildonan Park Trail (asphalt)/Kildonan Park Golf Course Trail (crushed limestone);** cycle the Kildonan Park Trail as it follows along the edge of the Red River. At the edge of the golf course the trail changes from asphalt to crushed limestone and becomes the Kildonan Park Golf Course Trail. At the end of the golf course, the Chief Peguis Greenway Trail begins.
1.52	6.50	Left	**Chief Peguis Greenway Trail (asphalt);** cycle to the second right turn, just before Main Street, which leads over the Kildonan Settlers Bridge. Just past the top of the bridge, the trail moves off the bridge and veers to the right. The trail splits, but stay to the right and cycle under the bridge to the north side of Chief Peguis. Continue straight and cross Henderson and Gateway, to Lagimodière Boulevard.

			At Lagimodière, you must cross to the south side of Chief Peguis before crossing Lagimodière. Continue straight on Chief Peguis Greenway Trail and follow it as it veers to the right and through Sunrise Park. The trail exits onto Shauna Way. ***Pursuit* Art Installations:** Stop and take a look at these magnificent wolves depicted running in packs by Henderson Highway. On the way back, you will cycle past the ones at the Lagimodière end. **Chief Peguis Loop:** Turn around before crossing Chief Peguis at Lagimodière Boulevard and return to Kildonan Park Trail. Continue, where indicated below, to return to start. Distance – 14.4 km.
8.02	0.03	Left	**Shauna Way;** cycle to the first street, Silver Fields Lane.
8.05	0.45	Right	**Silver Fields Lane/McLellan Drive;** cycle across Jacques and Grassie, at which point the street name changes from Silver Fields Lane to McLellan Drive. Cycle past Williamson and Rutledge Crescents. Archambault Park is immediately to your right and has a trail running through it. **Caution:** There is no break in the curb to access this trail.
8.50	1.54	Right	**Archambault-Inderjit-De Graaf Trail (crushed limestone);** cycle through Archambault Park, across Grantsmuir and through Inderjit Claire Park. When the trail splits turn right, cycle across Reg Wyatt, through the greenspace and across Reg Wyatt again, through De Graaf Nature Reserve and exit to Concordia Avenue E.
10.04	0.26	Left	**Concordia Avenue E;** cycle past Reg Wyatt to Peguis Street.
10.30	1.53	Right	**Peguis Multi-use Path (asphalt);** cycle past Prairie Crocus, Ravelston, and El Tassi to Almey Avenue/Cal Gardner Drive. There is a multi-use path on the south side of Cal Gardner Drive.

		⚠	**Caution:** There is a small section, just before Ravelston where the multi-use path is interrupted and there is no sidewalk. Use caution till you get back to where the path resumes.
11.83	0.19	Left	**Cal Gardner Multi-use Path (asphalt);** cycle past the Prairie Landing apartment block and parking lot to the park path on your right.
12.02	0.36	Right	**Devonshire Park Path (asphalt);** cycle through the park keeping the pond to your left. The path exits onto the Transcona Trail.
12.38	6.41	Left	**Transcona Trail (asphalt);** cycle past the back of Club Regent and across Transcona Road. The trail then turns to the right, over the railway tracks and turns left. Cross Plessis, Hoka, Day and Redonda to the end of the trail which is almost at the Perimeter Highway. **Tim Hortons:** Located on Regent Avenue E near the beginning of the Transcona Trail. To get there, turn right when you exit Devonshire Park Path and cycle to the trailhead on Regent. Tim's is to your left. **Transcona Loop:** This loop is of the Transcona Trail only. Refer to Quick Notes for parking directions. The trail begins from Regent Avenue, just past Costco. Cycle to the end of the trail and U-turn and return to start. Distance – 13.4 km.
18.79	0.89	U-turn	**Transcona Trail (asphalt);** at the end of the trail, turn around. Before you cross the first street, the Cordite Trail East starts to your right. It is a dirt and grass trail and you will notice the start of the trail by the bench and some information signs at the trailhead. **Note:** If you enter this trail here, when you get to the first street, Redonda, you must go down and up through the ditch. If you wish to skip this, stay on the Transcona Trail to Redonda, then turn right to the continuation of this trail on your left.
19.68	1.66	Right	**Cordite Trail East (dirt/grass);** cycle across Redonda and continue on the trail. The trail does not continue to the next cross street, instead, there is a post at the end of the trail, at which point you turn left and head back to the Transcona Trail.

			Cordite Trail: This trail has signage about the cordite plant built here during the Second World War. A truly fascinating piece of Winnipeg's history.
21.34	1.38	Right	**Transcona Trail (asphalt);** cycle across Day Street and look for the entrance into Transcona Bioreserve. There is an opening in the fence and there is a small sign, but it can be easy to miss.
22.72	1.03	Right	**Transcona Bioreserve Trail (crushed limestone);** shortly after entering the bioreserve, the trail splits. You can either go right or left as the trail forms a loop through the reserve with an exit at the opposite end to Gunn Road. **Transcona Bioreserve:** Take a moment to listen for songbirds or frogs croaking and to enjoy the colourful foliage and fluttering butterflies.
23.75	0.97	Left	**Gunn Road;** this can be a very busy street. Cross to the north side and cycle on the paved shoulder to Plessis Road.
24.72	0.73	Right	**Plessis Road;** cycle past Grassie Boulevard and just before the ditch and the next road is the entrance to the Cordite Trail to your left. **Caution:** This short stretch requires caution. Traffic can be heavy on Plessis and although there is a shoulder, it is rough.
25.45	1.87	Left	**Cordite Trail West (dirt/grass);** follow this trail along the edge of the Cordite Ditch. It turns right to get around an off-shoot of the ditch and then turns left to get back to the edge of the Cordite Ditch and continues left. The trail exits to Ham Street.
27.32	0.09	Left	**Ham Street;** cycle to Chief Peguis Greenway Trail which intersects with Ham Street by the lights to cross Lagimodière Boulevard.
27.41	0.92	Right	**Chief Peguis Greenway Trail (asphalt);** cycle across Lagimodière Boulevard and continue straight. Just before the end of the trail and where the community fence begins, is an exit to the left to Springfield Road.

			***Pursuit* Art Installation:** Stop and take a look at these magnificent wolves depicted running in packs at the Lagimodière end of the trail.
28.33	2.61	Left	**Springfield Road;** cycle across Gateway, Raleigh, Rothesay, and across Henderson Highway to the sidewalk of the west side.
30.94	0.05	Left	**Henderson Highway;** cycle past the Cambrian Credit Union to the trail to your right. **Henderson Highway Coffee Stop Options:** If you would like to take a break, there are options both left and right on Henderson. Right is Tim Hortons and McDonald's and left is Pizza Hut and Salisbury House.
30.99	0.69	Right	**Bergen Cutoff Path (crushed limestone/dirt);** follow the path along the embankment and just before the end of the trail, it veers right and exits to Kildonan Drive.
31.68	0.27	Straight	**Kildonan Drive/Kildonan Parkway Trail (asphalt);** cycle to the end of Kildonan Drive and continue on Kildonan Parkway Trail to where it intersects with the Chief Peguis Greenway Trail just before the underpass for Kildonan Settlers Bridge.
31.95	1.01	Right	**Chief Peguis Greenway Trail (asphalt);** cycle to where the path splits and turn left and left again to cycle up and over the Kildonan Settlers Bridge. Just before Main Street the trail splits, turn left and continue to Kildonan Park Golf Course Trail.
32.96	0.83	Right	**Kildonan Park Golf Course Trail (crushed limestone)/Kildonan Park Trail (asphalt);** cycle behind the golf course and into Kildonan Park. The Kildonan Golf Course Trail is made of crushed limestone and when you pass the Golf Course, the trail is asphalt. This is the beginning of the Kildonan Park Trail. Take the second exit right from the trail, just after Lord Selkirk Creek, to Peguis Drive, by the Witch's Hut. **Caution:** There is a steep dip at the end of the trail as it exits to the road. **Chief Peguis Loop continued:** Follow the directions from this point to return to the start.

33.79	0.05	Left	**Peguis Drive;** the first street to your right is Lord Selkirk Drive.
33.84	0.41	Right	**Lord Selkirk Drive;** follow this road back to the parking lot.
34.25	0.17	Left	**Kildonan Park parking lot;** cycle through the lot to the southeast corner by the children's playground and to McKay Drive.
34.42	0	End	**McKay Drive.**

The bike will transform anyone
who is willing to let it happen.

— Ina-Yoko Teutenberg

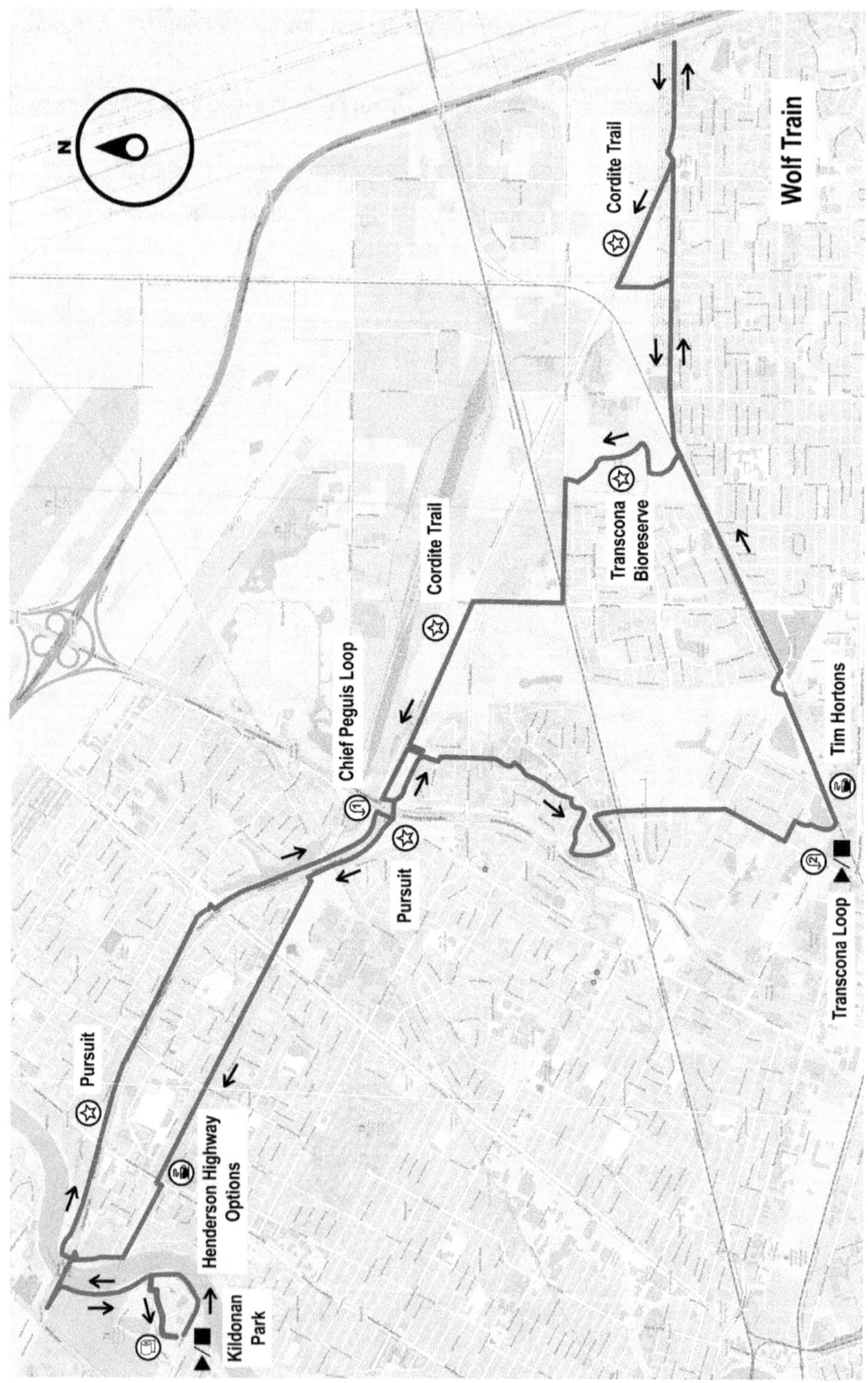
N
Wolf Train
Cordite Trail
Cordite Trail
Transcona Bioreserve
Transcona Loop
Tim Hortons
Chief Peguis Loop
Pursuit
Pursuit
Pursuit
Henderson Highway Options
Kildonan Park

Exchange Exploration

Northwest Winnipeg

The Exchange District is an interesting and unique part of Winnipeg. It extends from parts of Adelaide Street to the Red River and from James Avenue to Notre Dame Avenue. With 150 heritage buildings, it is recognized as a National Historic Site of Canada. This wealth of early 20th century structures of warehouses, office buildings, financial institutions and early skyscrapers, has made it a popular location for shooting films wanting to recreate that era.

The Exchange was Winnipeg's original downtown. Today it is an eclectic mixture of businesses, art galleries, shopping and restaurants. An example of some of the unique shops: Tiny Feast (stationary store), Toad Hall Toys (toy store), The Haberdashery (hat store) and Across the Boards (café where you can play board games). A complete listing of everything in the area, along with location and contact information can be found at https://www.exchangedistrict.org.

Exchange District

This ride starts in Assiniboine Park, heads north to Red River Community College and then east to the Exchange District with a little circle over the Disraeli Active Transportation Bridge and back over the Louise Bridge. The route continues back through the Exchange District to Ellen Street, through the downtown and eventually to Maryland Street and over the bridge to Wellington Crescent and back to Assiniboine Park. I chose this name because the ride goes through the Exchange District and all the way to its eastern edge as we cross the Disraeli; two of the three points of interest, plus one of the coffee stop suggestions, are in the Exchange; and, if you decide to stop and poke around a bit, it will be a true Exchange Exploration!

Forth

Although there are some bike paths on this route, much of the ride is on streets designated as Neighbourhood Greenways or low to medium stress roads, so it is quite an enjoyable ride.

I have two suggestions for coffee stops, Forth Café and The Tallest Poppy. Both are great places to stop. Forth Café, located at 171 McDermot Avenue, is close to the middle of the ride and can be visited before or after the loop

Tallest Poppy

around the Disraeli Active Transportation Bridge and Louise Bridge. Or, if you would like to wait a bit, The Tallest Poppy, at 103 Sherbrook Street, is closer to the end of the ride. If neither of these suggestions appeal to you, there are no shortages of other options in both areas where these two are located. Here are links for Forth Café and The Tallest Poppy. https://www.forth.ca/ and https://www.thetallest poppy.com/menu

There are three points of interest, each an art installation. The first, *Agassiz Ice*, is made up of three polished stainless-steel icebergs which grab your attention as you cross the Assiniboine River Park Bridge. The sculptures stand five metres at their tallest point, weigh 2000 kg, and are a nod to Lake Agassiz, a glacial lake which covered most of Manitoba in prehistoric times. The icebergs' changing reflection of light and landscape at different times of the day and year are the vision of the artist, Gordon Reeve, who wanted to suggest a sense of beginning and a moment of change.

The second, *Light Through* by Bernie Miller, is located along the Disraeli Active Transportation Bridge. *Light Through* consists of sixteen stainless steel structures showcasing historic photographs of the bridge and its surroundings. What makes the pictures unique is the artist developed software to translate the images into patterns of holes, which when light shines through them, gives a new perspective on the pictures.

The third art installation is what looks to be a streetcar embedded in the sidewalk outside the Pantages Theatre on Main and Market. You will have to take a short detour, detailed in the directions below, to see this work. Bernie Miller, the same person who did *Light Through*, and Noam Gonick, are the creators of this piece, entitled *Bloody Saturday*, and it is a nod to the events of the 1919 General Strike. This tilted and half-sunken, bronze and glass streetcar is set within footsteps of the location of the bloodiest clash during that strike. On Saturday, June 21, 1919, during a six-week strike of 30,000 workers, a large gathering of strikers and their supporters were demonstrating near city hall to protest the arrest of several of the strike leaders when a streetcar approached. The strikers were angry at the replacement workers hired to run the transit system in their place. Several in the crowd started to rock the streetcar and when unable to tip it over entirely, set it on fire. Mounties on horseback arrived and clashed with the strikers. Soon military personnel from Fort Osborne Barracks arrived with machine gun units. At the end of the encounter, two people died and 35 – 45 people, both strikers and police, had been injured. The day became known as *Bloody Saturday* and this art installment is an iconic image from that day. If you are interested in the strike, check out the link from the Canadian Encyclopedia for a more complete picture of all the events contributing to the strike and the final outcome.   https://www.thecanadianencyclopedia.ca/en/article/winnipeg-general-strike

Winnipeg General Strike

I hope you enjoy your exploration!

Quick Notes

Distance – 30.0 km

Parking –Assiniboine Park by the Duck Pond

Option to shorten – yes

> Exchange Loop – 12.5 km *For this loop, park on Pacific Avenue close to McPhillips Street

Bike repair station – Assiniboine Park between the Lyric Theatre and the Duck Pond

Suggested coffee stops – Forth Café located at 171 McDermot Avenue, The Tallest Poppy at 103 Sherbrook Street

Bathrooms – Assiniboine Park in the Duck Pond Shelter, coffee stop

Points of Interest –

> *Agassiz Ice* Art Installation in Assiniboine Park, north side of the Assiniboine River Park Bridge
>
> *Light Through* Art Installation on the Disraeli Active Transportation Bridge
>
> *Bloody Saturday* Art Installation at the corner of Main Street at Market Avenue

Trails

North Assiniboine Trail – asphalt

Berry Bike Path – asphalt

Sherwin Multi-use Path – asphalt

Pacific Industrial Trail – asphalt

North Winnipeg Parkway Trail – asphalt/crushed limestone

Disraeli Active Transportation Bridge – asphalt

Midwinter Multi-use Path – asphalt

Ernie O'Dowda Path – asphalt

Assiniboine Multi-use Path – asphalt

Wellington Multi-use Path – crushed limestone

Assiniboine Parkway Trail – asphalt

Safety Cautions

Detailed Directions

Km Total	Km Leg	Direction	Location, notes
0	0	Start	**Assiniboine River Park Bridge;** this is a pedestrian bridge located north of the duck pond. **Assiniboine Park:** Bathrooms are located in the Duck Pond Shelter which is open from 7am to 10pm. **Bike Repair Station:** Located between the Lyric Theatre and the Duck Pond, this is a good place to pump up your tires, if needed.
0	0.19	Straight	**Assiniboine River Park Bridge;** cross the bridge to the north side of the Assiniboine River. Once over the bridge, the trail splits three ways. *Agassiz Ice* **Art Installation:** Located just past the park bridge, this striking sculpture draws your attention.
0.19	1.45	Right	**North Assiniboine Trail (asphalt);** this is a collection of trails and streets all running along the north side of the Assiniboine River. As you cycle, you exit Assiniboine Park, continue straight on Deer Lodge Place, go through Bruce Park and over Truro Creek, exit right onto Douglas Park Road, cycle through Bourkevale Park and exit onto Assiniboine Avenue. There are bike route signs along the way. Cycle past Ferry, Collegiate, Roseberry, Parkview, Riveroaks, and Bourkevale to Cavell Drive.
1.64	0.38	Left	**Cavell Drive;** cycle to Portage Avenue.
2.02	0.03	Right	**Portage Avenue;** cycle to the lights at Berry Street.
2.05	2.98	Left	**Berry Bike Path (asphalt)/Berry Street;** just past Portage, a protected bike lane starts on the boulevard. Cycle across Ness, Silver and St. Matthews, at which point the lane on the boulevard ends and a painted bike lane continues on the street. Continue across Ellice, Sargent and Wellington to Saskatchewan Avenue. **Note:** Be mindful of pedestrians at the floating bus stop near Wellington.

5.03	0.25	Left	**Saskatchewan Avenue;** cycle to Sherwin Road and cross to the west side of the street to access the multi-use path.
5.28	1.24	Right	**Sherwin Multi-use Path (asphalt);** cycle over Omand's Creek and past Stevenson Road to Notre Dame Avenue.
6.52	0.33	Right	**Notre Dame Avenue;** cycle to King Edward Street.
6.85	0.11	Left	**King Edward Street;** cycle to the first block, McDermot Avenue West.
6.96	0.14	Right	**McDermot Avenue West;** cycle to Oddy Street.
7.10	0.41	Left	**Oddy Street;** cycle past Legion, Lismore, Bannatyne, and William to Elgin Avenue West.
7.51	1.54	Right	**Elgin Avenue West;** cycle past Juba, Keewatin, Worth, Cecil, and Langford streets to the end of Elgin at Jordan Street.
9.05	0.23	Left	**Jordan Street;** cycle along the edge of Pascoe Park to Pacific Avenue W/Pascoe Avenue.
9.28	0.14	Right	**Pascoe Avenue;** cycle along the edge of the park and then the road curves left, ending on Alexander Avenue.
9.42	0.44	Right	**Alexander Avenue;** cross Weston and Blaine to Winks Street.
9.86	0.06	Right	**Winks Street;** cycle across the back lane to the opening in the fence leading to the Pacific Industrial Trail.
9.92	0.71	Right	**Pacific Industrial Trail (asphalt);** cycle almost a complete circle around the pond. As heading back towards where you entered the trail, there is an exit trail to the right which runs along the fence, curves right and runs through the parking lot and exits to Pacific Avenue.
10.63	0.64	Left	**Pacific Avenue;** cycle across McPhillips to Xante Street. **Exchange Loop:** Refer to Quick Notes for parking directions. Start from this step and continue as follows until indicated below. Distance – 12.5 km.
11.27	0.07	Left	**Xante Street;** this street curves right where it becomes Alexander Avenue.

11.34	1.63	Right	**Alexander Avenue;** cycle across Arlington, Sherbrook and Salter to Princess Street.
12.97	0.58	Right	**Princess Street;** cycle in the bike lane on the east side of the street. It is a painted bike lane up to William and then becomes a protected bike lane. Cycle past Pacific, Ross, Elgin, William, and Bannatyne to McDermot Avenue.
13.55	0.77	Left	**McDermot Avenue;** cycle in the protected bike lane past King, Arthur, Albert, and Main Street. Continue past Rorie in the painted bike lane to Waterfront Drive. Cross Waterfront to access the North Winnipeg Parkway Trail on the east side boulevard of Waterfront. **Forth Café:** This popular coffee stop, in a gorgeous old building, is located on McDermot just past Main Street. You can stop here either at this time or on the way back.
14.32	1.19	Left	**North Winnipeg Parkway Trail (asphalt/crushed limestone);** follow the trail along the Red River through Steven Juba Park, past Cibo Waterfront Café and the Alexander Docks and through Fort Douglas Park. The trail curves right following the river and at this point becomes crushed limestone. Cycle to the end of the trail, just past Louis Bakó River Landing, to exit on Annabella Street.
15.51	0.62	Left	**Annabella Street;** cross Higgins and Sutherland to Rover Avenue.
16.13	0.09	Left	**Rover Avenue;** before the next street is the Disraeli Active Transportation Bridge, a cycling and pedestrian bridge, over the Red River.
16.22	0.21	Right	**Disraeli Active Transportation Bridge (asphalt);** cycle across the bridge to the Midwinter Multi-use Path. ***Light Through* Art Installation:** Notice the historic pictures of the bridge and surroundings in the stainless-steel structures located along the span of the Disraeli Active Transportation Bridge.

16.43	0.23	Right	**Midwinter Multi-use Path (asphalt);** cycle a short distance to Ernie O'Dowda Park and its park path.
16.66	0.35	Right	**Ernie O'Dowda Path (asphalt);** follow the path, which is part of the Kildonan Parkway, through the park to the exit on Stadacona Street at the Louise Bridge.
17.01	0.38	Right	**Louise Bridge/Higgens Avenue;** cycle over the Louise Bridge, at which point Stadacona Street changes to Higgins Avenue. Continue to the first street, Sutherland Avenue. **Note:** Louise Bridge is a narrow two-lane bridge. I would recommend crossing the bridge on the sidewalk.
17.39	0.51	Right	**Sutherland Avenue;** cycle past Angus, Stephens, Syndicate and McFarlane to the stop sign at Annabella Street.
17.90	0.34	Left	**Annabella Street;** cycle across Higgins to the entrance of the North Winnipeg Parkway Trail.
18.24	1.08	Right	**North Winnipeg Parkway Trail (asphalt/crushed limestone)/Waterfront Drive;** cycle the crushed limestone trail along the Red River. When you reach Waterfront Drive, the trail turns left and becomes an asphalt path through Fort Douglas Park, past the Alexander Docks and Cibo Waterfront Café, and Stephen Juba Park. The trail curves right to Waterfront Drive at the roundabout. Exit to the road to go around the right side of the roundabout and onto Bannatyne Avenue.
19.32	1.02	Right	**Bannatyne Avenue;** cycle in the painted bike lane to the first road, Rorie Street. Here you have three options: continue straight on with the route and perhaps stop in the Exhange District for shopping, turn right to take in a point of interest, or turn left for coffee. To continue on the route, cycle straight across Rorie, and continue in the protected bike lane across Main, Arthur, King, Princess, Adelaide, Hargrave and Dagmar to Ellen Street. ***Bloody Saturday* Art Installation:** To take in the sight of the burning tramway carriage, a nod to the 1919

			General Strike, turn right at Rorie Street, pass John Hirsch to Market Avenue. Turn left on Market and cycle to Main Street. The carriage is in front of the Pantages Playhouse Theatre at the corner of Market and Main. Once done, return to Rorie and Bannatyne and continue the ride. **Forth Café:** If you chose to skip this place when you first went by, you can go there now by turning left at Rorie and then cycle one block to McDermot and turn right. Once done, return to Rorie and Bannatyne and continue the route. **Exchange District:** Once across Main Street, you are in the heart of the Exchange District. There are a lot of unique shops in the area, well worth a look.
20.34	1.97	Left	**Ellen Street/Carlton Street;** cycle in the painted bike lane and cross Notre Dame at which point Ellen Street becomes Carlton Street. Cycle past Cumberland, Central Park, Qu'Appelle, Ellice, Portage, Graham, St. Mary, York and Broadway to Assiniboine Avenue. **Exchange Loop continued:** Turn right on Ellen Street and cycle across William to Elgin. Turn left and cycle to Ellen which continues to your right. Cycle across Ross and Pacific to Alexander. Turn left on Xante, right on Pacific and cross McPhillips Street to return to your car.
22.31	0.63	Right	**Assiniboine Avenue/Assiniboine Multi-use Path (asphalt);** cycle in the two-way protected bike lane on the south side of the road. The bike lane goes to Kennedy Street at which point you veer left onto Assiniboine Multi-use Path, cycle past the Riel Statue and then veer right towards Assiniboine Avenue and follow the trail across Assiniboine to the lights at Granite Way.
22.94	0.34	Left	**Granite Way;** cycle past the Granite Curling Club to Balmoral Street.
23.28	0.18	Left	**Balmoral Street;** cycle past Spence to Young Street.
23.46	0.11	Left	**Young Street;** cycle to the end of the road and at curve Young Street becomes Westminster Avenue.

23.57	0.37	Right	**Westminster Avenue;** cycle past Langside, Furby and Sherbrook to Maryland Street. **The Tallest Poppy:** This trendy eatery is located on Sherbrook Street just north of Westminster Avenue.
23.94	0.58	Left	**Maryland Street;** cycle over the Maryland Bridge to Wellington Crescent.
24.52	2.83	Right	**Wellington Crescent/Wellington Multi-use Path (crushed limestone);** after the first block, Wellington becomes divided with a centre boulevard which has a path. Cycle either on the street or the path. The centre boulevard stretches from Guelph to Lindsay Street. Pass Currie Park and look for the start of the Assiniboine Parkway Trail to your right. **Note:** Wellington Crescent, from Academy Road to Guelph Street, is designated as a Sunday/Holiday Bicycle Route, from 8am to 8pm, by the city of Winnipeg. This means, on those days, motor vehicle traffic is restricted to one block. **Water:** There are two water stops along this stretch. The first water stop is on the boulevard, close to where Guelph Street enters Wellington and a second water stop is in Andrew Currie Park, located on the south side of Wellington Crescent, just after the centre boulevard ends.
27.35	2.70	Right	**Assiniboine Parkway Trail (asphalt);** follow the trail back into Assiniboine Park. Once in the park the trail splits, turn right. Continue as the path runs along the edge of the Assiniboine River and returns to the Assiniboine River Park Bridge.
30.05	0	End	**Assiniboine River Park Bridge.**

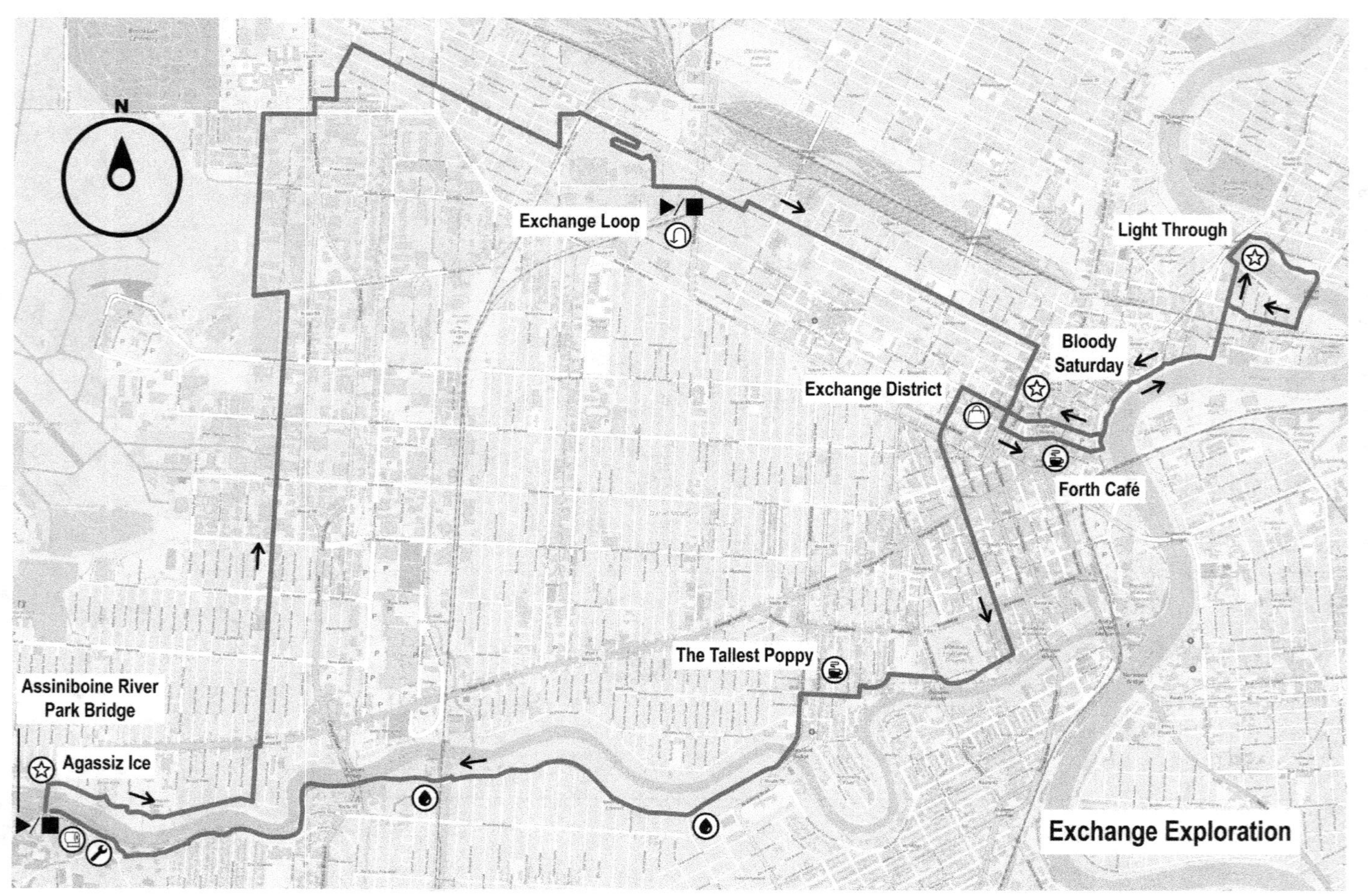

N
Exchange Loop
Light Through
Bloody Saturday
Exchange District
Forth Café
The Tallest Poppy
Assiniboine River Park Bridge
Agassiz Ice
Exchange Exploration

Saskatoon Pie

Northwest Winnipeg

This ride is meant to be done from mid-July to mid-August to take advantage of the peak season for saskatoon berries. Saskatoon bushes are abundant in Manitoba and are in many parks, one being Little Mountain Park. In case you are unaware of saskatoons, they are a berry similar in look to blueberries and grow in bunches on tall shrubs. This plant is related to the apple tree, and in describing the taste, some describe it as between a blueberry and an apple. The berries can be eaten as is, or served with cream or ice cream or made into wonderful pies or jams. If you decide to pick enough to go home and make them into a delicious pie, I have added my husband's favourite Saskatoon Pie recipe below. Now you know how I picked the name!

This route goes by Little Mountain Park specifically so you can stop and pick some saskatoons. From there, the route tours some of the countryside in the area before returning to Kildonan Park. Because most of this ride is on roads, be sure to wear reflective clothing.

If you will be picking berries, be sure to bring some mosquito spray because they can be vicious, and bring a container to put your berries in so they don't get squished. The bushes are easy to spot along the walking trails. Chances are you will see others picking while in the park, but if not, and you are unsure of what saskatoons look like, visit the Saskatoon Berry Institute website. http://www. saskatoonberryinstitute.org/saskatoons/

If you're not picking berries, this is simply a nice ride which spans between city streets and a touch of country roads.

Happy eating!

Quick Notes
Distance – 32.1 km
Parking – Kildonan Park at 2015 Main Street, park in lot by the Chief Peguis Pavilion
Option to shorten – yes
    Amber Trails Loop – 18.9 km
Suggested coffee stop – Tim Hortons at 2360 McPhillips Avenue
Bathrooms – Kildonan Park in Chief Peguis Pavilion, Walmart at 2370 McPhillips
    Avenue
Point of Interest –
    Saskatoon Picking at Little Mountain Park

Trails

Ambergate Park Path – asphalt
Morava Multi-use Path – asphalt
Foxwarren Lake Path – asphalt
Chief Peguis Greenway Trail – asphalt
Kildonan Park Golf Course Trail – crushed limestone
Kildonan Park Trail – asphalt

Safety Cautions

Detailed Directions

Km Total	Km Leg	Direction	Location, notes
0	0	Start	**McKay Drive;** this ride starts on McKay Drive by the children's playground at the southeast corner of Kildonan Park parking lot. **Kildonan Park:** Bathrooms are in the lower level of the Chief Peguis Pavilion located just off the parking lot. They are open daily from 8am to 9pm.
0	0.14	Left	**McKay Drive;** cycle to the first exit to the left, Scotia Street, which leaves the park.
0.14	0.32	Right	**Scotia Street;** exit the park and continue straight on Scotia, past Armstrong and Newton, to Leila Avenue.
0.46	1.11	Right	**Leila Avenue;** cycle across Marymound, Main and Aikins to Salter Street.
1.57	0.49	Right	**Salter Street;** cycle to the four-way stop sign at Templeton Avenue.
2.06	0.41	Left	**Templeton Avenue;** cycle across the railway tracks to the first street to your right, Ferrier Street.
2.47	0.18	Right	**Ferrier Street;** cycle to Beecher Avenue.
2.65	1.44	Left	**Beecher Avenue;** cycle past Diplomat and Sinclair, Tokarz Park, and Yanofsky to Drimes Place.

4.09	0.16	Left	**Drimes Place;** cycle to Templeton Avenue.
4.25	0.92	Right	**Templeton Avenue/Service Road;** cycle straight across McPhillips Street and stay on the service road as it curves left behind Walmart and ends at Court Avenue. **Walmart:** Bathrooms are located inside, at the front of the store.
5.17	1.08	Right	**Court Avenue/Ambergate Drive;** cycle straight across Pipeline at which point Court Avenue becomes Ambergate Drive. This road ends at Amber Trails and across this street is Ambergate Park Path.
6.25	1.42	Straight	**Ambergate Park Path (asphalt);** cycle along the edge of a pond through Ambergate Park, cross Novara and continue straight through the greenspace, do not turn off. Cross Danube Drive, cycle along the edge of a pond and exit to Strasbourg Drive.
7.67	0.15	Left	**Strasbourg Drive;** cycle to the first street, Morava Way, and cross to access Morava Multi-use Path.
7.82	0.76	Right	**Morava Multi-use Path (asphalt);** cycle to next corner, Massalia, and the path crosses diagonally to the other side of Morava and continues along the edge of a pond, across Lakebourne and exits to Amberstone Road.
8.58	0.31	Left	**Amberstone Road/Ritchie Street;** cycle past Leila, at which point Amberstone Road becomes Ritchie Street. Cycle to the next street, Foxwarren Drive. **Amber Trails Loop;** when exit trail, turn left on Amberstone Road, cycle to first street, Morava Way. Turn left on Morava and cycle across Massalia and Strasbourg. Once past Strasbourg, Morava Way becomes Tessler Bay. The street curves to the right and exits on Amber Trail. Stay on Amber Trail till Ambergate Drive, turn right. Cross Pipeline, at which point, Ambergate Drive becomes Court Avenue.

			Continue, where indicated below, to return to start. Distance – 18.9 km.
8.89	0.13	Right	**Foxwarren Drive;** cycle to the greenspace and the Foxwarren Lake Path.
9.02	0.49	Left	**Foxwarren Lake Path (asphalt);** cycle along the edge of Foxwarren Lake and exit to Foxwarren Drive at Burnside Way. **Note:** There is no break in the curb from the street leading to the path.
9.51	0.11	Straight	**Burnside Way;** cycle to the stop sign at Jefferson Avenue.
9.62	4.34	Right	**Jefferson Avenue/Farmer Road;** stay on Jefferson past Dr. Jose Rizal, King Edward and Brookside Boulevard/Route 90. Once past Brookside, Jefferson becomes Farmer Road. Cycle past Mountainview, Wheatfield and Little Mountain Park to Klimpke Road. **Saskatoon Picking:** Stop at Little Mountain Park and pick some saskatoons to either eat on the spot or take home and serve with cream or ice cream or perhaps make a pie or jam. Saskatoons are in season from mid-July to mid-August. Enjoy!
13.96	1.61	Right	**Klimpke Road;** cycle to Road 66/Mollard Road.
15.57	6.77	Right	**Road 66/Mollard Road;** cross Brookside/Route 90 and King Edward to Pipeline Road.
22.34	1.75	Right	**Pipeline Road;** pass Storie and Templeton to the four-way stop sign at Court Avenue.
24.09	1.46	Left	**Court Avenue/Service Road;** cycle to the service road just before Walmart and turn left. The road curves right and heads to the lights at McPhillips. Cross McPhillips and now the service road becomes Templeton Avenue. **Tim Hortons;** If you are not full from the saskatoons, you can stop at the Tim's located at 2360 McPhillips Street. To get there, before crossing McPhillips, turn right at the at the parking area for McMunn and Yates and Tim Hortons is located past a lane, next to this lot.

		↻	When done, return to McPhillips and Templeton to continue. **Amber Trails Loop continued:** Follow directions from this point on to return to start of ride.
25.55	0.25	Straight	**Templeton Avenue;** cycle past Holiday Place to Drimes Place/Meredith Bay.
25.80	0.16	Left	**Drimes Place;** cycle to Beecher Avenue.
25.96	1.42	Right	**Beecher Avenue;** cycle past Yanofsky, Tokarz Park, Sinclair and Diplomat to Ferrier Street.
27.38	1.21	Left	**Ferrier Street;** cycle to Murray Avenue.
28.59	0.91	Right	**Murray Avenue;** cycle past Carsdale to Endcliffe Place.
29.50	0.09	Right	**Endcliffe Place;** cycle one block to Frog Plain Way.
29.59	0.09	Left	**Frog Plain Way;** cycle to the greenspace and access to Chief Peguis Greenway Trail.
29.68	0.93	Right	**Chief Peguis Greenway Trail (asphalt);** cycle through the park, across Main and turn right to cross Chief Peguis. The trail splits, turn left. Cycle past the two turnoffs to the left and continue towards the river and to Kildonan Park Golf Course Trail.
30.61	0.83	Right	**Kildonan Park Golf Course Trail (crushed limestone)/Kildonan Park Trail (asphalt);** cycle behind the golf course and into Kildonan Park. The Kildonan Golf Course Trail is made of crushed limestone and when you pass the Golf Course, the trail is asphalt. This is the beginning of the Kildonan Park Trail. Take the second exit right from the trail, just after Lord Selkirk Creek, to Peguis Drive, by the Witch's Hut. **Caution:** There is a steep dip at the end of the trail as it exits to the road.
31.44	0.05	Left	**Peguis Drive;** the first street to your right is Lord Selkirk Drive.
31.49	0.41	Right	**Lord Selkirk Drive;** follow this road back to the parking lot.

31.90	0.17	Left	**Kildonan Park parking lot;** cycle through the lot to the southeast corner by the children's playground and to McKay Drive.
32.07	0	End	**McKay Drive.**

Saskatoon Pie
Recipe by Sanford Larson

This recipe is for two 9-inch double-crust pies. I tend to make my crust less fatty and the filling less sugary, than usual, resulting in a relatively healthy, but still delicious pie.

Ingredients:
- Pastry – use your own recipe or mine as below
- 8 cups (approx. 1 kg.) saskatoon berries
- ½ cup sugar
- 2 tbsp flour
- 1 tsp cinnamon (optional)
- 2 tbsp lemon juice

Instructions:
1. Place the bottom crusts in two 9-inch pie plates. Trim edges.
2. Place 4 cups of berries in each pie. Mix sugar, flour and cinnamon and pour half of the mixture over berries in each pie. Sprinkle 1 Tbsp of lemon juice over berries in each pie.
3. Moisten the rims of crusts. Place the top crusts on each pie, crimp-seal around the edges and trim. Make a small hole in the centre top to let the steam escape.
4. Bake in 350 F oven for 45 minutes, or until the pies look done.
5. Serve as is or with ice cream.

Pastry
Ingredients:
- 2 ½ cup plain flour
- 2/3 cups (approx.) margarine or other shortening
- 1 large egg (or 2 egg whites)
- 1 Tbsp. vinegar

Instructions:

1. Knead the flour with sufficient margarine to make a fairly dry loose crumble.
2. Add the egg and vinegar, and knead to a stiff dough. Add a splash of water, if required, to knead to a rollable pastry.
3. Divide into four parts. Roll out two top and two bottom crusts.

Enjoy!

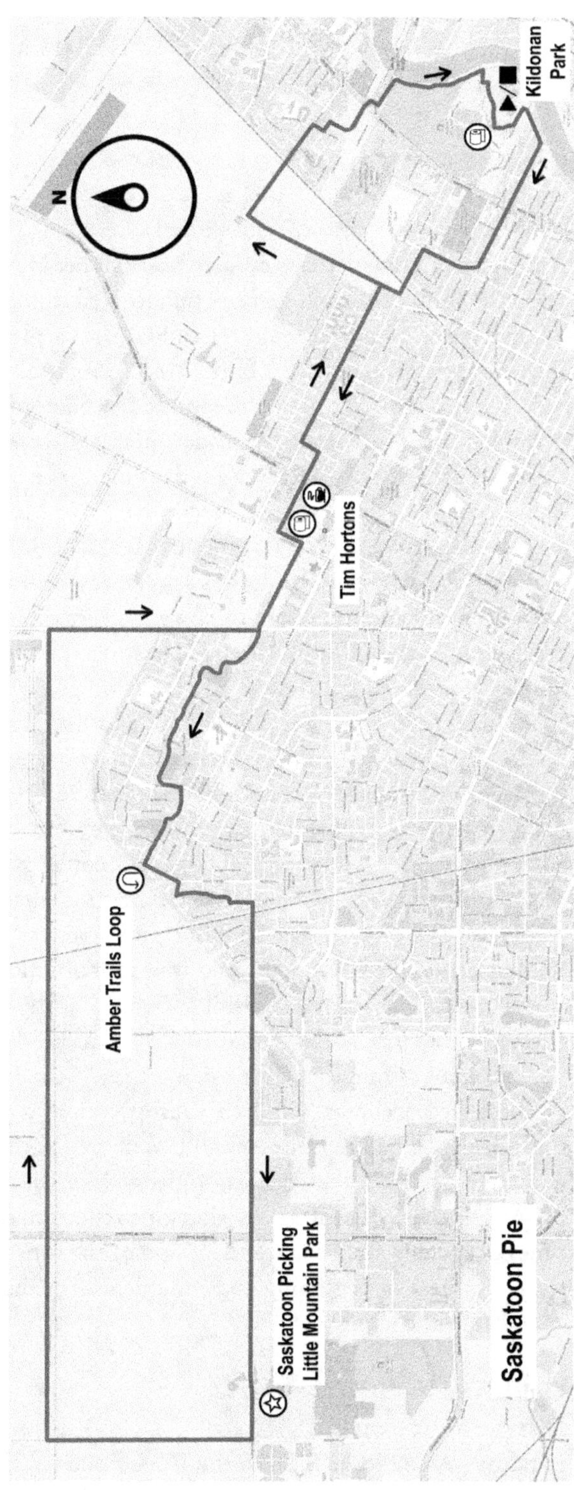

Two Mountain Climb

Northwest Winnipeg

I can already hear the question you're asking, "What mountains?" I concede, it is a bit of a stretch, perhaps even an outright lie. However, we do have a big hill, kind of, in the form of the old garbage hill, located in the west end of the city, now called Westview Park. For the second "mountain", since I couldn't think of another big hill, I decided to use our steepest bridge, the Arlington Street Overpass.

I was tempted to name this route the Sanford-Craig Trail, only because these two small streets are along the route and my husband's name is Sanford and my son's name is Craig. I thought it was a neat coincidence but realized that name would only mean something to me, so the descriptive, Two Mountain Climb, won.

Be sure to stop for a few minutes when at the top of both "mountains" to take in the views. Westview Park offers a great view of the west end of the city and the Arlington Street Overpass offers a good view of the CP rail yards. Interestingly, Westview Park is considered an historic site in Winnipeg. At one time, this spot was the city dump and has had an interesting history. If you would like to know more about it, check out this page by the Manitoba Historical Society, http://www.mhs.mb.ca/docs/sites/winnipegdump.shtml

There are a few opportunities for a coffee stop on this ride. If you are worn out after the first mountain, you can get sustenance at the corner of Keewatin Street and Burrows Avenue, where you can choose between Starbucks or A&W. Or you could wait till both mountains are climbed and stop for a break on the way back at Freshii or Subway at the corner of St. James Street and St. Matthews Avenue.

A point of interest for this ride is the *Agassiz Ice* art installation. Three polished stainless-steel icebergs will grab your attention as you cross the Assiniboine River Park Bridge. The sculptures stand five metres at their tallest point, weigh 2000 kg, and are a nod to Lake Agassiz, a glacial lake which covered most of Manitoba in prehistoric times. The icebergs' changing reflection of light and landscape at different times of the day and year are the vision of the artist, Gordon Reeve, who wanted to suggest a sense of beginning and a moment of change.

Enjoy the climb!

Quick Notes
Distance – 29.9 km
Parking – Assiniboine Park by the Duck Pond

Option to shorten – yes
    Westview Loop – 16.4 km
Bike repair station – Assiniboine Park between the Lyric Theatre and the Duck Pond
Suggested coffee stops – Starbucks in the Safeway in Tyndall Square at 850 Keewatin Street, A&W at 817 Keewatin Street, Freshii or Subway at 900 St. James Street
Bathrooms – Assiniboine Park in the Duck Pond Shelter, Tyndall Square at 850 Keewatin Street, coffee stops
Point of Interest –
    Agassiz Ice Art Installation in Assiniboine Park, north side of the Assiniboine River Park Bridge

Trails

North Assiniboine Trail – crushed limestone/asphalt
Westview Park Path – crushed limestone/asphalt
Keewatin-Park Lane Link Path – asphalt
Albina Park Path – asphalt
Yellow Ribbon Greenway Trail – asphalt

Safety Cautions

Detailed Directions

Km Total	Km Leg	Direction	Location, notes
0	0	Start	**Assiniboine River Park Bridge, north of the duck pond.** **Assiniboine Park:** Bathrooms are located in the Duck Pond Shelter which is open from 7am to 10pm. **Bike Repair Station:** Located between the Lyric Theatre and the Duck Pond, this is a good place to pump up your tires, if needed.
0	0.18	Straight	**Assiniboine River Park Bridge;** cross the bridge to the north side of the Assiniboine River and to the North Assiniboine Trail.

		★	***Agassiz Ice* Art Installation:** Located just past the park bridge, this striking sculpture will draw your attention.
0.18	3.72	Right	**North Assiniboine Trail (crushed limestone/asphalt)/Wolseley Avenue;** this is a collection of trails and streets which connect and run along the north side of the Assiniboine River. The trail exits Assiniboine Park onto Deer Lodge Place, through Bruce Park, onto Douglas Park Road, through Bourkevale Park and onto Assiniboine Avenue. Assiniboine curves left and becomes Parkside Drive. Before Parkside curves left, take the continuation of the North Assiniboine Trail to the right as it goes along the edge of Jae Eadie Park. The trail exits onto Riverbend Crescent which curves to the left. Just before Portage, turn right onto Wolseley Avenue W. Wolseley curves right and then left past Herzing College. The road continues under the Route 90 Bridge and continues straight, ending at the St. James Cemetery. Cycle on the trail which runs behind the cemetery and continues along the edge of the river into Omand Park and Halter Park and then curves left and climbs up to and exits at Wolseley Avenue. Cycle one block to Craig Street.
3.90	0.32	Left	**Craig Street;** cycle to Portage Avenue.
4.22	0.04	Right	**Portage Avenue;** cycle half a block to Valour Road.
4.26	0.07	Left	**Valour Road;** cross at the lights and cycle to the back lane behind the businesses on Portage Avenue.
4.33	0.22	Right	**Back lane of Portage Avenue;** cycle past Bruce and the back of Taco Bell to Clifton Street.
4.55	1.91	Left	**Clifton Street;** cycle across St. Matthews, Ellice and Sargent to Wellington Avenue.

6.46	0.41	Left	**Wellington Avenue;** cycle past Spruce, Valour, Ashburn and Strathcona to the back lane of Strathcona Street.
6.87	0.38	Left	**Back lane of Strathcona Street;** cycle to Sargent Avenue.
7.25	0.19	Right	**Sargent Avenue;** cycle across the railroad tracks to Sanford Street.
7.44	0.38	Right	**Sanford Street;** cycle to the end of the street to Wellington Avenue.
7.82	0.08	Left	**Wellington Street;** before the first street is an entrance road into Westview Park.
7.90	0.84	Right	**Westview Park Path (asphalt/crushed limestone);** cycle up the road to the top of the mountain (hill) and then down the other side on the crushed limestone trail to exit onto Midland Street. **Westview Loop:** At the top of Westview Park hill, turn around and head back down exiting to Wellington. To retrace the steps back to Clifton Street, turn left at Wellington, right at Sanford, left at Sargent, left at the back lane of Strathcona, and right at Wellington to Clifton Street. Continue, where indicated below, to return to start. Distance – 16.4 km.
8.74	0.33	Straight	**Midland Street;** cycle to the parking lot entrance of the Canadiana Motor Inn, just before Notre Dame Avenue. Note: There is a sign for Canadiana Thriftlodge at the entrance into the parking lot.
9.07	0.12	Right	**Parking lot of Canadiana Motor Inn;** turn into the parking lot and turn left to cycle past the inn to reach Notre Dame Avenue. At this spot, Flint Street intersects with Notre Dame and there is a street light.
9.19	0.44	Straight	**Flint Street;** cross Notre Dame at the lights and cycle on Flint till ends at William Avenue W.
9.63	0.12	Left	**William Avenue W;** cycle to the first road, Langford Street.
9.75	0.08	Right	**Langford Street;** cycle to Elgin Avenue W.

9.83	0.98	Left	**Elgin Avenue W;** cycle across Cecil, Worth and Keewatin to Juba Street.
10.81	0.28	Right	**Juba Street;** cycle to the end of the street at Alexander Avenue.
11.09	0.21	Left	**Alexander Avenue;** cycle over railroad tracks to Dee Street.
11.30	0.16	Right	**Dee Street;** cycle across Logan to Gallagher Avenue W.
11.46	0.27	Right	**Gallagher Avenue W;** cycle past Midmar to Keewatin Street.
11.73	0.39	Left	**Keewatin Street;** stay on the sidewalk, go under the railroad track and just before the entrance into the first parking lot is the Keewatin-Park Lane Link Path.
12.12	2.19	Left	**Keewatin-Park Lane Link Path (asphalt)/Park Lane Avenue/King Edward Street;** cycle up the incline on the link path and exit to Park Lane. Continue straight as Park Lane curves around Woodsworth Park to Selkirk. Cross Selkirk and Park Lane becomes King Edward Street. Cycle across Manitoba, past Tyndall Park Community School and across Burrows to access the Albina Park Path.
14.31	0.69	Straight	**Albina Park Path (asphalt);** cycle along the edge of the pond and when the trail splits at the end of the pond, veer right and when splits a second time, veer right again and exit to Albina Way.
15.00	0.49	Right	**Albina Way;** cycle past Raber to Burrows Avenue.
15.49	2.50	Left	**Burrows Avenue;** cycle across Keewatin and Sheppard, and past Lawrence to Shaughnessy Street. **Starbucks or A&W:** Coffee or a burger? These two choices are across the street from each other at Keewatin Street. Starbucks is located in the Safeway in Tyndall Square. **Public Bathroom:** A public bathroom is located in Tyndall Square.
17.99	0.25	Right	**Shaughnessy Street;** cycle past Magnus and Manitoba to Pritchard Avenue.

18.24	1.85	Left	**Pritchard Avenue;** cross McNichol, McPhillips, Sgt. Tommy Prince, Battery and Sinclair to Arlington Street.
20.09	2.21	Right	**Arlington Street;** straight ahead is the second mountain, the Arlington Street Overpass. Cycle on the street to the bridge and then cycle over the bridge. Cross Logan and continue straight, on the road, past the National Microbiology Laboratory, across William, past Burton Cummings Community Centre, across Notre Dame Avenue and past St. Edward the Confessor Church to Adele Avenue. **Caution:** Use caution coming down the bridge. **Note:** I recommend cycling on the sidewalk. I have never seen a bike in the traffic lane on the bridge as it is very narrow.
22.30	0.09	Right	**Adele Avenue;** cycle one block to Alverstone Street.
22.39	0.23	Left	**Alverstone Street;** cycle to Wellington Avenue.
22.62	1.10	Right	**Wellington Avenue;** cycle past Daniel McIntyre Collegiate Institute, the stop sign at Garfield, past Sargent Park, Wall and Erin to Clifton Street.
23.72	1.15	Left	**Clifton Street;** cycle across Sargent and Ellice to St. Matthews Avenue. **Westview Loop continued:** Continue from this step to return to start. **Note:** Because you approach Clifton from the opposite direction, turn right onto Clifton.
24.87	2.35	Right	**St. Matthews Avenue;** this street has a combination of a painted bike lane and once past Route 90, a protected bike lane. Stay on St. Matthews past the Polo Park area and Route 90 to its end at Ferry Road. Cross Ferry to access the Yellow Ribbon Greenway. **Freshii or Subway:** Both are located side by side at the corner of St. Matthews Avenue and St. James Street.

27.22	0.96	Straight	**Yellow Ribbon Greenway Trail (asphalt);** follow the trail as it curves left, skirts the edge of the St. James Memorial Sports Park and curves right at Silver Avenue. Cycle past the Community Gardens and one block before the end of Silver is Linwood Street.
28.18	0.73	Left	**Linwood Street;** cycle across Ness to Bruce Avenue.
28.91	0.20	Right	**Bruce Avenue;** cycle past Winchester to Overdale Street.
29.11	0.54	Left	**Overdale Street;** cycle across Portage to Assiniboine Park and the trail straight ahead.
29.65	0.25	Straight	**North Assiniboine Trail (asphalt, crushed limestone);** cycle straight to go over the Assiniboine River Park Bridge.
29.90	0	End	**Assiniboine River Park Bridge.**

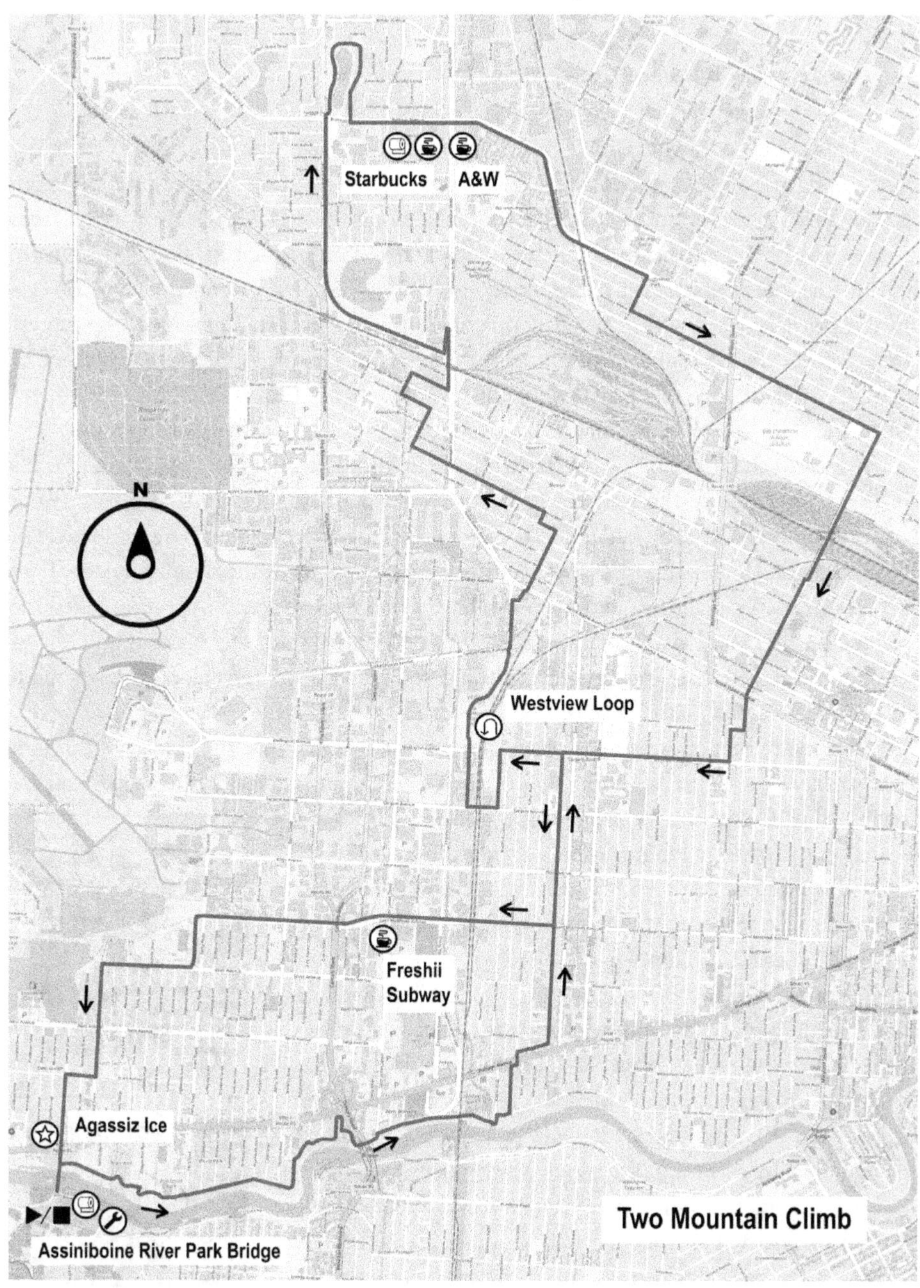
N
Starbucks   A&W
Westview Loop
Freshii
Subway
Agassiz Ice
Two Mountain Climb
Assiniboine River Park Bridge

Cottonwood Trail

North and Central Winnipeg

This is a pleasant ride which mostly follows the banks of the Red River. Part of the route, along the Brooks and Towering Cottonwood trails, run through a river bottom forest. What's a river bottom forest? It's a forest along the edge of the river where trees are sustained by the deposit of nutrient rich silt from annual spring floods. In return, healthy tree roots stabilize the banks reducing erosion. Willows, maples and cottonwoods are the primary trees which grow in this environment, and in Winnipeg, the largest cottonwoods can be found here. Because of this fact, I named this ride in honour of them. Of note, if you are a bird watcher, be on the lookout for eagles, in the spring and fall, as the Red River is along their migration route.

Many of the trails in this ride have several names. For example, the system of trails along the west side of the Red River, from Chief Peguis to The Forks are part of the North Winnipeg Parkway and when you cross the Norwood Bridge to the other side of the river is the Boni-Vital Parkway. Both sides are also part of the Trans Canada Trail and smaller sections of these parkways also have a trail name. Generally, I have called the sections by their trail name or by some other descriptive name to make it as clear as possible in the detailed directions. But should you see various signs along the way with different names, that is the reason.

There are two options for a coffee stop on this route. Since the ride goes through The Forks, it is a natural stopping point which offers many choices for whatever you are craving. But if you want to wait till the finish, an A&W is located in the parking lot at the end of the ride.

This ride has many points of interest. Most are a quick stop to look at something, but there is also a park and two museums worthy of a stop.

Seven Oaks House Museum is a two-story log dwelling and is a designated Provincial Heritage Site. Built from 1851-5, it is the oldest house in Winnipeg. The museum, with many period artifacts, depicts what life would have been like in the Red River Settlement in the 19th century. Admission is by donation. http://www.sevenoakshouse.ca

Fort Gibraltar is a replica of the North West Company fur trading post which was originally built in 1809-10. The purpose of this historical museum is to commemorate the early history of Western Canada when fur trading was the main industry. Entering Fort Gibraltar is like stepping back in time; interpreters are dressed in period costumes creating

Seven Oaks House

Fort Gibraltar

characters who lived there in 1815. A guided tour can be taken which recounts the fort's historical significance. https://www.fortgibraltar.com/en/

St. John's Park, located on Main Street, at Mountain Avenue, has a colourful history. The land was purchased from the Anglican Church for $15,000 by the Winnipeg Parks Board in 1893. At the time, it was located in the suburbs of Winnipeg. When the city took possession, the land was wild, but soon afterwards was transformed with a formal garden in the shape of a six-pointed star with radiating pathways and a wooden bandstand was built. More information on the park's history, with pictures, is located at the northwest corner of the park on some information boards. St. John's Park is also home to the Healing Forest, a memorial to Indigenous children lost to the residential school system, missing and murdered Indigenous women and girls, and Indigenous children lost in the child welfare system. It is located on the north side of the park, west of the wading pool. It is a circular learning space with several huge rocks with Aboriginal artwork surrounding the circle. The Healing Forest is meant to be a place where those who have been affected can come for reflection, meditation and healing.

The Oodena Celebration Circle is located at The Forks. The word Oodena is Ojibwe for "heart of the community". This natural amphitheatre was designed to pay homage to 6,000 years of Aboriginal peoples in the area. The Celebration Circle features ethereal sculptures, a sundial, interpretive signage, a naked eye observatory and a ceremonial fire pit. https://www.theforks.com/attractions/oodena-celebration-circle

Oodena Circle

Phare Ouest, which translates to west lighthouse, is an art installation on the pedestrian belvédère, a 100-metre-long walkway, suspended off the Tache Promenade. This stainless steel with LED lighting installation is by Marcel Gosselin. Gosselin's inspiration for this piece came from an event in 1844 when Bishop Provencher waited along the riverbank at night, with a lantern in hand, for the arrival of four members of the Grey Nuns order from Montreal. Inscribed on the ground next to the sculpture is a quote from Gabrielle Roy's 1945 novel, *The Tin Flute*: "Where could you find a light to guide the world?" While at the lookout, take in the great views of The Forks, the Canadian Museum of Human Rights, Riel Esplanade and the downtown skyline. http://winnipegarts.ca/wac/artwork/phare-ouest-far-west

Phare Ouest

Life Journey is an art installation located along the Northeast Pioneers Greenway Trail. These colourful glass tile mosaic sculptures, created by Denise Préfontaine with the Kildonan-East Collegiate Girls' Club, captures the stages of growth and transformation in a butterfly's life cycle.

Lots to see, enjoy!

Quick Notes
Distance – 32.2 km
Parking – Parking lot at the corner of Main Street and Red River Boulevard
Option to shorten –
    Forks Loop – 22.5 km
Suggested coffee stops – The Forks, A&W at 2585 Main Street
Washrooms – Sobeys or A&W at the corner of Main Street and Red River Boulevard,
    the Pavilion in Kildonan Park, St. John's Park, The Forks, Whittier Park at 836
    Rue Saint Joseph, coffee stop
Points of Interest –
    Seven Oaks House Museum at 50 Mac Street
    St. John's Park on Main Street at Mountain Avenue
    Oodena Celebration Circle at The Forks
    Phare Ouest Art Installation on the pedestrian belvédère along Tache Avenue
    Fort Gibraltar at 866 Rue Saint Joseph in Whittier Park
    Life Journey Art Installation along the Northeast Pioneers Greenway Trail

Trails
Rivergrove Park Path – asphalt
Brooks Trail – asphalt
Towering Cottonwood Trail – crushed limestone/woodchip
River Ridge-River Grove Link Path – crushed limestone
Scotia Street Link Path – crushed limestone
Chief Peguis Greenway Trail – asphalt
Kildonan Golf Course Park Trail – crushed limestone
Kildonan Park Trail – asphalt
St. John's-Redwood-Aberdeen Park Path – asphalt/crushed limestone
Alfred-Burrows Link Path – crushed limestone
North Winnipeg Parkway Trail – crushed limestone
Old St. Boniface Route – crushed limestone/asphalt
Sentier La Liberté Trail – asphalt/crushed limestone
Montcalm-Nairn Overpass Parks Path – dirt/asphalt
Northeast Pioneers Greenway Trail – asphalt
Kildonan Parkway Trail – asphalt

Safety Cautions

Detailed Directions

Km total	Km Leg	Direction	Location, notes
0	0	Start	**Parking lot at Main Street and Red River Boulevard.** **Sobeys or A&W:** Bathrooms are located in both these locations.
0	0.32	Left	**Red River Boulevard;** exit parking lot and cycle past Knotwood to River Grove Drive.
0.32	0.37	Left	**River Grove Drive;** cycle past McBeth Park and Summerview to Rivergrove Park.
0.69	0.30	Right	**Rivergrove Park Path (asphalt);** follow the path through the park and exit to Summerview Lane.
0.99	0.06	Right	**Summerview Lane;** at the curve left, between houses, #78 and #82, is Brooks Trail.
1.05	1.09	Left	**Brooks Trail (asphalt)/Towering Cottonwood Trail (crushed limestone/woodchip);** follow Brooks Trail as it runs along the river edge of McBeth Park. When the trail curves to the right, away from the river, look for a woodchip trail which continues straight, this is the Towering Cottonwood Trail. Follow the Cottonwood Trail through the river bottom forest and when it emerges, look for a small trail to the right which leads straight up to River Ridge Drive and the River Ridge-Rivergrove Link Path.
2.14	0.20	Straight	**River Ridge-River Grove Link Path (crushed limestone);** cycle across River Ridge to the link path and to River Grove Drive.
2.34	0.49	Left	**River Grove Drive/Ridgecrest Avenue;** cycle past River Ridge and when the road curves right, River Grove Drive becomes Ridgecrest Avenue. Cycle to the first street, Scotia Street.
2.83	0.37	Left	**Scotia Street/Scotia Street Link Path (crushed limestone)/Scotia Street;** Scotia Street is not continuous, but there is a link path from one part of the street to the next. At the end of Scotia, to your left, is access to Chief Peguis Greenway Trail.

3.20	0.32	Straight	**Chief Peguis Greenway Trail (asphalt);** follow the trail under the Kildonan Settlers Bridge to the south side of Chief Peguis. The trail curves right and splits before Main Street. At the split turn left and just before the river the trail turns right onto Kildonan Golf Course Park Trail.
3.52	1.36	Right	**Kildonan Golf Course Park Trail (crushed limestone)/Kildonan Park Trail (asphalt);** follow the trail along the Red River as it goes behind the golf course. Once past the golf course, the trail becomes the Kildonan Park Trail and continues along the edge of the river and exits onto Scotia Street within the park. **Kildonan Park:** Bathrooms are in the lower level of the Chief Peguis Pavilion located just off the parking lot. They are open daily from 8am to 9pm.
4.88	0.29	Left	**Scotia Street;** exit the park and continue straight, past Armstrong and Newton to Leila Avenue.
5.17	0.34	Right	**Leila Avenue;** cycle to Marymound Way.
5.51	0.15	Left	**Marymound Way;** cycle to street end at Forest Avenue.
5.66	2.46	Left	**Forest Avenue/Scotia Street;** Forest Avenue curves right and becomes Scotia Street. Stay on Scotia until it ends at Cathedral Avenue. **Seven Oaks House Museum:** turn right on Rupertsland Boulevard which runs into Mac Street and the Museum. There is a sign on Scotia indicating the museum.
8.12	0.17	Right	**Cathedral Avenue;** cycle one block to St. Cross Street.
8.29	0.45	Left	**St. Cross Street;** just before St. Cross turns right and becomes Anderson Avenue, is a bike trail into St. John's Park.
8.74	0.69	Left	**St. John's-Redwood-Aberdeen Park Path (asphalt/crushed limestone);** this trail is part of the North Winnipeg Parkway and runs along the Red River at the back of St. John's Park.

			Near the end of the park, at the southeast corner, the trail splits. Veer left and go under the Redwood Bridge, through Redwood Park and Aberdeen Playground and exit onto Alfred Avenue. Cross Alfred and between houses #146 and #150 is a link path to Burrows Avenue. **Note:** If the river is flooding the path, there are two alternatives to get to the next segment: 1. If the water is not too high, you can still exit at the same point from St. John's Park towards the river but rather than going down next to the river, when the path slits, take the path which veers back up, before the bridge, towards a parking area. From here, cross Redwood and continue straight on the path as it merges with the path which went under the bridge. 2. At the point where you would exit St. John's Park towards the river, instead, follow the trail as it curves right towards Main Street. At Main, turn right, cycle past Holy Trinity Ukrainian Orthodox Cathedral into the parking lot of Shoppers Drug Mart. Cycle through the lot and turn left before KFC, continue cycling through the lot to the farthest point possible. Cross Redwood and continue straight on the path as it merges with the path which went under the bridge. **St. John's Park:** Take a few minutes to enjoy this historic park and view the Healing Forest. **St. John's Park:** Bathrooms are located by the wading pool but are only open when the pool is open.
9.43	0.09	Straight	**Alfred-Burrows Link Path (crushed limestone);** exit to Burrows and go straight across the boulevard to the south side of the street. **Caution:** The opening in the fence by the back lane is quite narrow.
9.52	0.08	Left	**Burrows Avenue;** at the end of Burrows is a trail veering to the right.
9.60	0.52	Right	**North Winnipeg Parkway Trail (crushed limestone);** cycle the trail along the edge of the Red River through

			Pritchard Point Park, Michelle Jean Parc and the Norquay Community Centre to exit at Rover Avenue.
10.12	0.48	Straight	**Rover Avenue;** cycle to the second street after you pass under the Disraeli Freeway which is Annabella Street.
10.60	0.63	Right	**Annabella Street;** cycle across Sutherland and Higgins to the end of this street to access the North Winnipeg Parkway Trail.
11.23	2.45	Right	**North Winnipeg Parkway Trail (crushed limestone);** this part of the North Winnipeg Parkway runs along the Red River, through Fort Douglas and Stephen Juba Parks. After you cycle under a railway bridge and are near Provencher, the trail splits. Veer to the left, towards the river. After you cycle over the bridge, with wood sides, the trail splits once more and again, veer to the left to cycle under the Provencher Bridge and into The Forks grounds. Stay on the trail closest to the river, but do not go down to the river level. Just past the Children's Museum and the Oodena Celebration Circle is a bridge to your left and the start of the Old St. Boniface Route. **Oodena Celebration Circle:** This amphitheatre features ethereal sculptures, a sundial, interpretive signage, a naked eye observatory and a ceremonial fire pit. **The Forks:** With a wide selection of food venues, you should be able to find whatever beverage or snack you are craving. **The Forks:** There are many bathrooms located throughout The Forks area. **Forks Loop:** At this point, turn around and retrace steps back to the start of the ride. Distance – 22.5 km.
13.68	2.47	Left	**Old St. Boniface Route (asphalt)/Sentier La Liberté Trail (asphalt);** cycle over the bridge, through South Point Park and the trail exits to Main Street at the Norwood Bridge. Cycle over the bridge on the north side of Main using the multi-use path.

			Just before the end of the bridge, turn left on a path which leads down to the river. This path splits, stay left on the path closest to the river.
			Cycle north (downstream) along the banks of the Red River behind Asper Clinical Research Institute, St. Boniface Hospital, and up to the Tache Promenade with a multi-use path on the west side of Tache Avenue.
			Continue straight and note this section of the route is called Sentier La Liberté Trail.
			The trail zig-zags down to the river again just before the Provencher Bridge.
			Cycle under the bridge and straight through Parc Joseph Royal and Parc Elzéar Goulet.
			Just before the overhead railway line, the trail splits, turn right to exit on Tache Avenue.
			Phare Ouest Art Installation: This stainless steel, LED lighting installation pays homage to the colonial history of St. Boniface.
16.15	0.27	Left	**Tache Avenue;** cycle to the end of the street and access to Sentier La Liberté Trail.
16.42	2.14	Straight	**Sentier La Liberté Trail (crushed limestone);** cycle the trail to the river where it curves right to follow along the Red River as it winds behind Fort Gibraltar and through Whittier Park. Although it may not be noticeable, when the trail curves right, it leaves the banks of the Red River and follows the Seine River. Just past the overhead CNR railway bridge, the trail splits in three, take the middle path. The trail continues through Lagimodiére-Gaboury Park. Near the Thibault Street exit, the trail splits again into three. Turn left, and left again, to cross the bridge over the Seine River. Continue through the park to exit on Notre Dame Street.

			Fort Gibraltar: Step back into time to the early 1800s and find out what daily life was like in this North West Company trading post. **Whittier Park:** Bathrooms are located in the shelter next to Fort Gibraltar. Open variable hours.
18.56	0.23	Straight	**Notre Dame Street;** cycle past Nadeau to La Fleche Street.
18.79	0.09	Left	**La Fleche Street;** cycle to the end of the street where it curves into La Verendrye Street.
18.88	0.16	Right	**La Verendrye Street;** cycle to Archibald Street.
19.04	0.62	Left	**Archibald Street;** cycle through the railway underpass and immediately after the Winnipeg Fire Paramedic Service Building and before Nairn, is Montcalm Park. There is a break in the curb at the corner of Archibald and Nairn to access the park entrance. **Caution:** This short stretch of cycling on Archibald requires extreme caution. Traffic is often quite heavy and there is no designated bike lane.
19.66	0.46	Right	**Montcalm-Nairn Overpass Parks Path (dirt/asphalt);** curve right along the embankment for the Nairn Overpass through Montcalm Park, then curve left under the bridge from Nairn Overpass South Park to Nairn Overpass North Park towards the beginning of the Northeast Pioneers Greenway Trail close to Talbot.
20.12	2.22	Straight	**Northeast Pioneers Greenway Trail (asphalt);** cycle past Talbot, Chalmers and Munroe to Kimberley Avenue. *Life Journey* **Art Installation:** These eye-catching colourful mosaic sculptures depict the life cycle of a butterfly.
22.34	2.07	Left	**Kimberley Avenue;** cycle across Raleigh, Golspie, Watt, Roch, Brazier and Henderson to Kildonan Drive.
24.41	4.14	Right	**Kildonan Parkway Trail (asphalt)/Kildonan Drive;** this section of the Kildonan Parkway Trail is made up mostly of Kildonan Drive and paths through two parks.

			Kildonan Drive ends at a stop sign at Helmsdale, turn left and when the road curves right, Helmsdale becomes Kildonan Drive. When you reach Fraser's Grove Park and Kildonan Drive turns right, continue straight on the path which runs through the park and exits back onto Kildonan Drive at Larchdale. Cycle to the end of Kildonan Drive and take the crushed limestone trail straight ahead which leads up an embankment and into Bergen Cutoff Park. The trail splits, turn left towards the river. The trail curves right and exits back onto Kildonan Drive. Turn left at the multi-use path just past Essar. This path intersects with Chief Peguis Greenway Trail just before the underpass at Kildonan Settlers Bridge.
28.55	1.13	Right	**Chief Peguis Greenway Trail (asphalt);** cycle to where the path splits and turn left and left again to cycle up and over the Kildonan Settlers Bridge. Just before Main Street the trail splits, turn left to head back to the river and left again when the trail splits to go under the Kildonan Settlers Bridge and to the trail end at Scotia Street.
29.68	0.37	Straight	**Scotia Street/Scotia Street Link Path (crushed limestone)/Scotia Street;** Scotia Street is not continuous, but there is a link path from one part of the street to the next. Cycle to the end of the street at Ridgecrest Avenue.
30.05	0.36	Right	**Ridgecrest Avenue;** after the road curves left, cycle to the first street, River Ridge Drive.
30.41	0.19	Right	**River Ridge Drive;** cycle to the beginning of the Towering Cottonwood Trail located between houses #46 and #62.
30.60	0.67	Right	**Towering Cottonwood Trail (crushed limestone/woodchip);** cycle the trail towards the river and then left along the river bank.

			When the Cottonwood Trail reaches McBeth Park, it merges with the Brooks Trail, an asphalt trail.
31.27	0.52	Left	**Brooks Trail (asphalt);** cycle through McBeth Park to exit on River Grove Drive.
31.79	0.15	Left	**River Grove Drive;** cycle one block to Red River Boulevard.
31.94	0.30	Right	**Red River Boulevard;** cycle past Sandalwood Crescent to the entrance of the parking lot at Red River Boulevard and Main Street.
32.24	0	End	**Parking lot at Main Street and Red River Boulevard.** **A&W:** Now that the ride is done, you might like to stop for lunch or a snack at A&W.

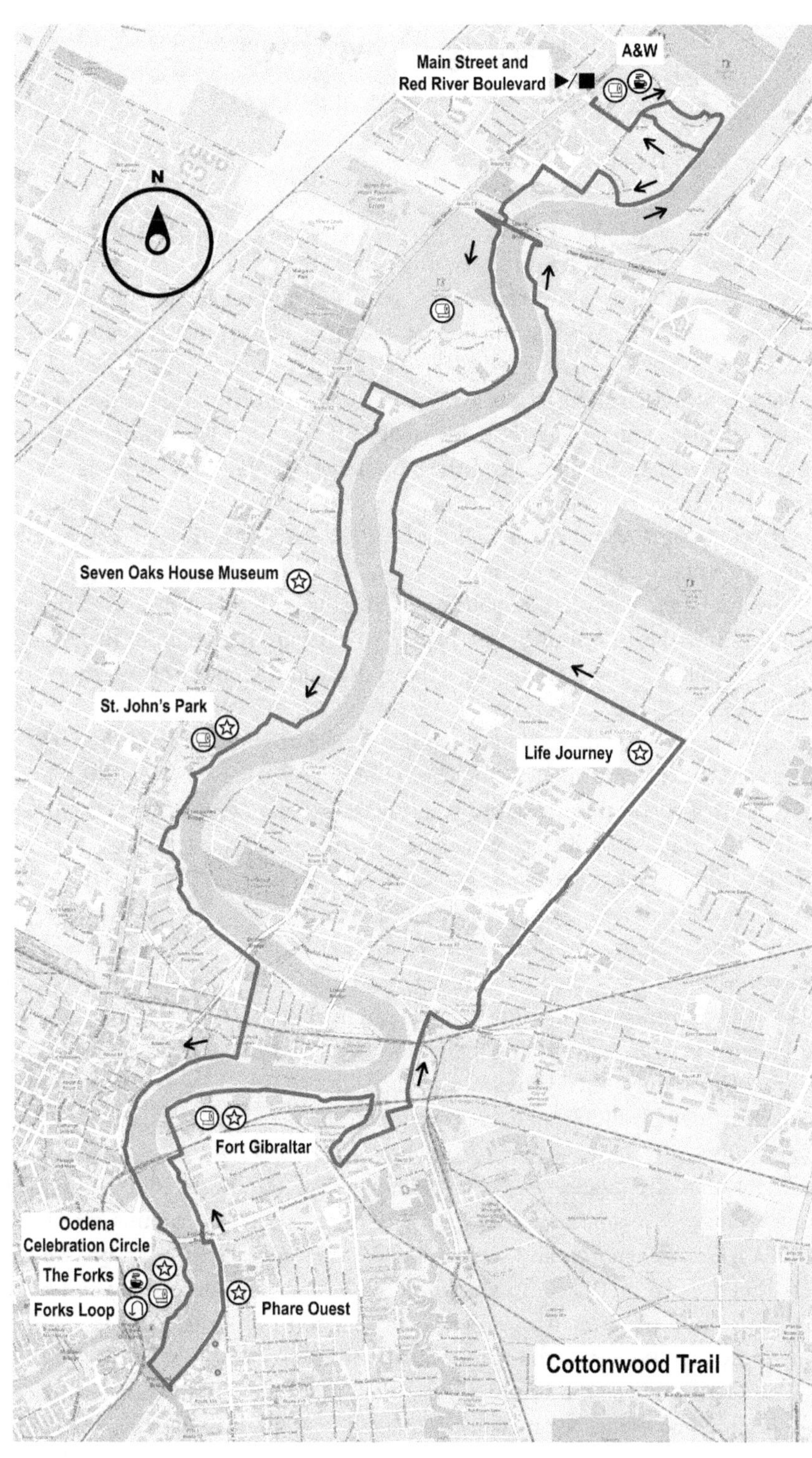
N
Main Street and
Red River Boulevard
A&W
Seven Oaks House Museum
St. John's Park
Life Journey
Fort Gibraltar
Oodena
Celebration Circle
The Forks
Forks Loop
Phare Ouest
Cottonwood Trail

Heading Downtown

Central and South Winnipeg

This ride starts and ends in Crescent Drive Park and goes through River Heights, Downtown, and St. Vital, among other suburbs. Most of the ride is done on streets considered low stress routes. The points of interest are all in the downtown area, around Broadway and Assiniboine, so Heading Downtown seemed like an apt title.

Because you are passing the downtown area with a plethora of coffee options, I didn't make any specific suggestions for venues. If you want to stop here, detour off Assiniboine Avenue and head to either Broadway or Portage and you can find whatever you fancy. You might like to explore your options on-line prior to the ride, if this is your plan. Or you could wait till near the end of the ride and stop at BDI, always a great place for an ice cream!

I always like to showcase something of Winnipeg in each ride and in this one I chose five sites, the Osborne Street Bridge, the Louis Riel Statue, the Manitoba Legislature Building, the Millennium Library Park and Upper Fort Garry Heritage Provincial Park.

Osborne Street Bridge – You can either cycle across the bridge in the bike lane on the road or take your time walking over the bridge on the sidewalk. I recommend the latter as it allows you to view the art installation *From Here to Until Now* by spbm (Eduardo Aquino and Karen Shanski), which is a celebration of the neighbourhoods on each side of the bridge. The sidewalk is meant to look like a street map and the panels below the handrails have text from consultations with citizens of Winnipeg with the end panels highlighting four important architectural achievements in the surrounding neighbourhoods; the Manitoba Legislature, the Granite Curling Club, the Roslyn Apartment Building and the Evergreen Towers. http://winnipegarts.ca/wac/artwork/from-here-until-now

The Louis Riel statue – This statue, situated on the Manitoba Legislative grounds facing the Assiniboine River, is quite majestic. It was commissioned by the Manitoba Metis Federation and sculpted by Miguel Joyal. This 11 ft. bronze statue depicts Riel dressed in 19th century clothing with moccasins on his feet and holding in his left hand a parchment meant to represent the Manitoba Act. It is a fitting tribute to the man known as the Father of Manitoba.

The Manitoba Legislature Building – This building, with the Golden Boy at its crown, is an iconic Winnipeg image. Completed in 1920, it is an example of Beaux-

Arts Classical architecture due to its Greco-Roman Styling. The building took about ten million bricks, made from Manitoba shale and clay, for its construction. The exterior of the building has many works of art referencing wisdom, justice, and courage. The Golden Boy is meant to be symbolic of Manitoba's eternal youth and progress. In the summer, free guided tours are offered. Guides show you around the building and explain its history and architecture. Check the website for details as it's worth a stop. Plus, if it is a really hot day for cycling, the coolness inside will be a welcome relief. https://www.gov.mb.ca/ legislature/visiting/index.html

Manitoba Legislature

Millennium Library Park – Winnipeg has many interesting art installations all over the city. In the greenspace behind the Millennium Library, known as the Millennium Library Park, are two installations worth seeing. The first one, known as *emptyful*, is by Bill Pechet, and is a large Erlenmeyer flask with colourful fog pouring out. It's meant to represent the idea that Winnipeg and the surrounding prairies are full of emptiness; a boundless space where weather, light, seasons and human endeavours come and go. The second installation is on the Smith and Graham corner of the library building itself and is entitled *Waterfall #2* by Theresa Himmer. This installation was created in Iceland and transplanted here. Manitoba has a large community of Icelandic Canadians and this piece alludes to a history of migration and longing.

Upper Fort Garry Heritage Provincial Park – This site was home to a fort established by the Hudson Bay Company. Unlike other forts in and around Winnipeg, there is no physical fort here, nor interpreters to guide you around. The only remaining physical structure is the Governor's Gate, at the north end of the park. The history of Upper Fort Garry and its buildings is relayed using interpretation, art and technology. The highlight of this park is a multi-layered, 440-foot-long steel sculpture entitled, Manitoba Liquor & Lotteries Heritage Wall. It depicts, through more than 7000 LED lights, along with sound, a 300-year timeline of important events and places of the area. This wall has been labeled "the largest piece of public art in Canada". If you do decide to spend some time here, on their website is an Upper Fort Garry App which can be downloaded. The app uses your location in the park to help explore the many symbols and stories of the fort. http://www.upperfortgarry.com

Upper Fort Garry

<u>**Quick Notes**</u>
Distance – 31.2 km
Parking – Crescent Drive Park at 781 Crescent Drive

Option to shorten – yes
    Harrow Loop – 19.3 km
Suggested coffee stop – Downtown options, BDI at 766 Jubilee Avenue
Bathrooms – Crescent Drive Park at 781 Crescent Drive, Real Canadian Superstore
    at 215 St. Anne's Road, coffee stop
Points of Interest –
    Osborne Street Bridge
    Louis Riel Statue on the Manitoba Legislative grounds facing Assiniboine River
    Manitoba Legislature Building at 450 Broadway Avenue
    Millennium Library Park at the corner of Smith Street and St. Mary Avenue
    Upper Fort Garry Heritage Provincial Park at 130 Main Street

Trails

Chevrier Multi-use Path – asphalt
Waverley Multi-use Path – asphalt
Archibald Multi-use Path – asphalt
Niakwa Trail – asphalt
Saint Vital Memorial Park Path – asphalt
Jubilee Multi-use Path – asphalt
Oakenwald Dike Path – crushed limestone

Safety Cautions

Detailed Directions

Km Total	Km Leg	Direction	Location, notes
0	0	Start	**Parking lot of Crescent Drive Park.** **Crescent Drive Park:** Bathrooms are located by the picnic shelters, just west of the parking lot.
0	3.73	Right	**Crescent Drive/Chevrier Boulevard/Chevrier Multi-use Path (asphalt);** turn right out of the parking lot onto Crescent Drive and follow as it curves along the Red River, goes past Thermea Spa, Fort Garry Roman Catholic Cemetery, and across Pembina Highway.

			Once across Pembina, the street becomes Chevrier Boulevard.
			Continue straight, past the lights at the Southwest Rapid Transit Corridor. Just past the corridor is a mutli-use path on the sidewalk extending to the lights at Waverley Street and access to the Waverley Multi-use Path.
3.73	3.50	Right	**Waverley Multi-use Path (asphalt);** cross McGillivray, Buffalo, Seel, Victor Lewis Drive, Wilkes, and Taylor, to Mathers Avenue.
7.23	0.20	Right	**Mathers Avenue;** cycle one block to Cambridge Street.
7.43	0.87	Left	**Cambridge Street;** cycle across Grant Avenue to the 4-way stop sign at Fleet Avenue.
8.30	0.34	Right	**Fleet Avenue;** cycle past Nathaniel to the 4-way stop sign at Thurso Street.
8.64	0.17	Left	**Thurso Street;** cycle past Mulvey to the roundabout at Warsaw Avenue.
8.81	2.23	Right	**Warsaw Avenue;** cycle past Rockwood, Wilton, Guelph, Harrow, Stafford, Wentworth, Lilac, Arbuthnot, Cockburn, Hugo, and Daly to Nassau Street N.
			Harrow Loop: At Harrow, turn right and cycle past Grant to Taylor Avenue. Cross Taylor to access the multi-use path on the south side of the street and turn right.
			Cycle to Waverley and turn left onto the Waverley Multi-use Path and retrace the steps back to Chevrier.
			Cross Chevrier and cycle on the multi-use path on the north side of the road. Shortly after the Southwest Rapid Transit Corridor, the multi-use path ends and you must cycle on the road.
			Cycle across Pembina Highway and Chevrier becomes Crescent Drive. Return to Crescent Drive Park parking lot. Distance – 19.3 km.
11.04	1.00	Left	**Nassau Street N;** cycle across Corydon and past a number of churches, Nassau Street Church, Evangelical Mennonite Mission, Trinity Baptist Church, and Crescent Fort Rouge United Church, then across

			Stradbrook and past The Parish Church of Saint Luke, and across River to the stop sign at Roslyn Road.
12.04	0.29	Right	**Roslyn Road;** cycle to the lights at Osborne Street.
12.33	0.32	Left	**Osborne Street;** cross the Osborne Street Bridge. You can either cycle on the road, or walk along the sidewalk and take in the point of interest. Once over the bridge is Assiniboine Avenue. **Osborne Street Bridge:** Take your time walking over the Osborne Bridge and viewing the art installation, *From Here to Until Now*.
12.65	1.17	Right	**Assiniboine Avenue;** this street has a protected bike lane. Stay on Assiniboine Avenue to its end at Main Street. **Downtown Options:** Turn left off Assiniboine, at any street, and head to either Broadway or Portage for many options for coffee or a meal. When done, return to Assiniboine to continue. **Louis Riel Statue:** This 11 ft. bronze statue by Miguel Joyal is a fitting tribute to the man known as the Father of Manitoba. **Manitoba Legislative Building:** Have you ever graced the halls of our seat of government? If not, they offer a free tour which allows a glimpse into this amazing building. To get here, as soon as you come off the Osborne Street Bridge, take the path straight ahead, across Assiniboine, which veers to the right and heads towards the Legislature Building. Return to Assiniboine Avenue when done. **Millennium Library Park:** To take in the park, turn left at Smith Street and cross Broadway and York to St. Mary Avenue. The park is located at this corner. Return to Assiniboine when done. **Upper Fort Garry Heritage Provincial Park:** This park is located to the left of Assiniboine before Main Street. Take in the Heritage Wall which has been labelled "the largest piece of public art in Canada". Return to Assiniboine when done.
13.82	0.67	Right	**Main Street/Queen Elizabeth Way;** cycle over the two bridges spanning the Assiniboine and then the Red

			River. Of Note, the span of the two bridges is known as Queen Elizabeth Way. As soon as you are off the second bridge is Lyndale Drive to your right.
14.49	0.39	Right	**Lyndale Drive;** cycle past the Norwood Community Centre to Walmer Street. **Note:** Lyndale Drive, from Cromwell Street to Gauvin Street, is designated as a Sunday/Holiday Bicycle Route, from 8am to 8pm, by the city of Winnipeg. This means, on those days, motor vehicle traffic is restricted to one block.
14.88	0.36	Left	**Walmer Street;** cycle past Lawndale to Ferndale Avenue.
15.24	0.06	Left	**Ferndale Avenue;** when the street curves to the right, it becomes Eugenie Street.
15.30	1.41	Right	**Eugenie Street;** cycle across St. Mary's Road at the lights and continue straight past Coronation Park, Tache, Kenny, Traverse, Braemar, Enfield, Hill, and Des Meurons to Youville Street.
16.71	0.09	Right	**Youville Street;** cycle one block to Edgewood Street.
16.80	0.28	Left	**Edgewood Street;** cycle to the end of the street and then follow the path straight ahead leading to the Tremblay Bridge, go over the Seine River and straight to Tremblay Street.
17.08	0.22	Straight	**Tremblay Street;** cycle one block to Evans Street.
17.30	0.49	Right	**Evans Street;** cycle past Deniset and at the back lane of Deniset, take the link path straight ahead to the continuation of Evans. Cycle past Cusson, Cote, and Gareau. Follow the road as it goes around Archwood Community Centre to Guilbault Street.
17.79	0.30	Left	**Guilbault Street;** cycle to Archibald Street.
18.09	2.18	Right	**Archibald Multi-use Path (asphalt);** the sidewalk on the west side on Archibald is a multi-use path. Cycle past Elizabeth Road to Fermor Avenue and the Niakwa Trail which runs along the north side of Fermor.

20.27	2.43	Right	**Niakwa Trail (asphalt);** cycle through Papoose Park, over the Seine River, past St. Vital Outdoor Pool, and across St. Anne's and St. Mary's. Just past the YMCA-YWCA is Saint Vital Memorial Park which has a trail heading north just after the parking area and the picnic shelter. **Note:** At Fermor the Niakwa Trail has two options to access, one before the business on the corner at Fermor, which is the older trail, and one after, which is the newer trail. You can take either path as after the Seine River the two paths merge. **Real Canadian Superstore:** Superstore is located at the corner of St. Anne's and Fermor and the bathrooms are located inside, at the front of the store.
22.70	0.18	Right	**Saint Vital Memorial Park Path (asphalt);** cycle through the park and the trail curves right and then left to exit to Sunset Boulevard.
22.88	0.52	Straight	**Sunset Boulevard/Killarney Street;** cross Glenlawn and Sunset curves to the right around Dean Finlay Park. At about the centre of the curve, as the road begins to curve left, Sunset becomes Killarney Street. Continue on Killarney past Springside, Cunnington, and Elm Park to the stop sign at Kingston Row.
23.40	1.63	Left	**Kingston Row;** cycle under the St. Vital Bridge and continue straight. When you reach Kingston Park the road splits, stay right. The street is now called Kingston Crescent. Look for Riverdale Avenue which is the first cross street.
25.03	0.28	Right	**Riverdale Avenue;** cycle to the end of the street and over the pedestrian Elm Park Bridge which crosses the Red River. Continue to Jubilee Avenue. The sidewalk on the south side is a multi-use path. **BDI:** Feeling like ice cream? This Winnipeg icon is the perfect place to stop and have a treat.
25.31	0.30	Left	**Jubilee Multi-use Path (asphalt);** cycle to Riverside Drive.

25.61	0.79	Left	**Riverside Drive;** cycle past the stop sign at Merriam and the stop sign at the spot where Riverside curves right. Shortly, Riverside turns left. Cycle past Toilers Memorial Park, and the stop signs at Windermere, and Somerset to North Drive.
26.40	0.60	Left	**North Drive/Netley Street;** follow the road as it curves right and becomes Netley Street. Cycle past Waterford, Viscount and Riverwood and just before Netley ends at Oakenwald, is the Oakenwald Dike Path to your left.
27.00	0.73	Left	**Oakenwald Dike Path (crushed limestone);** cycle the length of the path to exit onto North Drive.
27.73	0.68	Right	**North Drive;** cycle past the stop sign at Oakenwald and the Wildwood Park Community Centre to the stop sign at South Drive.
28.41	1.92	Right	**South Drive;** cycle past St. John's-Ravenscourt School. At the stop sign, South Drive turns right. Cycle across Point Road and Dowker to Crane Avenue.
30.33	0.88	Left	**Crane Avenue/Stretford Road/Crescent Drive;** follow the road as it curves right and becomes Stretford Road and once in Crescent Drive Park becomes Crescent Drive.
31.21	0	End	**Parking lot of Crescent Drive Park.**

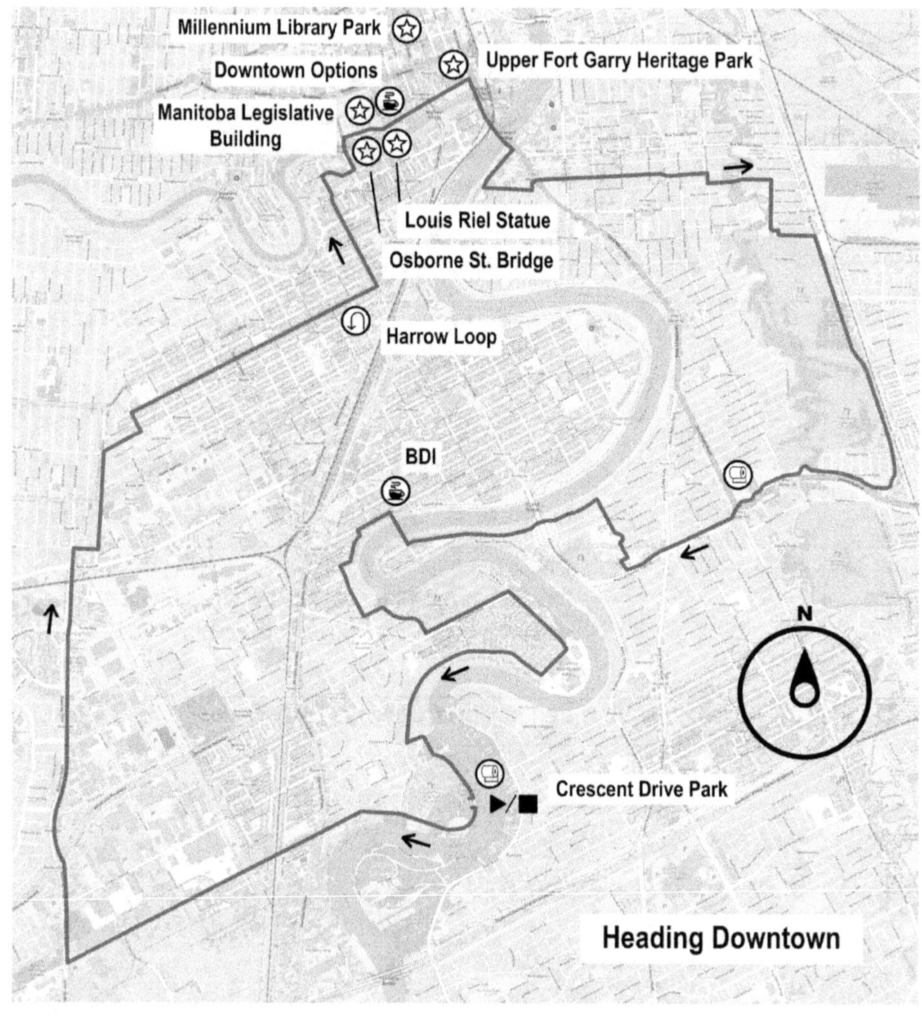
Millennium Library Park
Downtown Options
Upper Fort Garry Heritage Park
Manitoba Legislative Building
Louis Riel Statue
Osborne St. Bridge
Harrow Loop
BDI
Crescent Drive Park
N
Heading Downtown

Cruisin' Along the Red

Southeast Winnipeg

The Red River is 865 km long and originates in the United States, flowing along the border of Minnesota and North Dakota, continues northward into Manitoba, and empties into Lake Winnipeg. Part of this ride, mostly in the middle, follows along a small section of this river, hence the name Cruisin' Along the Red.

This is a scenic ride with a combination of paths and some cycling on quiet streets. Some paths and roads included are River Road, Kingston Row, Churchill Drive and Lyndale Drive, which are situated on either side of river's banks. In addition, the ride crosses the Red twice, first on the Elm Park Bridge and second on the Norwood Bridge. To get the most enjoyment from this ride, be sure to stop along the way and watch the river flow and observe any wildlife about.

There are a couple of great places to take a break. If you feel like ice cream, you have two choices; BDI, a Winnipeg institution, or Chaeban Ice Cream, started by Syrian refugees who have made Winnipeg their home. If ice cream is not your thing, there is also a Tim Hortons further along in the ride.

There are two points of interest worth noting on this ride. One is a public art installation and the second is a tourist site.

Along the stretch of Bishop Grandin Greenway Trail, as you cycle around a particular bend, you suddenly come face to face with huge moose antlers! It is quite striking. This is an art installation by Jacqueline Metz and Nancy Chew entitled *land/mark*. It represents an interpretation of the imprints left on the landscape by animals and humans. The antlers, of course, are the animal imprints, and the granite bench inscribed with a linear pattern is a nod to the historical "long lot" system of land division common to the area. To get even more insight into this piece, check out the link which includes further description and the artists' statement. http://winnipegarts.ca/wac/artwork/land-mark

land/mark

This ride also passes a popular Winnipeg tourist site, The Royal Canadian Mint, where all Canadian coins are produced. If you haven't already visited this site, you might like to make the time to take it in. They offer a short 45-minute guided tour which explains the process of making coins from beginning to end. In addition to the tour, there is an interesting boutique for coin enthusiasts and for unique gift ideas. It is well worth the stop and one of my favourite places to take visitors to Winnipeg. There is a small charge for the tour and reservations need to be made ahead of time; current information for pricing and tour times can be found on their website. http://www.mint.ca/store/mint/visit-the-mint/visit-the-mint-1200026

Quick Notes

Distance – 32.0 km
Parking – Near the end of Des Meurons Street by Windsor Park Golf Course
Options to shorten – yes
    1 – Dakota Loop – 14.9 km
    2 – Fermor Loop – 19.2 km
Bike repair station – Bishop Grandin Trail East at the corner of Dakota Avenue
Suggested coffee stops – BDI at 766 Jubilee Avenue, Chaeban Ice Cream at 390 Osborne Street, Tim Hortons at 19 Marion Street
Bathrooms – Real Canadian Superstore at 215 St. Anne's Road, by the exit gate of St. Vital Park at 190 River Road, public bathroom on Churchill Drive just east of the St. Vital Bridge, coffee stop
Points of Interest –
    land/mark art installation on Bishop Grandin Greenway Trail
    Royal Canadian Mint at 520 Lagimodière Boulevard

Trails

Niakwa Trail – asphalt
Lagimodière Multi-use Path – asphalt
Bishop Grandin Trail East– asphalt
Bishop Grandin Greenway Trail – asphalt
Dakota/Dunkirk Pathway – asphalt
Jubilee Multi-use Path – asphalt
Churchill Parkway Trail – crushed limestone
South Winnipeg Parkway Trail – crushed limestone, asphalt
Boni-Vital Parkway Trail – crushed limestone
Windsor Park Golf Course Trail – crushed limestone

Safety Cautions

Detailed Directions

Km total	Km Leg	Direction	Location, notes
0	0	Start	**Niakwa Trail (asphalt);** access located at the end of Des Meurons.
0	3.91	Left	**Niakwa Trail (asphalt);** cycle past St. Vital Pool to the main Niakwa Trail and turn left. Almost immediately the trail splits. If you veer to the left, the trail rides across a footbridge over the Seine River, if you veer to the right, the trail rides over the Seine River along the edge of Fermor Avenue. Shortly after, both trails merge and continue. You can take either path but, in the spring, the trail to the left, before the merge, is often flooded. Continue across Archibald, Autumnwood, Westmount and across Lagimodière Boulevard to the east side of the Boulevard to access the multi-use path. **Real Canadian Superstore:** This store is located at the corner of St. Anne's and Fermor. When you reach the main Niakwa trail, turn right towards St. Anne's. When done, return to this spot and resume ride.
3.91	1.92	Right	**Lagimodière Multi-use Path (asphalt);** cycle past E Mint Place, Glen Lawn Funeral Home and Cemetery and T&T Soils to Bishop Grandin Boulevard. **The Royal Canadian Mint:** If you have a chance to stop, you won't be disappointed. They offer a great tour and have a wonderful boutique to browse.
5.83	7.25	Right	**Bishop Grandin Trail East (asphalt)/Bishop Grandin Greenway Trail (asphalt);** this trail runs parallel to the boulevard, first on the south side, past De la

			Seigneurie, Island Shore and Shorehill to St. Anne's Road, at which point you cross to the north side. Cycle past Dakota and St. Mary's to River Road. **Note:** This whole section of trail, from Lagimodière Boulevard to the Red River is known as Bishop Grandin Trail East, but within it, from the Seine River, located close to St. Anne's Road, to the Red River, this trail is also known as Bishop Grandin Greenway Trail. *land/mark* **Art Installation:** This art installation will take you by surprise when you come around a bend in the trail just past St. Anne's Road. It is perfectly situated on the edge of a pond. **Dakota Loop:** Turn right at Dakota Street on the multi-use Dakota/Dunkirk Pathway on the east side of the road. Note the street name changes to Dunkirk Drive after crossing St. Mary's Road. Cycle across Fermor Avenue to the multi-use path on the north side and turn right. Cross St. Mary's and St. Anne's where you pick up the Niakwa Trail. Take the exit to your left from the main trail just past the Superstore and St. Vital Outdoor Pool to return to Des Meurons Street, and the start of this ride. Distance – 14.9 km. **Bike Repair Station:** Located on Bishop Grandin Trail East/Bishop Grandin Greenway Trail at the corner of Dakota Street. If your tires are getting low, this is a great place to pump them up!
13.08	1.91	Right	**River Road;** cycle past St. Vital Park, Parkville and Moore to St. Vital Road. **St. Vital Park:** There are bathrooms located close to the exit gate. They are open from 7:30am to 10pm.
14.99	0.97	Right	**St. Vital Road;** cycle past Pulberry and cross Dunkirk Drive to the multi-use path on the east sidewalk.
15.96	1.62	Left	**Dakota/Dunkirk Pathway (asphalt);** cycle past Fermor Avenue to Edinburgh Street located just before the St. Vital Bridge. **Fermor Loop:** Once across Fermor Street turn right on the multi-use path on the north side of the street. Cross

			St. Mary's and St. Anne's where you then pick up the Niakwa Trail. Take the exit to your left from the main trail just past the Superstore and St. Vital Outdoor Pool to return to Des Meurons Street, and the start of this ride. Distance – 19.2 km.
17.58	0.17	Veer Right	**Edinburgh Street;** veer right and follow Edinburgh as curves and ends at Kingston Row.
17.75	1.22	Left	**Kingston Row/Kingston Crescent;** cycle under the St. Vital Bridge and continue straight. When you reach Kingston Park the road splits, stay right, keeping the park to your left. The street is now called Kingston Crescent. Look for Riverdale Avenue which is the first cross street.
18.97	0.30	Right	**Riverdale Avenue;** cycle over the pedestrian Elm Park Bridge which crosses the Red River. Continue to Jubilee Avenue and the multi-use path on the sidewalk on the south side of the street. **BDI:** Feeling like ice cream? This Winnipeg icon is the perfect place to stop and have a treat.
19.27	0.16	Right	**Jubilee Multi-use Path (asphalt);** cycle one block to Cockburn Street S.
19.43	4.26	Right	**Cockburn Street S/Churchill Drive/Churchill Parkway Trails (crushed limestone);** Cockburn curves into Churchill. At the curve, take the crushed limestone trail on the south side of Churchill Drive going through the parkway between the road and the river. The trail runs through Churchill Drive Park and then exits onto Churchill Drive. Just past the community gardens the trail begins again through Don Gerrie Park before exiting once again onto Churchill Drive. Cycle to the end of Churchill to Brandon Avenue. **Public Bathroom:** There is a public bathroom located on this trail just east of the St. Vital Bridge. Open variable hours.
23.69	0.25	Left	**Brandon Avenue;** cycle one block to Osborne Street. **Caution:** There appears to be a trail leading along the river at the end of Churchill Drive, but I do not recommend taking this. It is very narrow and quite uneven, and not appropriate for the bike. The start of

			the next trail should be picked up a few blocks over from this point and instructions on how to get there follows.
23.94	0.17	Right	**Osborne Street;** cycle two blocks to Glasgow Avenue.
24.11	0.06	Right	**Glasgow Avenue;** cycle to the back lane behind the Winnipeg Transit building.
24.17	0.06	Left	**Back Lane;** lane exits on Togo Avenue.
24.23	0.03	Right	**Togo Avenue;** at the end of this street is the access to the South Winnipeg Parkway.
24.26	1.68	Left	**South Winnipeg Parkway Trail (crushed limestone);** continue on this trail for some distance as it runs alongside the Red River. As you approach the Norwood Bridge take the ramp to the left leading up to street level. **Chaeban Ice Cream:** Once on the South Winnipeg Parkway, almost immediately, just past the black iron fence, is a paved path to your left leading back to Osborne Street. This is the next street over from Togo, and here you will find Chaeban Ice Cream. If you've always gone to BDI, you might like to give this spot a try. They feature waffle cones, sundaes, milkshakes, and other delectables, yum!
25.94	0.24	Right	**Norwood Bridge;** cycle over the bridge to Lyndale Drive. **Tim Hortons:** If ice cream is not your thing, once over the Norwood Bridge, take the trail leading under the bridge to the north side of St. Mary's, or cross at the lights, to get to the Tim Hortons located in the Dominion Centre.
26.18	2.80	Right	**Lyndale Drive/Boni-Vital Parkway Trails (crushed limestone);** cycle the entire length of the drive to its end at St. Mary's Road. You can either cycle on the road or on the crushed limestone trails by the river going through Lyndale Drive Park North and then Lyndale Drive Park.
28.98	0.19	Right	**St. Mary's Road;** cycle two blocks to Carriere Avenue, a crosswalk is located at this corner.

29.17	0.51	Left	**Carriere Avenue;** cycle past Des Meurons, to the next cross street which is Youville Street.
29.68	0.29	Right	**Youville Street;** cycle past Fifth and Guay to Morier Avenue.
29.97	0.15	Left	**Morier Avenue;** cycle to the end of this street to Egerton Road.
30.12	1.40	Right	**Egerton Road;** this road winds its way beside the Seine River. Egerton is interrupted at some point by Blenheim Avenue. When you reach Blenheim, turn left, and then when Blenheim veers right, you are again on Egerton. There are bike route signs indicating the way. This road ends at Windsor Park Golf Course and to your right is a trail along the outer edge of the course.
31.52	0.26	Right	**Windsor Park Golf Course Trail (crushed limestone);** cycle to end where exits on Des Meurons Street.
31.78	0.19	Left	**Des Meurons Street;** cycle to the end of the street to Niakwa Trail.
31.97	0	End	**Niakwa Trail.**

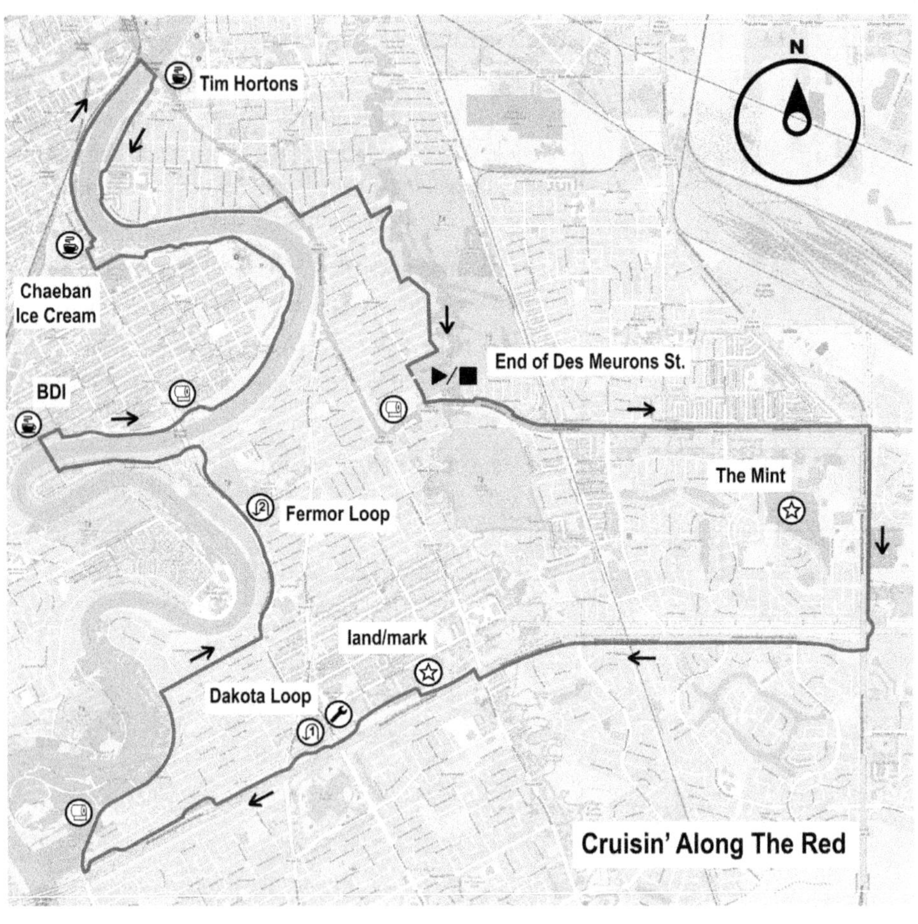
Tim Hortons
Chaeban
Ice Cream
BDI
Fermor Loop
End of Des Meurons St.
The Mint
land/mark
Dakota Loop
N
Cruisin' Along The Red

Le Quartiér Français

Southeast Winnipeg

Bishop Provencher founded St. Boniface in 1818 in order to provide a community to meet the cultural and religious needs of the French and Métis residents of the Red River Colony. Today, Old St. Boniface is known as the centre of Manitoba's French community and is one of the largest francophone communities west of the Great Lakes. It is filled with history, tourist sites, many unique shops and quaint cafés.

This ride starts and stops in Old St. Boniface and travels through a number of the communities included in the city ward of St. Boniface as the route winds its way as far south as Royalwood. The ride also follows various stretches of the Seine River. This river acts as the east-west boundary between St. Boniface and St. Vital in the southern part of Winnipeg. As we are exploring the ward of St. Boniface and the centre of Manitoba's French community, Le Quartiér Français seemed the perfect name for this ride.

Although I have given a suggestion for a coffee stop mid-way through the ride, I highly recommend you wait until the end of the ride and go for coffee in Old St. Boniface. There are numerous selections for coffee or French cuisine along Provencher Boulevard or the surrounding streets.

Writing up the points of interest and highlights for this ride was the most difficult of all the rides I've written up. I didn't know where to start and where to end. There is so much history and so much to see in Old St. Boniface. Most of the sites I mention are at the end of the ride. You can explore them while on the route, or, if you would like to spend more time in the area, park your bikes somewhere and wander around by foot. With all I mention below, I have just scratched the surface. If you are interested in spending more time in the area or exploring beyond what I have listed, I highly recommend you do some searching on the Internet before you head out to be sure you see what you want.

What follows is my, not so brief, list of points of interest and even some shopping suggestions!

But before I get to the sites related to St. Boniface, there are two wood carvings worth looking at in Bois-des-Esprit Forest. The first one you come to on the Bois-des-Esprit Trail is the *Great Grey Owl* located just after you enter into the wooded area. The artist, Murry Watson, is a self-taught Metis carver, and he has, in addition to the owl, transformed other dead branches and stumps with his carvings, so don't be surprised if you come across other carvings.

The second carving is *Woody the Tree Spirit*, located close to where you exit this trail. Walter Mirosh and Robert LeClaire carved two spirits from an elm tree. It is said there was a magical moment when the eyes were being carved. The normal forest sounds suddenly became quiet as the sculptors worked on the eyes and only when the outline of the eyes was complete, did the forest sounds resume. There is an interpretive sign next to this carving to learn more about this sculpture.

St. Boniface is the birthplace of Louis Riel and there are a number of sites commemorating him throughout the area. I have indicated them as points of interest in the detailed description below. Louis Riel (b.1844 – d.1885) is a significant historical figure in the history of the province of Manitoba. He was the leader of the Métis people in western Canada and led the 1869 Red River Rebellion against the government of Canada when they wanted to take over the land the Métis lived on and which was previously owned by the Hudson's Bay Company. Riel was worried the Métis would have to give up their French culture and language, along with the land, to the Anglophones and therefore sought to protect the Métis rights. The Rebellion led to a provisional government being established with Riel as president and he negotiated acceptable terms under which the province of Manitoba entered the Canadian Confederation. Because of this, Riel is frequently referred to as the Father of Manitoba. The sites related to Riel throughout this ride are:

- Louis Riel Sr Trail – Named in honour of Louis Riel Sr., the father of Louis Riel. He was known as the "miller of the Seine" after he established a mill in the area of this trail.

- Louis Riel Statue at Université de Saint-Boniface at 200 Avenue de la Cathedrale – This statue was originally placed on the grounds of the Legislative Building in 1971. It is an artistic abstract sculpture depicting Riel's tortured soul. It was a controversial statue and was eventually replaced in 1996 with a more statesmanlike statue of Riel and this original one was moved here, to the grounds of Université de Saint-Boniface.

- Louis Riel's Gravesite in St. Boniface Cemetery at 190 Avenue de la Cathedrale – Louis Riel was hanged in Regina on November 16, 1885, for his role as leader of the North-West Rebellion against the Canadian government, and his body was eventually interred here by the Cathedral.

- Louis Riel Bust at St. Boniface Museum at 494 Tache Avenue – This bust was erected in the late 1980s. It sits in front of the St. Boniface Museum which houses the largest collection of Riel artifacts in Canada.

- Esplanade Riel Footbridge – This cable pedestrian walkway, over the Red River, connects St. Boniface to The Forks.

In addition to all the sites related to Louis Riel, there are a number of other notable points of interest in Old St. Boniface:

- Université de Saint-Boniface at 200 Avenue de la Cathedrale – This is the oldest post-secondary educational institute in Western Canada.

- Saint Boniface Cathedral at 409 Tache Avenue – The Cathedral is considered one of Winnipeg's major architectural landmarks. The present building, the fifth built since 1818, was designed by Étienne Gaboury, a renowned Franco-Manitoban architect. The previous basilica, built in 1908, burned down in 1968, leaving behind an intact façade and some walls. Étienne combined these remaining structures in his new design, which was considered an unusual architectural achievement at the time.

- St. Boniface City Hall at 219 Provencher Boulevard – The City Hall was built in 1906 and is now a municipally-designated historic site. It is worthwhile to head over and take a look at the building and the surrounding grounds. Often there is artwork outside which changes from year to year. Also, if interested in more information on St. Boniface, the city hall has the Riel Tourism Bureau offering information for attractions and events throughout St. Boniface and other French communities in the province. In the summer time, guided tours of the French Quarter are offered. Check out their website for more information http://tourismeriel.com/en

Riel Tourism Bureau

I hope you have your panniers with you as you might like to explore some of the shopping. There are all kinds of wonderful shops to explore, but there are three I would like to draw your attention to:

- Chocolatier Constance Popp shop at 180 Provencher Boulevard – Feel like chocolate? I've got the answer. Constance is a premium artisan chocolatier who likes to bring a creative twist to her chocolates. Her chocolates have made their way to the Junos, Royal Visits in Winnipeg, the Golden Globes, the Oscars, the Toronto Film Festival and the Olympics. She sells a wide variety of chocolates, made-fresh daily Chocolate Beverages and ice cream treats. http://constancepopp.com

Constance Popp

- The Fromagerie Bothwell at 136 Provencher Boulevard – How about some cheese to go with the chocolate? This shop sells award winning cheese made right here in Manitoba. The Bothwell Cheese company is Canada's largest independently owned cheese maker and located in New Bothwell, Manitoba. It was founded in 1936 as a co-operative by local farmers. https://www.bothwellcheese.com

Bothwell Cheese

- La Belle Baguette at 248 Avenue de la Cathedrale – If you have cheese, you need bread, right? La Belle Baguette is a French bakery and café. You can either enjoy your treats in-house or take them home to savour later. https://www.labelle baguette.ca

La Belle Baguette

Quick Notes

Distance – 31.6 km

Parking –Whittier Park at 836 Rue Saint Joseph

Option to shorten – yes

    Windsor Park Loop – 17.1 km

Suggested coffee stops – Southdale Shopping Centre options at the corner of Lakewood Boulevard and Fermor Street, Old St. Boniface options along Provencher Boulevard or surrounding streets

Bathrooms – Whittier Park at 836 Rue Saint Joseph, Franco-Manitoban Cultural Centre at 340 Provencher Boulevard, Southdale Shopping Centre at the corner of Lakewood Boulevard and Fermor Street, Real Canadian Superstore at 215 St. Anne's Road, coffee stops

Points of Interest –

    Louis Riel Sr Trail located in Royalwood

    Great Grey Owl carving in Bois-des-Esprits

    Woody the Tree Spirit carving in Bois-des-Esprits

    Louis Riel Statue at St. Boniface College at 200 Avenue de la Cathedrale

    Université de Saint-Boniface at 200 Avenue de la Cathedrale

    Louis Riel's Gravesite at St. Boniface Cemetery at 190 Avenue de la Cathedrale

    Saint Boniface Cathedral at 409 Tache Avenue

    Louis Riel Bust at St. Boniface Museum at 494 Tache Avenue

    Esplanade Riel Footbridge spanning the Red River

    St. Boniface City Hall at 219 Provencher Boulevard

    Chocolatier Constance Popp at 180 Provencher Boulevard

    The Fromagerie Bothwell at 136 Provencher Boulevard

    La Belle Baguette at 248 Avenue de la Cathedrale

Trails

Sentier La Liberté Trail – asphalt/crushed limestone

Sentier Gabrielle-Roy Trail – crushed limestone

Archibald Multi-use Path – asphalt

Windsor Park Neighbourhood Path – grass

Frontenac Park Trail – asphalt

Culloden Multi-use Path – asphalt

Bois-des-Esprits Trail – crushed limestone
Louis Riel Sr Trail – asphalt
Bishop Grandin Trail East – asphalt
Lagimodiére Multi-use Path – asphalt
Niakwa Trail – asphalt
Windsor Park Golf Course Trail – crushed limestone

Safety Cautions

Detailed Directions

Km Total	Km Leg	Direction	Location, notes
0	0	Start	**Sentier La Liberté Trail starting from Whittier Park parking lot.** **Whittier Park:** Bathrooms are located in the shelter next to Fort Gibraltar. Open variable hours.
0	2.11	Straight	**Sentier La Liberté Trail (crushed limestone);** cycle the trail past Fort Gibraltar towards the river. Turn right and follow the trail as it winds through Whittier Park and along the banks of the Red River. The trail curves right and at this point has left the Red and begins to follow the Seine River. Just past the overhead CNR railway bridge, the trail splits in three, take the middle path. The trail continues through Lagimodiére-Gaboury Park. Near the Thibault Street exit, the trail splits again into three. Turn left, do not cycle across the bridge, continue straight to exit park near the corner of Provencher Boulevard and Des Meurons Street.
2.11	0.21	Left	**Provencher Boulevard;** cross Provencher Boulevard at the lights to the south side of the street.

			Just past the Shell Station, but before the river, is the Sentier Gabrielle Roy Trail, which is part of the Seine River Parkway. **Centre Culturel Franco-Manitobain:** Public bathrooms are located inside the Culturel Centre. When done, return to east side of Des Meurons and continue ride.
2.32	1.50	Right	**Sentier Gabrielle Roy Trail (crushed limestone);** cycle along the banks of the Seine River, passing under a CNR railway bridge and past Winnipeg's largest soil decontamination site. Near the end of the trail, it splits, with the wider trail exiting to a street, do not exit trail here. Veer to the left onto the narrower trail. Follow the trail as it remains along the river edge behind a condo and then splits again. Turn right and exit onto Rue Youville. **Caution:** This path is quite narrow and is rough in spots. Cycle with care.
3.82	0.86	Straight	**Rue Youville;** follow Youville past Bertrand, Goulet, Marion, Horace and Eugenie to Edgewood Street. **Note:** At Goulet, Youville does not continue until past Marion, and Goulet is a one-way street going in the wrong direction. You must use the sidewalk to the crosswalk, cross Marion and you are back onto Youville.
4.68	0.28	Left	**Edgewood Street;** cycle to the end of the street and then follow the path straight ahead leading to the Tremblay Bridge. Cross the bridge over the Seine River and straight to Tremblay Street.
4.96	0.22	Straight	**Tremblay Street;** cycle one block to Evans Street.
5.18	0.49	Right	**Evans Street;** cycle past Deniset and at the back lane of Deniset, take the link path straight ahead to the continuation of Evans. Cycle past Cusson, Cote, and Gareau. Follow the road as it goes around Archwood Community Centre to Guilbault Street.
5.67	0.30	Left	**Guilbault Street;** cycle to Archibald Street.

5.97	0.57	Right	**Archibald Multi-use Path (asphalt);** the sidewalk on the west side of Archibald is a multi-use path. Cycle one block to Elizabeth Road.
6.54	0.14	Left	**Elizabeth Road;** cycle past the train tracks to the grass path running behind the properties.
6.68	0.82	Right	**Windsor Park Neighbourhood Path (grass);** cycle past Autumnwood Drive and then look for a small greenspace. Take the right grass path exit to Blueberry Bay.
7.50	0.39	Right	**Blueberry Bay/Blackberry Bay;** cycle across Drake Boulevard, at which point the road is now Blackberry Bay. Blackberry curves to the left and in about the middle of this back stretch, between houses #29 and #31, is access to Frontenac Park Trail.
7.89	0.63	Right	**Frontenac Park Trail (asphalt);** when trail divides, turn right and cycle through Frontenac Park and exit to Cottonwood Road.
8.52	0.23	Left	**Cottonwood Road;** cycle past Cherry and Cypress to the four-way stop at Autumnwood Drive.
8.75	0.76	Right	**Autumnwood Drive;** cycle past Cherry, Coral, Conifer, Crestwood and across Fermor to Weatherstone Place, just past the Circle K Convenience Store. **Southdale Shopping Centre Options:** There are a number of choices for a coffee or snack; Pizza Hut, McDonald's, Tim Hortons, A&W, etc. Enjoy! **Southdale Shopping Centre:** Bathrooms are located in Walmart or any of the coffee stops. **Windsor Park Loop:** Do not cross Fermor Avenue. At Fermor, turn right on the Niakwa Trail and cycle past Archibald, over the small bridge crossing the Seine River and just before the St. Vital Outdoor Pool, turn right to exit this trail onto Des Meurons Street. Continue, where indicated below, to return to start. Distance – 17.1 km.

9.51	0.33	Right	**Weatherstone Place;** cycle to end of street and continue straight on the trail ahead over the railway tracks to Pebble Beach Road.
9.84	0.70	Left	**Pebble Beach Road;** cycle to the end of the road at Willowlake Crescent.
10.54	1.00	Right	**Willowlake Crescent;** cycle past Willowlake Park and stay on road as curves left and left again. Cycle past École Guyot and Bluewater Crescent to Culloden Multi-use Path.
11.54	2.05	Right	**Culloden Multi-use Path (asphalt)/Shorehill Drive;** cycle across Bishop Grandin Boulevard, at which point Culloden becomes Shorehill Drive. Cycle across Shorehill to be on the correct side of the street for traffic and continue straight. Cycle past Fountainview Park and the stop sign at John Bruce. Cycle to Eastoak Drive, which is just before the roundabout.
13.59	0.51	Right	**Eastoak Drive;** cycle to the end of the road and the access to Bois-des-Esprits Trail.
14.10	1.27	Right	**Bois-des-Esprits Trail (crushed limestone);** turn right from the access trail and enter the forest. Immediately to your left will be the *Great Grey Owl* carving. Continue on the crushed limestone path. Once past the dirt trail to *Woody the Tree Spirit*, the trail splits. Veer left and exit onto John Bruce Road E. *Great Grey Owl* **carving:** This carving is located to your left, just off the trail, as soon as you enter the forest. The artist, Murry Watson, is a self-taught Metis carver. *Woody the Tree Spirit* **carving:** Shortly before the trail splits for the last time, this carving can be found on a small trail to your left. Unfortunately, there is no signage on the trail in the direction you are cycling, but there is a small sign, nailed to a tree, at the dirt trail leading to *Woody* that can be seen from the other direction. This carving was created by Walter Mirosh and Robert LeClaire from an elm tree and is well worth the detour.

15.37	0.15	Left	**John Bruce Road E;** cycle to the end of the street and start of the Louis Riel Sr Trail.
15.52	0.62	Right	**Louis Riel Sr Trail (asphalt);** cycle the trail through Orchard Hill Park and exit onto Bishop Grandin Trail East. **Louis Riel Sr Trail:** This trail is named after the father of Louis Riel and is close to the site where he established a mill.
16.14	2.90	Right	**Bishop Grandin Trail East (asphalt);** cycle past Shorehill, Island Shore and De la Seigneurine to Lagimodiére Boulevard. Cross Lagimodiére to the multi-use path on the east side of the street.
19.04	1.88	Left	**Lagimodiére Multi-use Path (asphalt);** cycle past Glen Lawn Funeral Home and E Mint Place to Fermor Avenue. Cross Fermor to north side of street to Niakwa Trail.
20.92	3.96	Left	**Niakwa Trail (asphalt);** cycle past Westmount, Lakewood, and Archibald. Continue straight and when trail splits, take either path, one rides over a small bridge crossing the Seine River and the other goes along the edge of Fermor, both trails merge after the river. Turn right just before the St. Vital Outdoor Pool and exit onto Des Meurons Street. **Real Canadian Superstore:** Superstore is located at the corner of Fermor Avenue and St. Anne's Road. To get there, do not turn at exit path but instead, continue straight, Superstore is on your right. Bathrooms are located just inside, at the front of the store. When done, return to turn off and continue ride.
24.88	0.15	Straight	**Des Meurons Street;** on your right, just past the end of Windsor Park Golf Course is a trail. There is a bike route sign indicating the turn onto this trail. **Windsor Park Loop continued:** Follow the remaining directions to return to the start.

25.03	0.27	Right	**Windsor Park Golf Course Trail (crushed limestone);** trail ends on Egerton Road.
25.30	1.41	Left	**Egerton Road;** this road winds its way beside the Seine River. As you follow the road, Egerton turns left at the stop sign, and briefly becomes Blenheim Avenue, until you turn right at the next corner and you are again on Egerton. Cycle to the end of the road where Egerton meets Morier Avenue.
26.71	0.16	Left	**Morier Avenue;** cycle one block to Rue Youville.
26.87	0.97	Right	**Rue Youville;** cycle past St. Boniface Golf Club, Heather Curling Club and the stop sign at Dubuc. The Springs Christian Academy is at corner of Rue Youville and Eugenie Street.
27.84	0.36	Left	**Eugenie Street;** cycle across Des Meurons to the stop sign at Enfield Crescent.
28.20	0.97	Right	**Enfield Crescent/St. John Baptiste Street;** cycle across Marion and Goulet, use caution as there are no street lights at these corners. Continue past Bertrand, at which point the road becomes St. John Baptiste Street. Cycle past Dollard and Yelle to the stop sign at Hamel Avenue.
29.17	0.32	Left	**Hamel Avenue;** cycle to the end of Hamel at Rue Aulneau.
29.49	0.16	Right	**Rue Aulneau;** cycle to the first corner, Avenue de la Cathedrale. **Université de Saint-Boniface:** This is the oldest university in Western Canada. **Louis Riel Statue:** Located on the grounds of the Université de Saint-Boniface at the corner of Rue Aulneau and Avenue de la Cathedrale.
29.65	0.37	Left	**Avenue de la Cathedrale;** cycle past Université de Saint-Boniface and St. Boniface Cathedral to Tache Avenue. Cross Tache to the west side to the multi-use path on the sidewalk, which is the Sentier la Liberté Trail.

			Saint Boniface Cathedral: Take in the impressive view of the surviving façade from an earlier church building on this present-day Roman Catholic basilica. **Louis Riel's Gravesite:** Located in front of Saint Boniface Cathedral. **Louis Riel Bust:** Located in front of the St. Boniface Museum at 494 Tache Avenue, which is next to the cemetery. **La Belle Baguette:** This French bakery and café is a bit of a detour, but worth it. Turn right at Avenue de la Cathedrale, instead of left, and cycle one block to Langevin Street. The bakery is on the corner. When done, resume at beginning of this step.
30.02	0.72	Right	**Tache Avenue/Sentier la Liberté Trail (asphalt/crushed limestone);** follow the path along Tache and just before the Provencher Bridge, cycle the zigzag path down to the river. Cycle under the bridge, past a utility building and exit on the third trail to your left to Tache Avenue at the corner of Notre Dame Street. **Esplanade Riel:** If you feel like taking a little detour, cycle to the middle of the footbridge and take in the views of Old St. Boniface and The Forks.
30.74	0.20	Straight	**Notre Dame Street;** cycle one block to Rue Saint Joseph.
30.94	0.51	Left Or Right	**Rue Saint Joseph;** here you have a choice: To continue to end of ride; cycle past La Verendrye and Aubert to the entrance of the parking lot in Whittier Park. To explore the area; cycle two blocks to Provencher Boulevard and stop for coffee, shopping, and some sightseeing before returning to Whittier Park. **Saint Boniface City Hall:** Stop to look at this historic building and the art work in the surrounding grounds. The Riel Tourism Bureau is located here and can provide information about happenings around St. Boniface.

			**Chocolatier Constance Popp:** Stop at this unique boutique for chocolates, a freshly made chocolate beverage or ice cream. **The Fromagerie Bothwell:** If you like cheese, why not try some of Manitoba's award-winning varieties. **Old St. Boniface Options:** Why not check out one of the cafés on Provencher Boulevard or on the surrounding streets.
31.45	0.11	Right	**Entrance to parking area of Whittier Park;** cycle to the start of the Old St. Boniface Route.
31.56	0	End	**Old St. Boniface Route.**

Ride as much or as little,
as long or as short as you feel.
But ride.

— Eddy Merckx

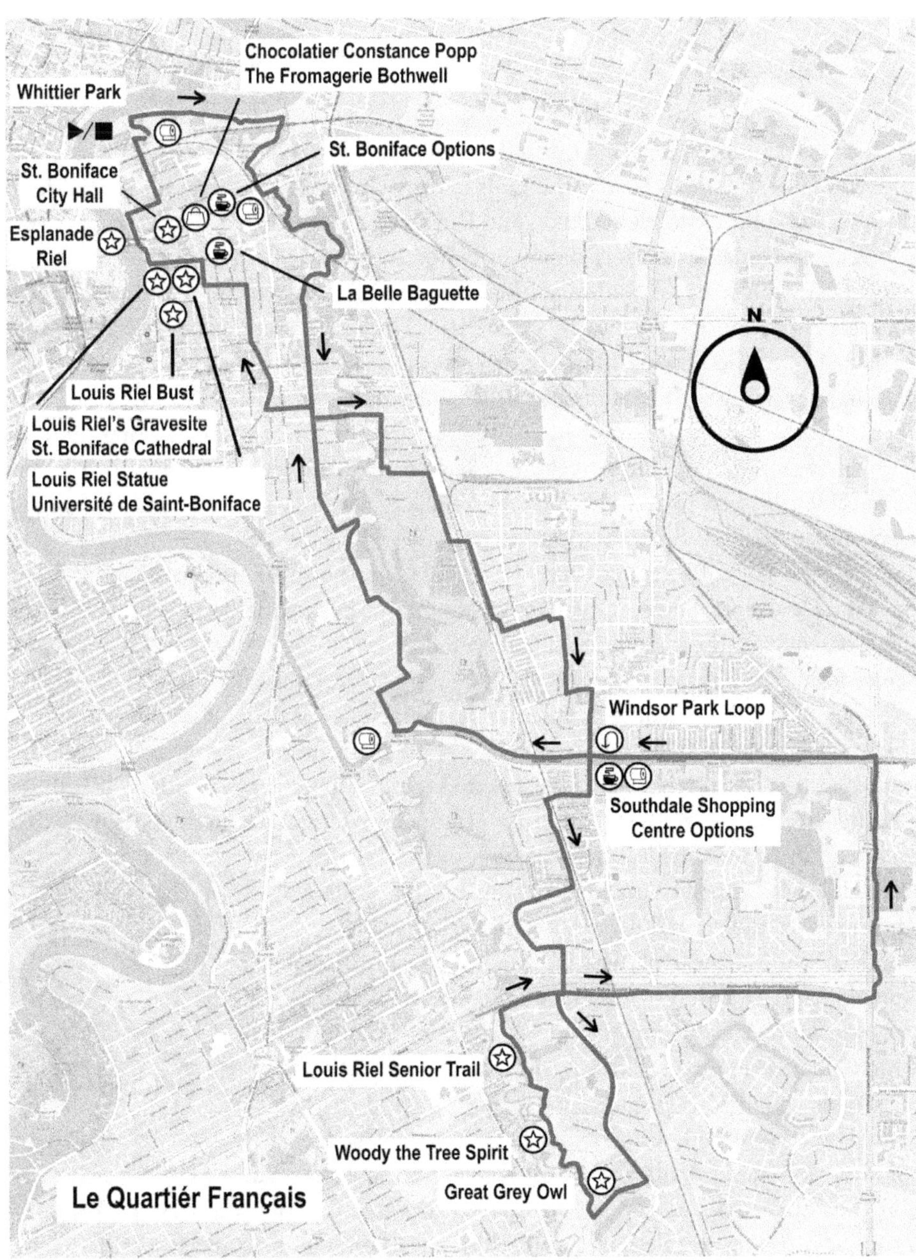
Chocolatier Constance Popp
The Fromagerie Bothwell
Whittier Park
St. Boniface Options
St. Boniface
City Hall
Esplanade
Riel
La Belle Baguette
Louis Riel Bust
Louis Riel's Gravesite
St. Boniface Cathedral
Louis Riel Statue
Université de Saint-Boniface
N
Windsor Park Loop
Southdale Shopping
Centre Options
Louis Riel Senior Trail
Woody the Tree Spirit
Great Grey Owl
Le Quartiér Français

South St. Vital Circuit

Southeast Winnipeg

This ride links together 11 different trails! It is a wonderful ride which starts in St. Vital Park and heads over to the trails in Sage Creek. From there, the route winds through the suburbs of Island Lakes and Royalwood to the banks of the Seine River. Along these banks is the Bois-des-Esprits Forest. Next the route continues through River Park South, across St. Mary's Road, and to the banks of the Red River, going through Normand Park and Van Hull Park. The route then leads back into River Park South, to the Dakota/Dunkirk Pathway and Bishop Grandin Greenway Trail, back to St. Vital Park. The trails along the banks of the Seine River and the Red River are quite different. Along the Seine River you are in a forest whereas along the Red River it is more open. I suppose I could have named this ride From River to River, but decided instead to call it South St. Vital Circuit, as you are essentially cycling from the west end of South St. Vital to the east end.

In terms of coffee stops, there is a Tim Hortons on Dakota Street, across from St. Vital Centre. If, however, you are wanting more substantial fare, you could go to the food court in the shopping mall. The food court is located just inside the doors across from Tim Hortons.

There are three points of interest on the ride, all artistic. The first is located along the stretch of Bishop Grandin Greenway Trail, where as you cycle around a particular bend, you suddenly come face to face with huge moose antlers! It is quite striking. This is an art installation by Jacqueline Metz and Nancy Chew entitled *land/mark*. It represents an interpretation of the imprints left on the landscape by animals and humans. The antlers, of course, are the animal imprints, and the granite bench inscribed with a linear pattern is a nod to the historical "long lot" system of land division common to the area. To get even more insight into this piece, check out the link which includes further description and the artists' statement. http://winnipegarts.ca/wac/artwork/land-mark

land/mark

The second and third points of interest are in the mystical Bois-des-Esprits Forest, the largest riverbank forest in the city. Shortly after you enter this trail is a wooden sign nailed to a tree pointing the way to *Woody the Tree Spirit*. It is a short detour and worth a look. Walter Mirosh and Robert LeClaire carved two spirits from an elm tree. It is said there was a magical moment when the eyes were being carved. The normal forest sounds suddenly became quiet as the sculptors worked on the eyes and only when the outline of the eyes was complete, did the forest sounds resume. There is an interpretive sign next to this carving to learn more about this sculpture.

At the east edge of the forest, Murry Watson, a self-taught Metis carver, created a carving of a *Great Grey Owl*. In addition to the owl, he has also carved other dead branches and stumps in the forest into works, so don't be surprised if you come across other carvings.

Enjoy the circuit!

Quick Notes

Distance – 33.6 km

Parking – St. Vital Park at 190 River Road in parking lot by the Duck Pond, off Lake Road

Option to shorten – yes

   Dakota Loop – 27.8 km

Bike repair station – Bishop Grandin Trail East at the corner of Dakota Avenue

Suggested coffee stops – Tim Hortons at 831 Dakota Street, St. Vital Centre food court

Bathrooms – St. Vital Park Pavilion by the duck pond in St. Vital Park, coffee stop

Points of Interest –

   land/mark art installation on Bishop Grandin Greenway Trail

   Woody the Tree Spirit tree carving, near the beginning of Bois-des-Esprits Trail

   Great Grey Owl wood carving, on the Bois-des-Esprits Trail running along the edge of the forest, close to Eastoak Drive

Trails

Bishop Grandin Greenway Trail – asphalt

Bishop Grandin Trail East – asphalt

Sage Creek Trail – crushed limestone

Warde Multi-use Path – asphalt

Lindsey Wilson Park Path – crushed limestone/asphalt

Coxswain-John Bruce Link Path – crushed limestone

Bois-des-Esprits Trail – crushed limestone

Seine River Greenway Trail – crushed limestone

South St. Vital Parks Trail – asphalt

Normand-Van Hull Parks Trail – crushed limestone

South St. Vital Pathway – asphalt

Dakota/Dunkirk Pathway – asphalt

Safety Cautions

Detailed Directions

Km total	KM Leg	Direction	Location, notes
0	0	Start	**Lake Road, St. Vital Park, at the entrance to the parking lot, facing the Duck Pond.** **St. Vital Park Pavilion:** The Pavilion is located by the Duck Pond. It is open from 7:30am to 10pm.
0	1.15	Left	**Lake Road;** cycle past the Duck Pond and follow the road as it curves left and joins with Perimeter Road and exits to River Road.
1.15	0.59	Right	**River Road;** cycle to the corner of Bishop Grandin to access the Bishop Grandin Greenway Trail/Bishop Grandin Trail East.
1.74	7.36	Left	**Bishop Grandin Greenway Trail (asphalt)/Bishop Grandin Trail East (asphalt);** cycle this trail, first on the north side of Bishop Grandin, past St. Mary's and Dakota to St. Anne's. Cross St. Anne's and then Bishop Grandin to continue on this trail on the south side of Bishop Grandin. Cycle across Shorehill, Island Shore and De la Seigneurie to Lagimodière Boulevard and cross to the east side to access Sage Creek Trail. **Note:** This whole section of trail, from the Red River to Lagimodière Boulevard is known as Bishop Grandin Trail East, but within it, from the Red River to the Seine River, located close to St. Anne's Road, this trail is also known as Bishop Grandin Greenway Trail. *land/mark* **Art Installation:** This art installation takes you by surprise when you come around a bend in the trail just before St. Anne's Road. It is perfectly situated on the edge of a pond. **Bike Repair Station;** located on Bishop Grandin Trail East at the corner of Dakota Street. If your tires are getting low, this is a great place to pump them up!
9.10	2.45	Right	**Sage Creek Trail (crushed limestone);** cycle past a pond to your left, cross Burning Glass and continue straight past a second pond, cross Des Hivernants into

			the green space, where the trail veers right and crosses Sage Creek into another green space. Continue straight and when trail splits, turn right and cross Des Hivernants. Continue past two more ponds on your left. The trail splits again, take the trail on the right, past another pond on your right and exit onto Warde Avenue.
11.55	0.71	Right	**Warde Avenue/Warde Multi-use Path (asphalt);** cross Lagimodière and continue straight on Warde Multi-use Path. Cycle to the first street, De la Seigneurie Boulevard.
12.26	0.33	Right	**De la Seigneurie Boulevard;** cycle past Frigate to Pauline Boutal Crescent/Dockside Way.
12.59	0.40	Left	**Dockside Way;** cycle to the end of the street to Lindsey Wilson Park.
12.99	0.40	Straight	**Lindsey Wilson Park Path (crushed limestone/asphalt);** the trail splits soon after entering the park, veer to the left. The trail splits a second time, and again veer to the left. Pass the tennis court and the trail exits beside Island Lakes Community School on Island Shore Boulevard and Pamela Road. Cross Island Shore to Pamela Road.
13.39	0.31	Straight	**Pamela Road;** cycle past Hacault to Coxswain Cove. At this corner, to your right is Coxswain-John Bruce Link Path.
13.70	0.20	Straight	**Coxswain-John Bruce Link Path (crushed limestone);** cycle across the railway tracks to John Bruce Road E/Wildfire Drive.
13.90	0.68	Straight	**John Bruce Road E;** cycle across Shorehill and past Lardon and Hardman Crescents. Immediately after Hardman is the Bois-des-Esprits Trial.
14.58	1.85	Left	**Bois-des-Esprits Trail (crushed limestone);** this trail runs west of the Seine River. Follow the limestone trail as it runs through the forest. At one point it will emerge from the forest and shortly

			after the trail will split, veer back into the forest. The trail ends at the sidewalk of Shorehill Drive.
			Take the trail to your right which leads under the Royalwood Bridge and curves to the left and up to the sidewalk on the north side of Shorehill Drive.
			Turn left, go over the bridge and on the east side of the river is Seine River Greenway Trail.
		⭐	***Woody the Tree Spirit* carving:** Shortly after you enter the trail, look for a small wooden sign, nailed to a tree, pointing the way to Woody the Spirit Tree. This carving was created by Walter Mirosh and Robert LeClaire from an elm tree and is well worth the detour.
		⭐	***Great Grey Owl* carving:** This carving is located past the Woody the Spirit Tree detour, beside the main trail, just before the trail merges out from the forest.
16.43	1.82	Left	**Seine River Greenway Trail (crushed limestone);** continue cycling along the banks of the Seine River, this time on the west side, past Morrow Gospel Church, Dr. Raj Pandey Hindu Centre and the Seine River Retirement Residence. The trail ends at Creek Bend Road.
18.25	0.27	Right	**Creek Bend Road;** cycle to the stop sign and then turn right to continue on Creek Bend to St. Anne's Road.
18.52	0.42	Right	**St. Anne's Road;** cycle to the traffic lights at Aldgate Road.
18.94	1.00	Left	**Aldgate Road;** cycle past Abbotsfield, John Forsyth, Erindale, Kamberwell, and Vogan's Run. Aldgate Park is to your right and access to South St. Vital Parks Trail.
19.94	2.49	Right	**South St. Vital Parks Trail (asphalt);** this trail starts at Aldgate Park, runs through John Forsyth Park, across Dakota, through Highbury Park, across Highbury, through a green space, across Paddington and finally through Burland Park. The trail splits near the end of Burland Park, turn right and cycle along the edge of the park exiting to the back lane and cycle to Burland Avenue. **Dakota Loop:** At Dakota Street turn right. Cycle past John Forsyth to Warde Avenue. At this intersection, the Dakota/Dunkirk Pathway, a multi-use path, begins on

			the sidewalk on the west side of Dakota. Cross to the other side of Dakota at this intersection to access. Continue straight past Paddington, Novavista and Meadowood to Bishop Grandin Boulevard. Cross Bishop Grandin to the Bishop Grandin Greenway Trail on the north side of the road. Continue, where indicated below, to return to start. Distance – 27.7 km.
22.43	0.48	Left	**Burland Avenue;** cycle to traffic lights on St. Mary's Road.
22.91	0.11	Left	**St. Mary's Road;** cycle to the first street, Redview Drive.
23.02	0.06	Right	**Redview Drive;** just before the street curves right is the start of the Normand-Van Hull Parks Trail.
23.08	2.33	Straight	**Normand-Van Hull Parks Trail (crushed limestone);** follow this trail as it goes along the edge of the Red River through Normand Park and turns right at Van Hull Park. As you near St. Mary's Road, the trail splits, turn right onto the wood chip path and exit on a road at St. Mary's Road. Use caution to cross St. Mary's and directly ahead is South St. Vital Parkway. **Note:** When you cross St. Mary's, there is no break in the curb on the other side.
25.41	1.44	Straight	**South St. Vital Pathway (asphalt);** cycle across Paddington, Charing Cross, John Forsyth and Ashford to Dakota Street.
26.85	2.35	Left	**Dakota/Dunkirk Pathway (asphalt);** cycle on the multi-use path which runs along the west side of Dakota. Cycle past Paddington, Novavista, and Meadowood to Bishop Grandin. Cross Bishop Grandin to the Bishop Grandin Greenway Trail/Bishop Grandin Trail East on the north side of the road. **Tim Hortons or St. Vital Food Court:** Ready for a break? Tim's is located on Dakota, across from St. Vital Centre. Or if you prefer, you could always go to St. Vital food court for more selections.

29.20	2.53	Left 	**Bishop Grandin Greenway Trail (asphalt)/Bishop Grandin Trail East (asphalt);** cycle past St. Mary's to River Road. **Dakota Loop continued:** Continue from this step to return to the start.
31.73	0.92	Right	**River Road;** cycle past St. Vital Cemetery to the entrance of St. Vital Park and Perimeter Road.
32.65	0.77	Left	**St. Vital Park, Perimeter Road;** enter park and follow the road to the Lake Road turn-off.
33.42	0.15	Left	**Lake Road;** cycle to parking lot.
33.57	0	End	**Lake Road at the parking lot.**

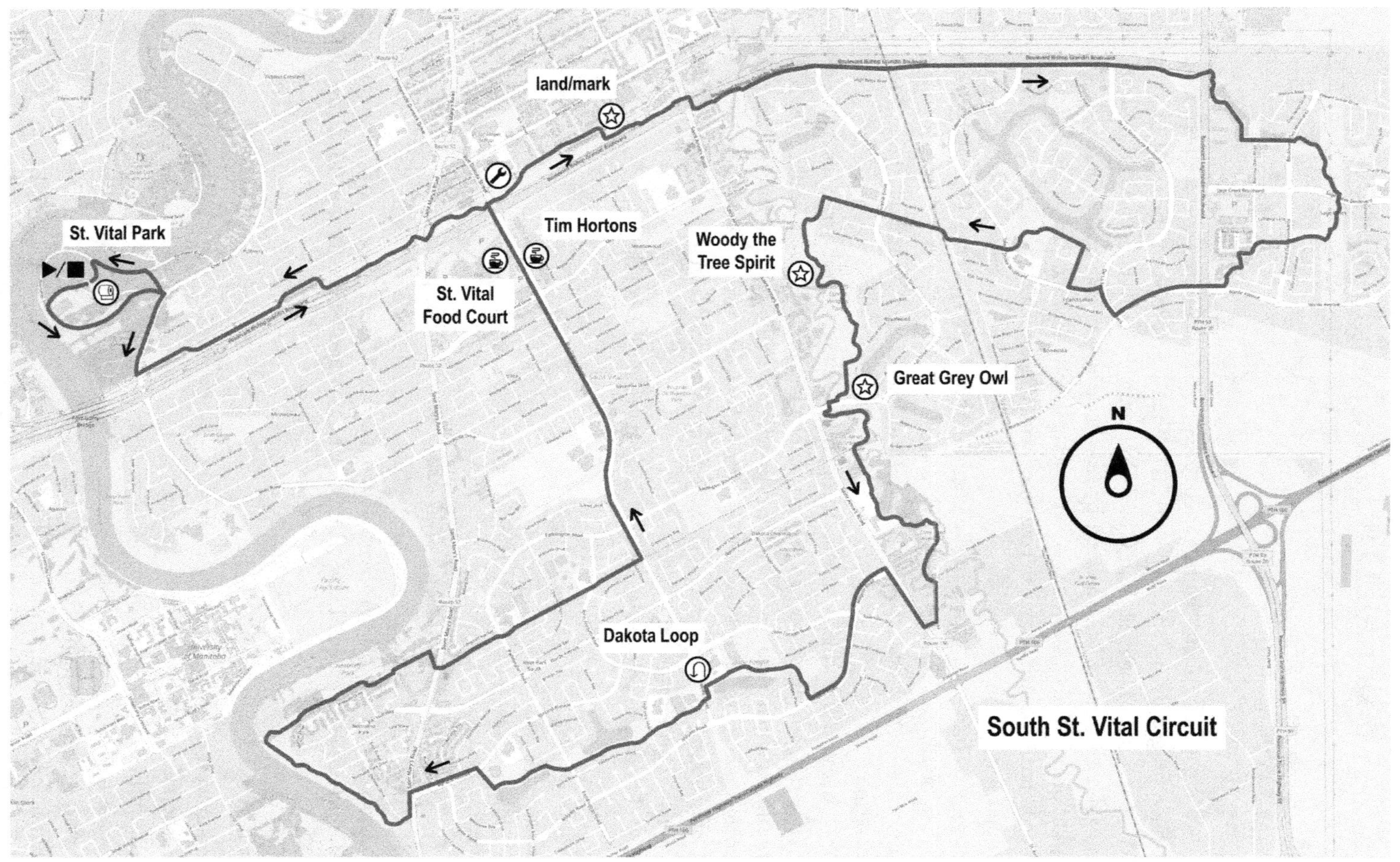
land/mark
St. Vital Park
Tim Hortons
Woody the Tree Spirit
St. Vital Food Court
Great Grey Owl
N
Dakota Loop
South St. Vital Circuit

Beautiful Day in the Neighbourhoods

Southwest Winnipeg

What I like about the newer communities in Winnipeg is the incorporation of wonderful greenways and trail systems. When I first took my bike out to Waverley West and rode along the Ken Oblik Greenway, I was wishing I could move to that neighbourhood! I was impressed by how long it was and how beautiful it was. In addition to this trail, there are several other great trails in surrounding neighbourhoods which, when combined with this Greenway, makes a most charming route.

This ride covers trails in the neighbourhoods of Waverley Heights, Richmond West, South Pointe, Bridgwater Lakes and Bridgwater Forest. I think you will agree, after you do this ride, the name, Beautiful Day in the Neighbourhoods, is a good descriptive.

Because this ride is mostly through residential neighbourhoods, there are no coffee stops on the route, so a short detour is required if you would like to take a break. At about the middle of the ride, when heading towards Bridgwater Lakes, a small detour into Bridgwater Centre offers up many options. Good Earth Coffeehouse, Le Beaux Tea, Lucky Duck Chinese Restaurant, Freshii, Winnie Sweets, Tim Hortons and more.

I hope you enjoy this ride and find it as beautiful as I do!

Quick Notes
Distance – 28.2 km
Parking – Crescent Drive Park at 781 Crescent Drive
Option to shorten – yes
    Neighbourhoods Loop – 17.7 km *For this loop, park on Swan Lake Bay at Albrin Park
Suggested coffee stops – A selection of options on Centre Street in Bridgwater Centre
Bathrooms – Crescent Drive Park, Real Canadian Superstore at 80 Bison Drive, coffee stops

Trails
Southwest Corridor Trail – asphalt
Bishop Grandin West Trail – asphalt
Albrin Park Path – asphalt
Lindero-Syracuse Link Path – asphalt
Syracuse-Augusta Link Path – asphalt
Fairfield-Comdale-Barnes Link Path – asphalt

Kirkbridge Park Path – asphalt
Ken Oblik Greenway Trail – crushed limestone/asphalt
Kenaston Multi-use Path – asphalt
Bison Multi-use Path – asphalt
Bridgwater Lakes Community Path – asphalt
Bridgwater Forest Trail – asphalt

Safety Cautions

Detailed Directions

Km Total	Km Leg	Direction	Location, notes
0	0	Start	**Parking lot of Crescent Drive Park.** **Crescent Drive Park:** Bathrooms are located by the picnic shelters, just west of the parking lot.
0	1.78	Right	**Crescent Drive/Chevrier Boulevard;** follow Crescent Drive as it curves along the Red River, and goes past Thermea Spa, and the Fort Garry Roman Catholic Cemetery. Cross Pembina Highway, at which point the road becomes Chevrier Boulevard, and go to Hudson Street.
1.78	0.27	Left	**Hudson Street;** cycle to the end of the street and the entrance to the Southwest Corridor Trail.
2.05	1.21	Straight	**Southwest Corridor Trail (asphalt);** cycle the trail along the east side of the bus corridor, at Plaza Station the trail crosses to the west side. Watch for buses before crossing. Immediately after the bridge over Bishop Grandin Boulevard is an exit trail to your right leading to Bishop Grandin Trail West.
3.26	1.40	Right	**Bishop Grandin Trail West (asphalt);** the exit trail merges into the main Bishop Grandin Trail West.

			Continue straight, past the hydroelectric station and two exits on your left to the third exit which leads up to Albrin Park.
4.66	0.11	Left	**Albrin Park Path (asphalt);** at the park, the trail splits, turn left and when splits again, turn left again, to exit onto Swan Lake Bay.
4.77	0.64	Left	**Swan Lake Bay/Lake Lindero Road;** Swan Lake curves right and right again and crosses Chancellor, at which point Swan Lake Bay becomes Lake Lindero Road. As the road curves and passes Lake Green, there is Lindero-Syracuse Link Path to your left, located between #54 and #62 Lake Lindero Road. **Neighbourhoods Loop:** Refer to Quick Notes for parking directions. Start from this step and continue as follows until indicated below. Distance – 17.7 km.
5.41	0.17	Left	**Lindero-Syracuse Link Path (asphalt);** cycle the bridge over the pond and exit to Syracuse Crescent.
5.58	0.08	Straight	**Syracuse Crescent;** cycle to the Syracuse-Augusta Link Path located between 56 and 52 Syracuse Crescent.
5.66	0.09	Right	**Syracuse-August Link Path (asphalt);** cycle to Augusta Drive.
5.75	0.70	Right	**Augusta Drive;** Augusta splits and curves left almost immediately. Follow Augusta past Lakelea, Santa Clara, Quincy, Lowell and Salisbury to Chancellor Drive.
6.45	0.18	Left	**Chancellor Drive;** cycle past Chancellor School to Markham Road.
6.63	0.79	Right	**Markham Road/Barnes Street;** cycle across Bison Drive, at which point Markham Road becomes Barnes Street. Cycle past Lee and Colby to the end of Barnes at Fairfield Avenue. **Real Canadian Superstore:** Bathrooms are located in the Superstore at 80 Bison Drive. There is an entrance

			into the lot from Barnes Street once you are across Bison.
7.42	0.01	Left	**Fairfield Avenue;** immediately to your right, between #1206 and #1154 Fairfield Avenue is Fairfield-Comdale-Barnes Link Path.
7.43	0.19	Right	**Fairfield-Comdale-Barnes Link Path (asphalt);** cycle across Comdale and exit to Barnes Street.
7.62	0.53	Right	**Barnes Street/Firbridge Crescent;** cycle across Colebrook and Bairdmore at which point Barnes Street becomes Firbridge Crescent. Continue on Firbridge as it curves right and exits to Marrington Road.
8.15	0.24	Left	**Marrington Road;** to your right is Kirkbridge Park. Turn into the parking lot entrance to access the sidewalk and just past the parking lot is a path into the park.
8.39	0.80	Right	**Kirkbridge Park Path (asphalt);** follow the trail as it runs along the left (south) edge of the park and exits at the corner of Bairdmore Boulevard and Sandusky Drive.
9.19	0.29	Straight	**Sandusky Drive;** cross Bairdmore and continue straight. **Note:** If you stay on the south side of Sandusky, just past the first house is a cut-in lane off the main road. Continue straight, and at the end of it you are just about at the corner of Sandusky and Waverley. Cross Waverley to the beginning of the Ken Oblik Greenway Trail.
9.48	3.19	Left	**Ken Oblik Greenway Trail (crushed limestone/asphalt);** cycle the trail to the pond and when the trail splits, turn right and continue cycling along the edge of the pond. Near the end of the pond, as you approach Waverley, the trail splits, take the path which ends at the corner of Waverley Street and John Angus Drive. Cross Waverley to get to the south side of the street and turn left. The Ken Oblik Greenway Trail continues just past the black fence surrounding the grounds of South Pointe

			School. Note there is no break in the curb to access the trail. Turn right onto the trail, cross Kirkbridge and Tim Sale, and stay on the path which keeps the water to your left. The trail crosses Stan Ballie and then veers right as it runs parallel beside Kenaston. The trail exits at the corner of Kenaston Boulevard and Waverley Street. Cross Kenaston to the multi-use path on the west side of the street.
12.67	2.08	Right	**Kenaston Multi-use Path (asphalt);** cycle across Waverley and South Town to Bison Drive. There is a multi-use path on the south side of Bison.
14.75	0.72	Left	**Bison Multi-use Path (asphalt);** cycle past the first roundabout to the second and turn right onto Appleford Gate. **Bridgwater Centre Options:** The development between the split in Kenaston Boulevard is called Bridgwater Centre and here are a number of coffee options. To enter into this development, turn right at Bison Drive. At the roundabout at Centre Street turn left. The restaurants flank both sides of Centre Street plus there are a few more options behind Shoppers Drugmart. There is a walkway beside Good Earth Coffeehouse to reach this area. After your coffee return to the beginning of this step and continue.
15.47	0.40	Right	**Appleford Gate;** cycle past Eagleview and before the next street, is a community path running behind the houses.
15.87	2.41	Left	**Bridgwater Lakes Community Path (asphalt);** follow the path across Bluemeadow, Wood Glen, North Town, Creekside, Creekside (again) and exit on Creekside Road (yes again!). Turn left and pick up the community path at the bend of the road. The path curves left and exits to Kenaston Multi-use Path.

18.28	1.37	Left	**Kenaston Multi-use Path (asphalt);** cycle to Bishop Grandin and turn right to cross to the east side of Kenaston. Turn right to continue along this side of Kenaston. Cycle to the first exit left, leading into Bridgwater Forest. This exit is almost opposite where you exited from Bridgwater Lakes on the other side of Kenaston.
19.65	1.69	Left	**Bridgwater Forest Trail (asphalt);** when the trail splits, turn left. Cycle to the Bridgwater Forest Fountain and turn right. Cross Highland Creek Road and cycle over the bridge between the two ponds. Continue straight keeping the pond to your left. Cross Highland Creek and turn right, again keeping the pond to your left side. The trail exits to Bridgeland Drive N.
21.34	0.16	Right	**Bridgeland Drive N;** cycle past Lake Forest Road to the roundabout. To the left is the Bishop Grandin West Trail.
21.50	3.65	Left	**Bishop Grandin West Trail (asphalt);** when the trail splits, turn right. Cycle across Waverley and continue straight, under the pedestrian bridge over Bishop Grandin, and across Pembina. As you come to the bridge over the Red River, take the trail which veers right and goes under the bridge to the north side of Bishop Grandin. The trail turns left and exits to Plaza Drive. **Neighbourhoods Loop continued:** Just after Waverley Street, Bishop Grandin West Trail has two exits into Albrin Park. Take the second exit. The trail splits twice but always take the left to exit onto Swan Lake Bay and return to your car.
25.15	0.55	Right	**Plaza Drive;** follow Plaza as it turns left after the shopping strip and heads to Pembina Highway.

25.70	1.06	Right	**Pembina Highway;** use the protected bike lane and be mindful of pedestrians at the floating bus stops. Cycle to Crescent Drive.
26.76	1.43	Right	**Crescent Drive;** cycle past Thermea and into Crescent Drive Park.
28.19	0	End	**Crescent Drive Park parking lot.**

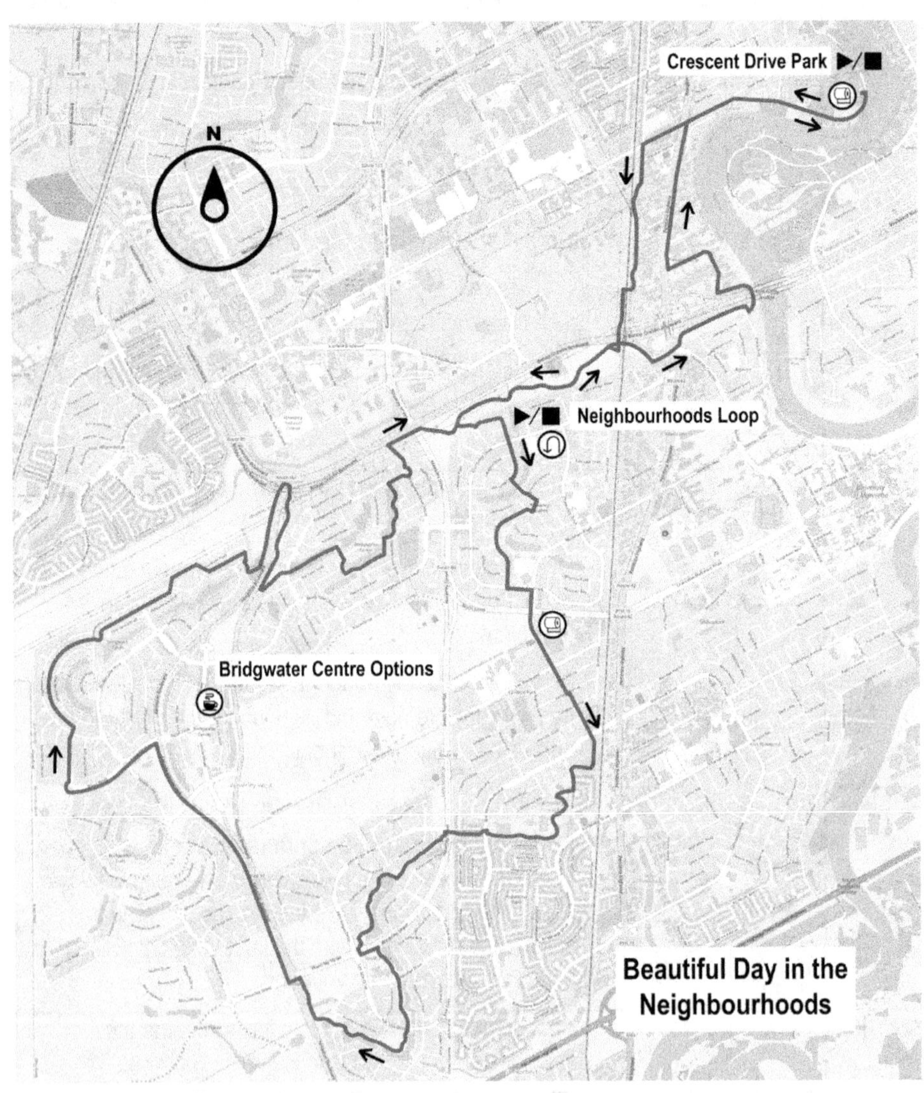

Bike Alive

Southwest Winnipeg

This bike ride starts in St. Vital Park and takes you to FortWhyte Alive. Yes, FortWhyte is one word, I did not spell it wrong! If you haven't been there before, you might like to stop for a while and check it out. At one time, this was an industrial site for mining clay and gravel to make cement, but today FortWhyte is an environmental, educational and recreational area. There is lots to see with an interpretive centre, bison lookout, interpretive nature trails, and floating boardwalks, among other things. The area is populated with a variety of songbirds, waterfowls and deer. For more information about FortWhyte, visit their website. http://www.fortwhyte.org

If you don't have time to explore the park, you might, at the very least, like to stop at Alloway Reception Centre, suggested below as a possible coffee stop. Here you can browse through The Nature Shop, have a snack at the Buffalo Stone Café, and use the bathrooms before continuing on the ride.

From FortWhyte the route heads east, across Pembina Highway, and through Wildwood and Crescent Park, back across Pembina to the Southwest Corridor Trail, to Bishop Grandin Trail West and back to St. Vital Park.

I'm sure you have figured how I came up with the name for this ride. It's definitely lifted from FortWhyte Alive, but I actually like the "Alive" descriptive for another reason. I think cycling makes you feel more alive because you are exercising and out in nature; it just doesn't get any better. So, go out there and feel more alive and do this ride!

Quick Notes
Distance – 34.5 km
Parking – St. Vital Park at 190 River Road in parking lot by the Duck Pond, off Lake
    Road
Option to shorten – yes
    FortWhyte Loop – 15.0 km *For this loop, park by Whyte Ridge Community
        Centre at 170 Fleetwood Road
Suggested coffee stops – Buffalo Stone Café in the Alloway Reception Centre in
    FortWhyte Alive at 1961 McCreary Road, IKEA at 500 Sterling Lyon
    Parkway, Tim Hortons at 860 Waverley Street
Bathrooms – St. Vital Park Pavilion by the duck pond in St. Vital Park, Alloway
    Reception Centre in FortWhyte Alive, coffee stop

Point of Interest –
> FortWhyte Alive at 1961 McCreary Road

Trails

Bishop Grandin Greenway Trail – asphalt
Bishop Grandin Trail West – asphalt
McGillivray Multi-use Path – asphalt
Whyte Ridge Community Centre Trail – asphalt/crushed limestone
FortWhyte Alive Trail – crushed limestone
Carolyn Sifton Trail – crushed limestone
Thundering Bison Trail – asphalt
Waverley Multi-use Path – asphalt
Southwest Corridor Trail – asphalt

Safety Cautions

Detailed Directions

Km total	Km Leg	Direction	Location, notes
0	0	Start	**Lake Road, St. Vital Park, at the entrance to the parking lot, facing the Duck Pond.** **St. Vital Park Pavilion:** The Pavilion is located by the Duck Pond. It is open from 7:30am to 10pm.
0	1.15	Left	**Lake Road;** cycle past the Duck Pond and follow the road as it curves left and joins with Perimeter Road and exits to River Road.
1.15	0.59	Right	**River Road;** cycle to the corner of Bishop Grandin to access the Bishop Grandin Greenway Trail.
1.74	5.79	Right	**Bishop Grandin Greenway Trail (asphalt)/Bishop Grandin Trail West (asphalt);** the trail curves left to go under the bridge to the south side of Bishop Grandin and then curves left and left again to go over the bridge. The trail name becomes Bishop Grandin Trail West in the middle of the bridge.

			At Pembina Highway, cross University Crescent and then Pembina at the lights to continue on the trail. Cycle across Waverley and Kenaston. Here the trail splits, stay on the trail which turns right and runs beside Bishop Grandin, now called Kenaston, and cycle to Scurfield Boulevard.
7.53	1.15	Left	**Scurfield Boulevard;** cycle past Columbia and Monticello to Fleetwood Road.
8.68	0.67	Right	**Fleetwood Road;** cycle past Wittenberg and Scurfield. On your right, just after the railway tracks is Whyte Ridge Community Centre, enter the parking lot to access the Whyte Ridge Community Centre Trail.
9.35	0.46	Straight	**Whyte Ridge Community Centre Trail (asphalt/crushed limestone);** cycle the trail as it goes past the community centre and runs along the edge of the property. When the trail splits, turn left. The trail exits at the end of Cloverwood and continues immediately to your right, exiting at the corner of Sigma Avenue and Front Street. **FortWhyte Loop:** Refer to Quick Notes for parking directions. Start from this step and continue as follows until indicated below. Distance – 15.0 km.
9.81	0.15	Straight	**Front Street;** cycle across McGillivray to the FortWhyte Alive Trail.
9.96	4.93	Left	**FortWhyte Alive Trail (crushed limestone)/Carolyn Sifton Trail (crushed limestone);** cycle between two bodies of water and then veer left, staying along the edge of the ponds. Cycle past FortWhyte's Interpretive Centre to the Alloway Reception Centre and take the trail to the right. This section of the trail is called the Carolyn Sifton Trail and runs along the edge of the bison enclosure to the Bison Viewing Mound. From here, the trail curves right and when intersects with a trail running along the edge of a lake, turn left. At this point you are leaving the Carolyn Sifton Trail. Proceed north though open parkland, and exit at Sterling Lyon Parkway/Thundering Bison Trail.

				FortWhyte Alive: A nice place to take a walk, look at the bison, and do some bird watching. **Buffalo Stone Café:** Located in the Alloway Reception Centre, it is a nice spot to grab a coffee and sit outside. Be sure to check out the gift shop next to the café. **FortWhyte Alive:** Bathrooms are located in the Alloway Reception Centre.
14.89	3.69	Right		**Thundering Bison Trail (asphalt);** this trail runs along the south side of Sterling Lyon Parkway/Wilkes Avenue. Cycle across Kenaston and Victor Lewis to Waverley Street. Cross Waverley Street to the multi-use path on the east side of the road. **IKEA:** Swedish apple cake, anyone? **Tim Hortons:** Located past IKEA at the corner of Wilkes and Waverley.
18.58	1.91	Right		**Waverley Multi-use Path (asphalt);** cycle across Victor Lewis, Seel, and Buffalo to McGillivray Boulevard. Cross McGillivray to the multi-use path on the east side of the road. **FortWhyte Loop continued:** Do not cross McGillivray. Turn right at McGillivray and use the McGillivray Multi-use Path on the north side of the street. Cycle past Dovercourt to Kenaston Boulevard. Cross Kenaston, then McGillivray, to access Bishop Grandin Trail West. Cycle to Scurfield Boulevard and turn right. Cycle past Columbia and Monticello to Fleetwood Road. Turn right and cycle past Wittenberg and Scurfield. On your right, just after the railway tracks, is Whyte Ridge Community Centre parking lot and back to the start of the ride.

20.49	2.36	Left	**McGillivray Multi-use Path (asphalt);** cycle across Hamelin, Irene, Beaumont, and Pembina to Oakenwald Avenue.
22.85	2.01	Straight	**Oakenwald Avenue;** cycle past the stop signs at Woodgrove, Wicklow and Point to the end of the road at North Drive.
24.86	0.65	Right	**North Drive;** cycle to the stop sign at South Drive.
25.51	2.56	Right	**South Drive;** cycle past St. John's Ravenscourt School to the stop sign, turn right to stay on South Drive. Cycle past the stop signs at Point, Dowker and Crane to Crescent Drive.
28.07	1.02	Right	**Crescent Drive/Chevrier Boulevard;** cycle across Pembina Highway at which point Crescent becomes Chevrier Boulevard. Cycle to Hudson Street.
29.09	0.24	Left	**Hudson Street;** cycle to the end of the street and to the Southwest Corridor Trail.
29.33	1.26	Straight	**Southwest Corridor Trail (asphalt);** cycle the trail along the east side of the corridor, at Plaza Station, the trail crosses the corridor to the west side. Continue straight and once over Bishop Grandin Boulevard, to the right is an access path to Bishop Grandin Trail West.
30.59	2.08	Right	**Bishop Grandin Trail West (asphalt)/Bishop Grandin Greenway Trail (asphalt);** the link path intersects with the main trail, turn right to go under the bridge you just crossed and cycle to Pembina. Cross Pembina and University Crescent and cycle over the bridge to cross the Red River. In the middle of this bridge, Bishop Grandin Trail West becomes Bishop Grandin Greenway Trail. Once over the bridge, the trail curves right and right again leading back under the bridge to the north side of Bishop Grandin. The trail curves right and goes to River Road.
32.67	0.93	Left	**River Road;** cycle past St. Vital Cemetery to the entrance of St. Vital Park and Perimeter Road.

33.60	0.77	Left	**St. Vital Park, Perimeter Road**; enter park and follow the road to the Lake Road turn-off.
34.37	0.15	Left	**Lake Road**; cycle to parking lot.
34.52	0	End	**Lake Road at the parking lot.**

Your bike is discovery; your bike is freedom.
It doesn't matter where you are,
when you're on the saddle, you're taken away.

— Doug Donaldson

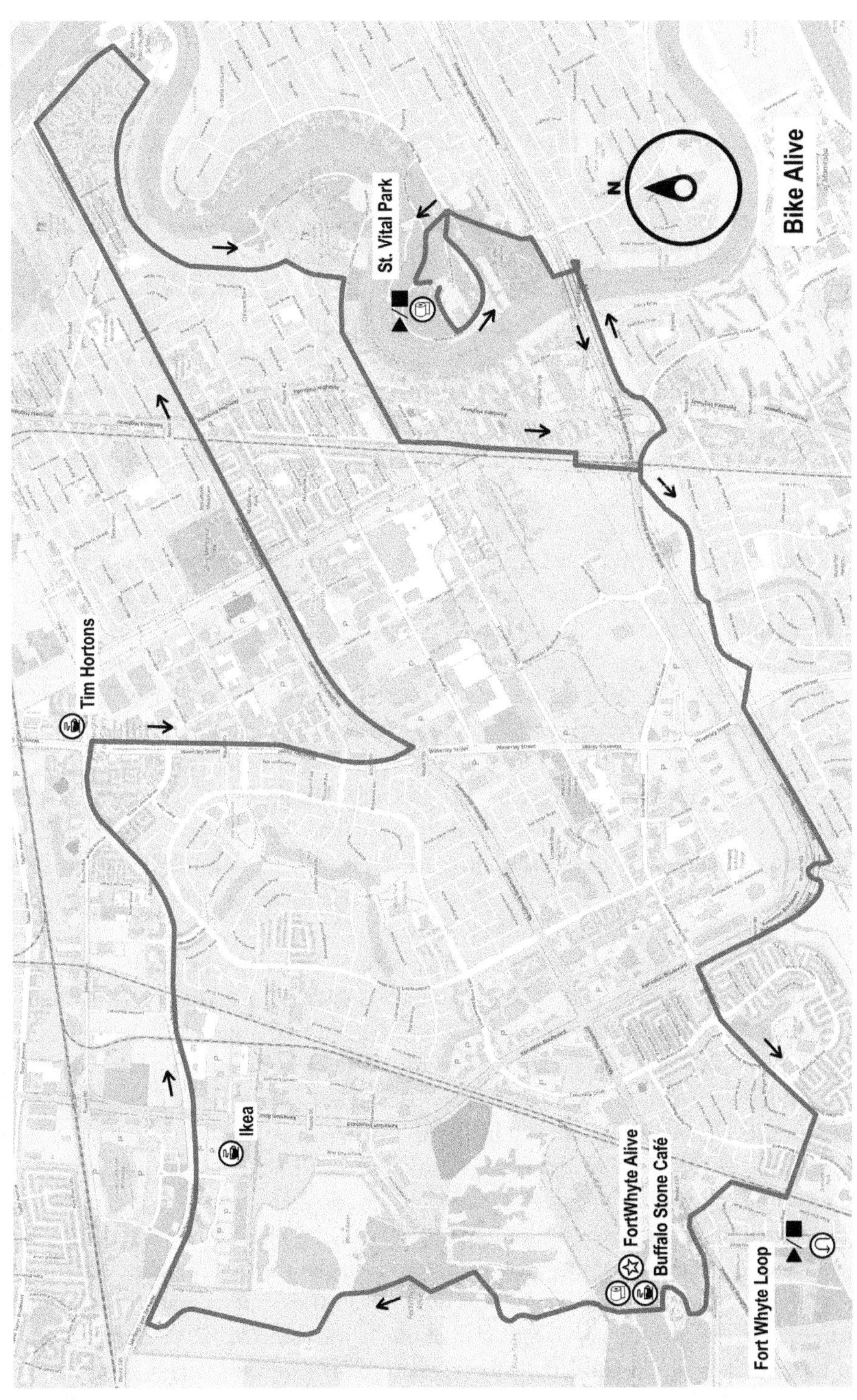
Bike Alive
N
St. Vital Park
Tim Hortons
Ikea
FortWhyte Alive
Buffalo Stone Café
Fort Whyte Loop

Rapid Transit

Southwest Winnipeg

A section of this bike route follows the Southwest Rapid Transit Corridor. This Corridor is an 11 km dedicated roadway, separated from regular traffic, where buses can travel up to 80 km/h. It runs from Queen Elizabeth Way and Stradbrook Avenue, near The Forks, to Bison Drive and the University of Manitoba. At the time of its inception, the expectation of a large population growth in the southwest corner of the city was one of the driving factors to get this project underway. The Corridor was considered essential to decrease future traffic congestion and to improve the overall bus transportation system in the city. This ride does not cover the entire length of the Corridor, never-the-less, I've named the ride Rapid Transit, in honour of this achievement in Winnipeg.

Part of this route also goes through the suburb of Lindenwoods, through Muys Park and VanWalleghem Park along the edge of a pond. While cycling along this stretch, watch for pelicans, as they can be seen here.

There are many options for coffee, a meal or an ice cream. As you pass through Bridgwater Centre, options include Good Earth Coffeehouse, Le Beaux Tea, Lucky Duck Chinese Restaurant, Freshii, Winnie Sweets, Tim Hortons and more.

If you didn't stop in Bridgwater Centre, the corner of Kenaston and McGillivray has shopping plazas at all four corners, each full of possibilities: A&W, Taco del Mar, Subway, Nuburger, Starbucks, Mucho Burrito, Swiss Chalet, Qdoba Mexican Eats, Umi Sushi, Quiznos, and Freshii, just to name a few. The hard part will be determining where you want to stop! Or, if you prefer, you can wait till closer to the end of the ride where there is a choice between Starbucks or BDI.

As a point of interest, there is some fascinating history attached to the area along Churchill Parkway, where this ride starts. In 1891, Albert William Austin, the founder of Winnipeg's first streetcar system, built a year-round playground called River Park on this site. The park occupied 150 acres and stretched roughly from Elm Park Bridge to the end of Claire Avenue. River Park featured a midway with rides including the largest roller coaster in North America at the time, called the Deep Dipper, a Crazy House, and a carousel. Also on site were a race track, sports facilities, a grass air strip, wildlife enclosures for various prairie animals such as elk, bison and even bears, and picnic areas. In the winter, there were toboggan slides, ice skating and snow shoeing. Many Winnipeggers would travel to the park via the Park Line street car which ran from Main Street and was the first electric car to operate in Canada. In its heyday it was a thriving, vibrant attraction. It was considered *the centre* of social life in Winnipeg and according to records, up to 50% of Winnipeg's population of about 25,000 in the 1890s, would be at River Park on a day. Unfortunately, this park eventually declined and disappeared in the early 1940s.

On the west side of the public bathroom on Churchill Parkway Trail, you can see some stonework embedded into the ground, these remnants are thought to be part of a 20-foot-deep bear pit!

If you would like to read up more about this park or see a layout of the grounds, there are three interpretive plaques in Elva Fletcher Way, located on the northwest corner of Osborne and Jubilee.

Enjoy!

Quick Notes

Distance – 30.3 km

Parking – Park on residential streets near the corner of Churchill Drive and Montgomery Avenue

Option to shorten – yes

Corridor Loop – 14.9 km

Suggested coffee stops – Centre Street in Bridgwater Centre or at the corner of Kenaston and McGillivray Boulevard each offer a smorgasbord of options, Starbucks at 1144 Pembina Highway, BDI at 766 Jubilee Avenue

Bathrooms – Public Bathroom on Churchill Parkway Trail, coffee stop

Point of Interest –

River Park Historic Site by Churchill Drive

Trails

Churchill Parkway Trail – crushed limestone
Southwest Corridor Trail – asphalt
Chevrier Multi-use Path – asphalt
Bishop Grandin Trail West – asphalt
Kenaston Multi-use Path – asphalt
Bison Multi-use Path – asphalt
Bridgwater Forest Trail – asphalt
McGillivray Multi-use Path – asphalt
Lindenwood Parks Trail – asphalt
Jubilee Multi-use Path – asphalt

Safety Cautions

Detailed Directions

Km total	Km Leg	Direction	Location, notes
0	0	Start	**Churchill Parkway Trail by the Public Bathroom, just east of the St. Vital Bridge, facing the river.** **River Park:** This fairground and amusement park, was located along this stretch of land in the late 1800s to 1930s. One of the many attractions which drew in the crowds were the animal enclosures for bison, elk and even bears. There are virtually no traces left of this once popular attraction, but on the west side of the public bathroom, you can still see some stonework embedded into the ground, remnants of the bear enclosure! **Public Bathroom:** Located on Churchill Parkway Trail at the start of the ride. Open variable hours.
0	3.22	Left	**Churchill Parkway Trail (crushed limestone)/Churchill Drive;** cycle the trail through Churchill Drive Park to its exit on Churchill Drive. Continue right on Churchill past the community gardens and the South Osborne Community Orchard to Don Gerrie Park where the trail continues to the right and goes past the Manitoba Canoe and Kayak Center before exiting back onto Churchill Drive. Cycle past Hay and Churchill curves into Brandon Avenue.
3.22	0.41	Straight	**Brandon Avenue;** cycle across Osborne and to your right, at the edge of Winnipeg Transit's Brandon Garage area, is access to the multi-use path along Brandon's north sidewalk, which is part of the Southwest Corridor Trail.
3.63	5.58	Straight	**Southwest Corridor Trail (asphalt);** cycle past the Transit Garage, and follow the trail as it turns left and runs along the back edge of Hethrington Park, and then veers right. The trail runs along the left side of the Southwest Rapid Transit Corridor.

			Just past the Jubilee Station, the trail splits, turn right and cycle over Pembina Highway and continue straight, staying beside the corridor. The trail curves left and goes over McGillivary, across Clarence to Chevrier Boulevard. Cycle across Chevrier at the lights to the multi-use path.
9.21	0.24	Left	**Chevrier Multi-use Path (asphalt);** cycle past French and over the railway tracks to Hudson Street.
9.45	0.25	Right	**Hudson Street;** cycle to the end of the street and the continuation of the Southwest Corridor Trail.
9.70	1.26	Straight	**Southwest Corridor Trail (asphalt);** cycle along the east side of the bus corridor and at Plaza Station, the trail crosses to the west side. Be sure to check for buses before crossing. Cycle over Bishop Grandin Boulevard and the trail immediately to your right is Bishop Grandin Trail West. **Corridor Loop:** When you reach the beginning of the Bishop Grandin Trail, turn around and cycle the Southwest Corridor Trail back to Seel Station and then continue, where indicated below, to return to start. Distance – 14.9 km.
10.96	2.92	Right	**Bishop Grandin Trail West (asphalt);** the trail merges with the main trail, continue straight and cross Waverley. As you approach Kenaston, the trail splits, turn right and head for the lights to cross Kenaston. Once across the street, the trail turns left and soon splits again. Continue straight on the Kenaston Multi-use Path.
13.88	2.05	Straight	**Kenaston Multi-use Path (asphalt);** cycle past North Town to Bison Drive. Cross Bison Drive to access the Bison Multi-use Path on the south side of the street.
15.93	0.59	Right	**Bison Multi-use Path (asphalt);** cycle across Kenaston, straight through the roundabout, and cross Kenaston to the Kenaston Multi-use Path. **Bridgwater Centre Options:** The development between the split in Kenaston Boulevard is called

			Bridgwater Centre and here are a number of coffee options. At the roundabout at Centre Street turn left. The restaurants flank both side of Centre Street plus there are a few more options behind Shoppers Drugmart. There is a walkway beside Good Earth Coffeehouse to reach this area. After your coffee return to Bison Multi-use Path and continue.
16.52	0.39	Left	**Kenaston Multi-use Path (asphalt);** cycle to North Town Road.
16.91	0.20	Right	**North Town Road;** cycle past Hill Grove to the green space and the Bridgwater Forest Trail.
17.11	2.27	Right	**Bridgwater Forest Trail (asphalt);** the trail skirts along the end of a pond before splitting. Veer left as the trail runs through a greenspace behind the homes on North Town Road. There are some paths leading off this trail but continue straight and cross Coach Hill and North Town Road. The trail now follows along a pond to your left, do not cross over the water and continue on the trail next to the water until you cross Highland Creek Road. Here the trail splits, turn left. Continue straight as it runs through a forested area, past Bridgwater Forest Fountain, and across Bridgeland. Take the next exit after Bridgeland, which is to your right and exits onto Kenaston Multi-use Path.
19.38	0.85	Right	**Kenaston Multi-use Path (asphalt);** cycle to the lights at the corner of Bishop Grandin and Kenaston. Cross Kenaston and the trail turns left and then splits. The trail to your right is Bishop Grandin Trail West.
20.23	1.69	Right	**Bishop Grandin Trail West (asphalt);** cycle past Scurfield and across McGillivray Boulevard to the north side and the McGillivray Multi-use Path. **Note:** At the corner of Kenaston and Bishop Grandin, Bishop Grandin becomes Kenaston Boulevard. The trail, however, is still called Bishop Grandin Trail West.

			Kenaston and McGillivray Options: If you feel like having a coffee or want a snack or a meal, at this corner is a smorgasbord of choices. Enjoy and then return to this spot to continue the ride.
21.92	0.60	Right	**McGillivray Multi-use Path (asphalt);** cycle to Lindenwood Drive W.
22.52	0.67	Left	**Lindenwood Drive W;** cycle past Fairhaven and Lindenwood Drive E to Lindenshore Drive.
23.19	0.47	Right	**Lindenshore Drive;** cycle past Linden Terrace. The road curves to the left and just before it curves again, between houses #112 and #120, is the Lindenwood Parks Trail.
23.66	1.41	Left	**Lindenwood Parks Trail (asphalt);** the trail enters Muys Park and curves to the right along the edge of a pond, when the trail splits, turn left to cycle between the two ponds. The trail then follows along a second pond to your right and over a bridge into Van Walleghem Park. Continue straight to the exit at the corner of Lindenwood Dr E and Lindenwood Place.
25.07	2.25	Straight	**Lindenwood Place/Seel Avenue/Somerville Avenue;** cycle across Waverley Street and Lindenwood Place becomes Seel Avenue. Cross Otter, Fennel and the Southwest Rapid Transit Corridor. Continue straight onto Somerville Avenue. Cycle past Mars, Planet, Beaumont, and Daniel to Rockman Street. **Corridor Loop continued:** Just before the Seel Station, take the path to your right to Somerville Avenue. Cycle past Mars, Planet, Beaumont, and Daniel to Rockman Street. Follow the directions below to return to the start.
27.32	0.08	Left	**Rockman Street;** cycle one block to Windermere Avenue.

27.40	0.40	Right	**Windermere Avenue/Point Road;** cycle across Pembina Highway at the lights. The road veers towards the right and is now called Point Road. Cycle one block to Somerville Avenue. **Starbucks:** Here's another opportunity for coffee! Starbucks is located on Pembina Highway just right of this corner, beside Shoppers Drug Mart.
27.80	0.31	Left	**Somerville Avenue;** cycle to the end of the street to Riverside Drive.
28.11	0.60	Left	**Riverside Drive;** cycle past Toilers Memorial Park and follow Riverside as it turns right, then left, past Merriam to Jubilee Avenue. There is a multi-use path on the south sidewalk.
28.71	0.47	Right	**Jubilee Multi-use Path (asphalt);** cycle past BDI to the lights at Cockburn Street S. **BDI:** Feeling like ice cream? BDI has a great selection of treats to suit everyone's taste. Enjoy.
29.18	0.09	Right	**Cockburn Street S/Churchill Drive;** Cockburn curves into Churchill Drive and at the curve is the entrance to Churchill Parkway Trail.
29.27	1.00	Left	**Churchill Parkway Trail (crushed limestone);** follow the trail through the greenspace between the road and the river, under the St. Vital Bridge and back to the start of the ride by the Public Bathroom.
30.27	0	End	**Churchill Parkway Trail by the Public Bathroom.**

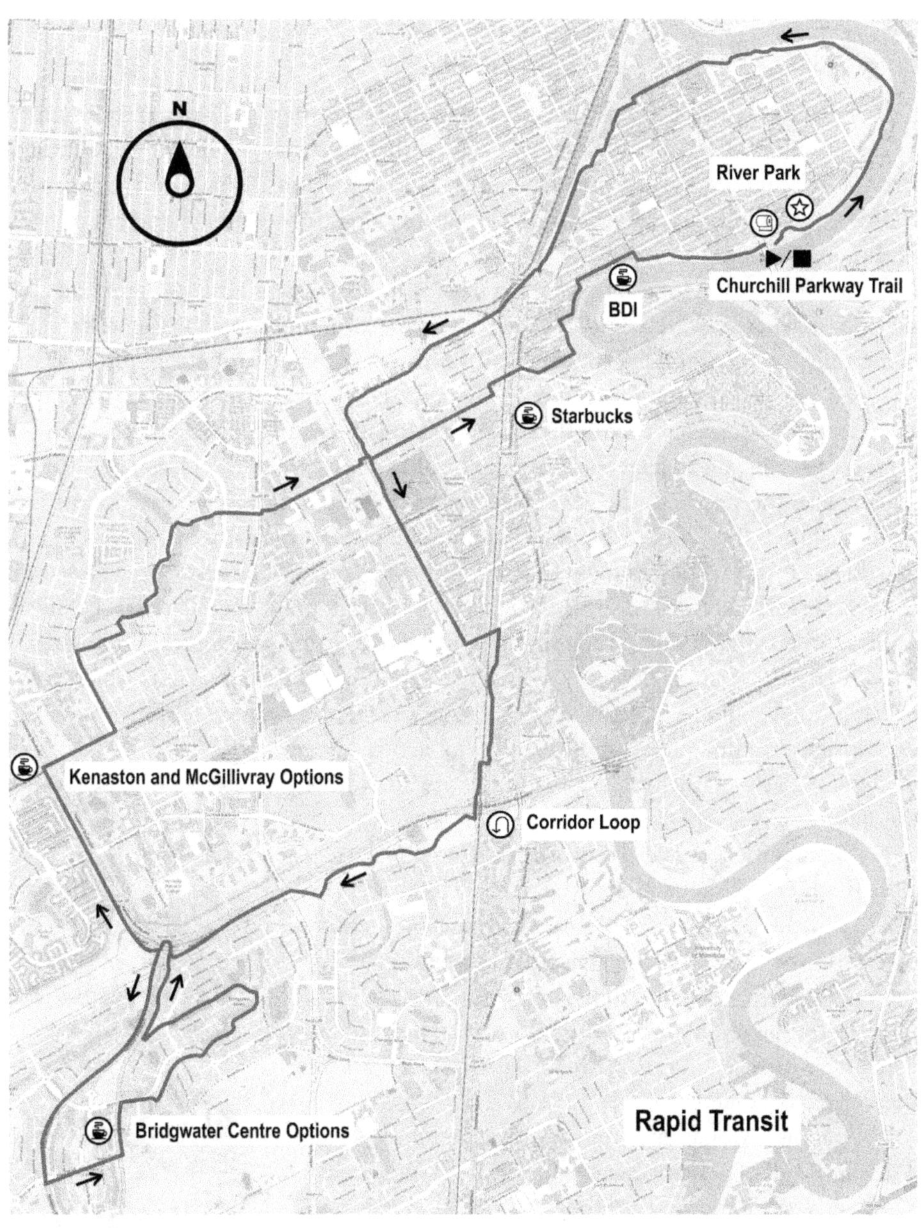
N
River Park
Churchill Parkway Trail
BDI
Starbucks
Kenaston and McGillivray Options
Corridor Loop
Bridgwater Centre Options
Rapid Transit

St. Norbert Exploration

Southwest Winnipeg

This ride takes you past the Perimeter into St. Norbert, a bilingual community of just over 5000 inhabitants. St. Norbert is rich in history with the St. Norbert Provincial Heritage Park and the Trappist Monastery and is home to the Farmers Market, the largest market of its kind in Manitoba. History and shopping, what a great combination!

St. Norbert Exploration cycles to a number of historical sites in the area and also up and down a few residential streets in quiet neighbourhoods. You enter this community on the Sentier Cloutier Trail which runs along river bottom forest, open tall grass prairie, oak and aspen forests and a wetlands area. Then you cycle through Ducharme Park on your way to the Trappist Monastery ruins. From there it is to St. Norbert Provincial Heritage Park and the turning point for the ride. On the way back you explore the neighbourhoods on the east side of Pembina Highway. There is a striking church, St. Norbert Parish, hidden there. I don't think I need to give you any details about it, you will know it when you see it. You exit the residential streets at the Farmers Market and then head back to the starting point. Because you see much of St. Norbert in this ride, I thought it appropriate to call it St. Norbert Exploration.

A large portion of this ride is done on St. Norbert Heritage Trails which are a collection of multi-use pathways, trails and residential streets. In the detailed description of the ride, I mostly refer to actual street names, for clarity, rather than calling the route St. Norbert Heritage Trails.

There are two good places to stop for coffee, one is at the Farmers Market and the other is at the Nobside Café located in the St. Norbert Hotel. This café has a varied menu, so you might wish to check it out before you get there. http://www.stnorberthotel.com/nobside-cafe

Nobside Café

I have suggested three points of interest: the Trappist Monastery ruins, St. Norbert Provincial Heritage Park and the Farmers Market.

Trappist Monastery Ruins – Five members of the Trappist Order in France came to reside in this area in 1892 and built a monastery here from 1903 – 1905. Over the decades, as urban sprawl started to affect their contemplative lifestyle, in 1978 the Trappists made the decision to move to a new location near Holland, Manitoba. Fire ravaged the vacated church and residential

Trappist Monastery

wing at this location in 1983. However, the ruins remain and there are interpretive signs about the Trappist monks and the monastery for interesting reading. This is a tranquil place to have a stroll and take in the view of the La Salle River and the surrounding countryside. The ruins are located in the Trappist Monastery Provincial Heritage Park. http://www.mhs.mb.ca/ docs/sites/trappist monastery.shtml

St. Norbert Provincial Heritage Park – This park is situated at the site where the La Salle River flows into the Red River, and is sometimes referred to as Winnipeg's "other forks". It features three 19th century log homes with exhibits which give a glimpse into Métis family life in the late 1800s. You can either do a self-guided tour or an hour-long guided tour. There is also a 1 km walking trail along the La Salle River. See website for more information. Admission is free. https://www.travelmanitoba.com/ directory/st-norbert-provincial-heritage-park/

St. Norbert Park

Farmers Market – This is a local market supporting Manitoba producers. They have items such as produce, eggs, baked goods, meats and crafts. The market is open year-round and if interested in stopping, check the days and times they are open on their website. http://www.stnorbert farmersmarket.ca

Farmers Market

Quick Notes

Distance – 33.7 km

Parking – Crescent Drive Park at 781 Crescent Drive

Options to shorten – yes

    1 – King's Park Loop – 17.2 km *For this loop, park in King's Park at 198 King's Drive

    2 – Farmers Market Loop – 21.7 km

Suggested coffee stops – Farmers Market at 3514 Pembina Highway, St. Norbert Hotel's Nobside Café at 3540 Pembina Highway

Bathrooms – Crescent Drive Park at 781 Crescent Drive, King's Park at 198 King's Drive, Trappist Monastery Provincial Heritage Park (non-modern) at Rue des Ruines du Monastere, St. Norbert Provincial Heritage Park (non-modern) at 40 Turnbull Drive, coffee stops

Points of Interest –

    Farmers Market at 3514 Pembina Hwy

    Trappist Monastery Ruins at 100 Rue des Ruines du Monastere

    St. Norbert Provincial Heritage Park at 40 Turnbull Drive

Trails

Southwest Corridor Trail – asphalt
Southpark Multi-use Path – asphalt
University Multi-use Path – asphalt
Sentier Cloutier Trail – asphalt
Pembina Multi-use Path – asphalt
St. Norbert Heritage Trails –asphalt
Ducharme Park Path – crushed limestone
Dysart Multi-use Path – asphalt
University Trail – crushed limestone/asphalt
Bishop Grandin Trail West – asphalt

Safety Cautions

Detailed Directions

Km Total	Km Leg	Direction	Location, notes
0	0	Start	**Parking lot of Crescent Drive Park.** **Crescent Drive Park:** Bathrooms are located by the picnic shelters, just west of the parking lot.
0	1.78	Right	**Crescent Drive/Chevrier Boulevard;** follow Crescent Drive as it curves along the Red River, and goes past Thermea Spa, and the Fort Garry Roman Catholic Cemetery. Cross Pembina Highway, at which point the road becomes Chevrier Boulevard, and go to Hudson Street.
1.78	0.27	Left	**Hudson Street;** cycle to the end of the street and the entrance to the Southwest Corridor Trail.
2.05	2.14	Straight	**Southwest Corridor Trail (asphalt);** cycle the trail along the east side of the bus corridor, at Plaza Station, the trail crosses to the west side. Watch for buses before crossing.

			Cycle the bridge over Bishop Grandin Boulevard and continue straight. At Chancellor Drive the trail moves back to the east side of the corridor. Cycle to the next street, Southpark Drive.
4.19	0.91	Left	**Southpark Multi-use Path (asphalt);** cycle across Pembina Highway, stay on the path to University Crescent.
5.10	1.33	Right	**University Multi-use Path (asphalt)/University Crescent;** cycle the multi-use path to the IG Field and then move onto the road. Continue straight past Chancellor Matheson, Dafoe and Freedman. Stay on University Crescent as it leaves the university grounds and goes into a residential area. Cycle past Grierson to Pasadena Avenue.
6.43	0.21	Left	**Pasadena Avenue;** cycle past April to King's Drive.
6.64	0.56	Right	**King's Drive;** cycle to King's Park and the road curves right and becomes Kilkenny Drive. **King's Park:** Bathrooms are located shortly after the entrance. They are open daily from 8am to 9pm. **King's Park Loop:** Refer to Quick Notes for parking directions. At the entrance to King's Park on King's Drive, turn left onto Kilkenny and follow the directions below until you return to King's Park. This loop does not cycle to St. Norbert Provincial Heritage Park. I have indicated below which steps to omit. Distance – 17.2 km.
7.20	2.03	Right	**Kilkenny Drive;** follow the drive as it winds along the Red River. This road ends at the beginning of the Sentier Cloutier Trail.
9.23	2.03	Left	**Sentier Cloutier Trail (asphalt);** the trail begins on the north shoulder of the road and as you approach the right turn to go under the Trans-Canada Highway, the trail crosses the road and a path begins on the west edge of the road, leading into the greenspace. Cycle this trail as it runs along Cloutier Drive to Pembina

			Highway and the multi-use path on the east sidewalk which is known as the St. Norbert Heritage Trail.
11.26	0.39	Left	**Pembina Multi-use Path (asphalt)/St. Norbert Heritage Trail (asphalt);** cycle to the light at Grandmont Boulevard. **Farmers Market Loop:** Continue straight another 0.53 km to the Farmers Market. When finished at the market, turn around and head back down Pembina Multi-use Path to Sentier Cloutier Trail and then continue, where indicated below, to return to start. Distance – 21.7 km.
11.65	0.68	Right	**Grandmont Boulevard;** cycle over the railway tracks and past Bellemer and Delorme to Ducharme Park. There is a park path to your left, but note there is no break in the curb to access.
12.33	0.72	Right	**Ducharme Park Path (crushed limestone);** the trail follows along the edge of a pond to your right, crosses Bellemer Drive and continues through another green space and exits at Avenue Ducharme. **Note:** There are breaks in the curbs at Bellemer Drive to easily cross the road, but there is no break in the curb when you reach Avenue Ducharme.
13.05	0.04	Left	**Avenue Ducharme;** cycle to the first block, Villeneuve Boulevard.
13.09	0.51	Left	**Villeneuve Boulevard;** cycle to the end of the road at Rue des Trappistes.
13.60	0.69	Right	**Rue des Trappistes;** cycle past Rue du Monastere to Rue des Ruines du Monastere.
14.29	0.75	Left	**Rue des Ruines du Monastere;** cycle to the end of the road to the Trappist Monastery Provincial Heritage Park. Take a few minutes to look around and then head back on the same road. **Trappist Monastery Ruins:** This is a tranquil place for a stroll and to find out the history of the Trappist Monks. **Trappist Monastery Provincial Heritage Park:** The bathrooms (non-modern) are located just off the parking area, close to the basilica.

15.04	0.75	U-turn	**Rue des Ruines du Monastere;** cycle back to Rue des Trappistes.
15.79	0.88	Right	**Rue des Trappistes;** cycle past Rue du Monastere, Villeneuve and across Pembina Highway to access the Pembina Multi-use Path on the east side of Pembina Highway. **Note:** There is a trail to your right, just before Pembina Highway which leads under the bridge to the east side of Pembina Highway that can be used, if prefer, and if not flooded. **King's Park Loop continued:** Omit the next two steps and continue with the step which turns right on Avenue de L'Eglise. However, you will already be on that street and don't have to turn, as once across Pembina Highway, Rue Des Trappistes becomes Avenue de L'Eglise.
16.67	1.32	Right	**Pembina Multi-use Path (asphalt)/St. Norbert Heritage Trail;** cycle over the La Salle River to Turnbull Drive. At this corner is St. Norbert Provincial Heritage Park. **St. Norbert Provincial Heritage Park:** Check out the 19th century log homes or walk along the trail by the La Salle River. **St. Norbert Provincial Heritage Park:** The bathrooms (non-modern) are located in the parking lot of the park.
17.99	1.32	U-turn	**Pembina Multi-use Path (asphalt)/St. Norbert Heritage Trail;** cycle back over the La Salle River bridge to Rue des Trappistes/Avenue de L'Eglise.
19.31	0.26	Right	**Avenue de L'Eglise;** cycle past Rue Landry to Rue Campeau. This section is still part of the St. Norbert Heritage Trails and meanders through some quiet residential streets.
19.57	0.11	Right	**Rue Campeau;** cycle to Avenue Ste Therese.
19.68	0.44	Left	**Avenue Ste Therese;** cycle past Saint Norbert Cemetery to Rue St. Pierre.
20.12	0.36	Left	**Rue St. Pierre;** cycle past the three churches clustered at the next corner; St. Norbert Parish, Eglise Church, and Chapelle de Notre-Dame-du-Bon Secours.

			Cycle past St. Norbert Nursing home to Lord Avenue.
20.48	0.40	Right	**Lord Avenue;** follow this road as it curves with the Red River and ends at Avenue Lemay.
20.88	0.77	Left	**Avenue Lemay;** cycle to Rue Landry, one block before Pembina Highway.
21.65	0.46	Right	**Rue Landry;** when the street ends, cycle straight, go through the parking area to a crushed limestone trail to your left in the green space behind École Noël-Ritchot. The trail turns right at the edge of the green space and just past the play structure is a path leading into the back of the Farmers Market parking lot. Go through the lot and exit onto the multi-use path on Pembina Highway. **St. Norbert Farmers Market:** Need some food items or crafts? Drop by the Farmers Market to check them out. **St. Norbert Farmers Market or Nobside Café:** Both of these eating options are close to each other with Nobside Café about one block south from the Farmers Market and located in the St. Norbert Hotel at 3540 Pembina Highway. You can't go wrong with either stop.
22.11	0.89	Right	**Pembina Multi-use Path/St. Norbert Heritage Trail (asphalt);** return to Sentier Cloutier Trail on the north side of Cloutier Drive.
23.00	2.03	Right	**Sentier Cloutier Trail (asphalt);** cycle the trail back under the Trans-Canada Highway to Kilkenny Drive. **Farmers Market Loop continued:** Follow details from this step onwards to return to Crescent Park.
25.03	2.03	Left	**Kilkenny Drive;** at King's Park, Kilkenny becomes King's Drive.
27.06	0.56	Left	**King's Drive;** cycle back to Pasadena Avenue. Fort Garry Evangelical Mennonite Church is on the corner.
27.62	0.25	Left	**Pasadena Avenue;** cycle past April to University Crescent.
27.87	0.92	Right	**University Crescent;** cycle back onto the university grounds, past Dafoe, to Dysart Road.

28.79	0.16	Right	**Dysart Multi-use Path (asphalt);** cycle to the crosswalk and the University Trail.
28.95	0.73	Left	**University Trail (crushed limestone/asphalt);** cross Dysart at the cross walk and follow the trail through the parking lot and across Sifton into the green space. At the end of the road is a trail to the right which shortly turns left. Cycle towards the Red River and when the trail splits, continue left. Follow the path next to the river to its exit onto D'Arcy Road.
29.68	0.49	Straight	**D'Arcy Road;** cycle to the end of the street and to an access on the right to the Bishop Grandin Trail West.
30.17	0.44	Right	**Bishop Grandin Trail West (asphalt);** cycle under the bridge to the north side of Bishop Grandin Boulevard. The trail curves left and exits at Plaza Drive.
30.61	0.55	Right	**Plaza Drive;** follow Plaza as it turns left after the shopping strip and heads to Pembina Highway.
31.16	1.06	Right	**Pembina Highway;** use the protected bike lane and be mindful of pedestrians at the floating bus stops. Return to Crescent Drive.
32.22	1.43	Right	**Crescent Drive;** cycle past Thermea and into Crescent Drive Park.
33.65	0	End	**Parking lot of Crescent Drive Park.**

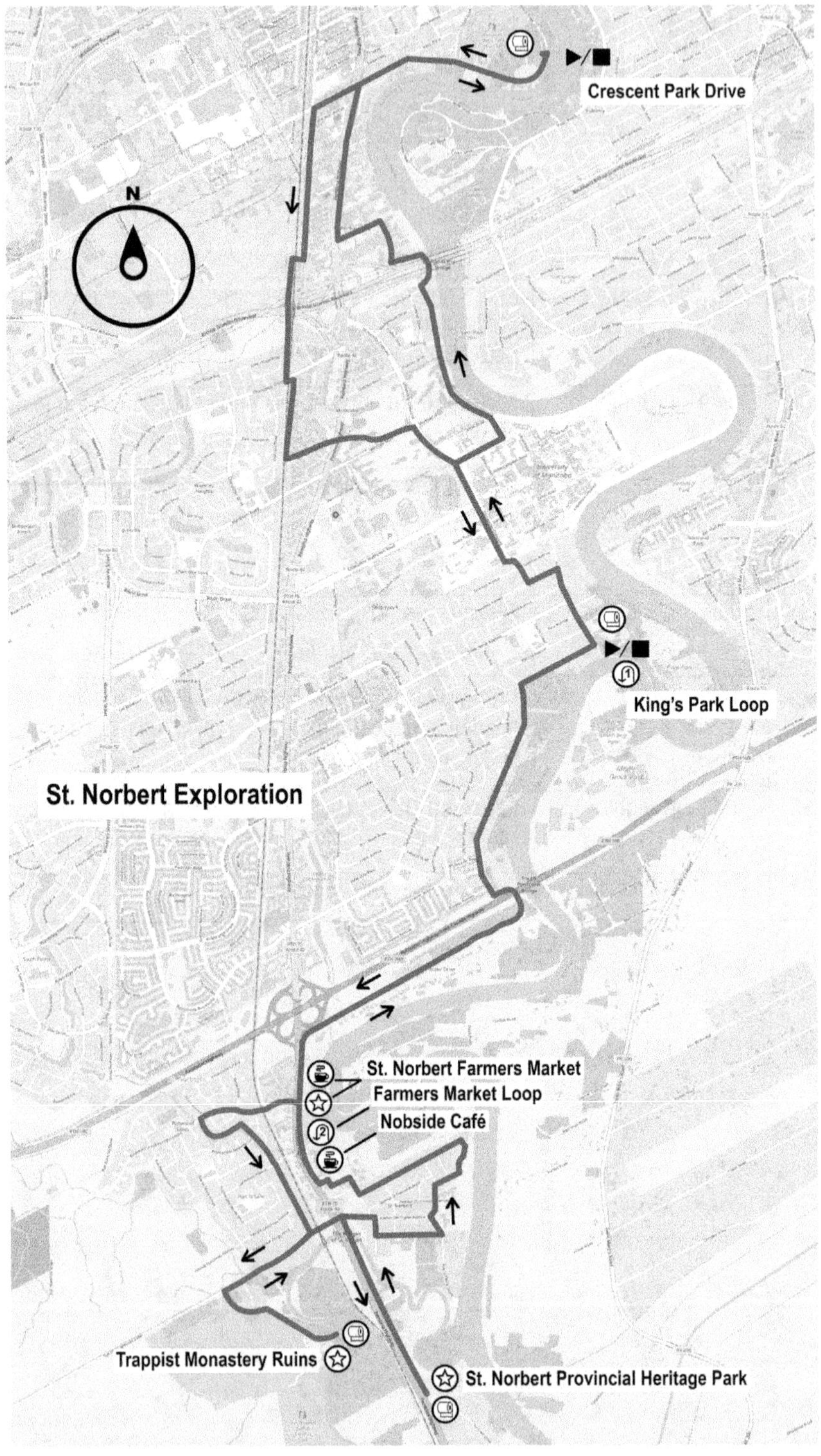
N
Crescent Park Drive
King's Park Loop
St. Norbert Exploration
St. Norbert Farmers Market
Farmers Market Loop
Nobside Café
Trappist Monastery Ruins
St. Norbert Provincial Heritage Park

Assiniboine Adventure

Southwest and Central Winnipeg

Winnipeg has a forest! Assiniboine Forest is one of Canada's largest urban nature parks comprising of 700-acres of aspen and oak trees. In this forest, we explore several of the trails running through it and one of the points of interest, the Eve Werier Memorial Pond. This pond was constructed in the late 1970s, by Ducks Unlimited, to supply a nesting habitat for waterfowl and water for wildlife. If you're lucky, depending on the time of day and the time of year, you may come upon deer or other small animals or birds at this watering hole.

If you're wondering how I picked the name, this ride covers Assiniboine Park, Assiniboine Parkway Trail, Assiniboine Forest, Assiniboine Avenue, and Assiniboine River…need I say more? Assiniboine Adventure is my most favourite ride in the book because it incorporates, what I consider, the best coffee stop in the city and has a surprise element in it.

The coffee stop I recommend is for a fresh, warm cinnamon bun from the original Tall Grass Prairie Bakery at 859 Westminster Avenue. It is a small shop with several tables outside. A perfect place to sit and watch the world go by. But, if that doesn't appeal to you, there are plenty of other options when you reach The Forks.

And what's the surprise element? Taking yourself and your bike on the River Spirit Waterbus from The Forks area on the Red River to Wellington Crescent on the Assiniboine River. Bikes are welcome on the Waterbus, and the fare for the service is reasonable. It's a fun element as it provides an opportunity to utilize this service, which you may otherwise never have considered trying. It's a pleasant five-kilometer cruise between the docks and provides wonderful views along the riverbanks. The Waterbus is seasonal, beginning Canada Day Weekend and closing after the September long weekend. This ride on the river is a real highlight. Just be sure to check their website http://www.splashdash.ca for current hours and fare prices so you can plan accordingly.

There are a number of points of interest. The Eve Werier Memorial Pond, mentioned above, is off the Sagimay Trail in Assiniboine Forest. Overlooking the wetland area is an observation mound which provides a good view of the area.

Back Alley Arctic is a fun little detour, not too far off the bike route, that takes you on an Arctic adventure. The artist Kal Barteski has used garage doors, fences and pavement as her canvas, painting a variety of Arctic animals in this alley. You can expect to see polar bears, herds of caribou, narwhals, a walrus, beluga whales, foxes, owls, puffins and more. Well worth the detour. https://www.travelmanitoba.com/blog/post/where-to-find-a-wild-polar-bear-in-a-winnipeg-alley/

Back Alley Arctic

The Louis Riel statue on the Manitoba Legislative Grounds facing the Assiniboine River is majestic. It was commissioned by the Manitoba Metis Federation and sculpted by Miguel Joyal. This 11 ft. bronze statue depicts Riel dressed in 19th century clothing with moccasins and holding in his left hand a parchment meant to represent the Manitoba Act. It is a fitting tribute to the man known as the Father of Manitoba.

The Manitoba Legislative Building on Broadway Avenue was constructed from Tyndall stone harvested right here in Manitoba. If you've never taken a tour through these hallowed hallways, it is well worth the time. Before visiting the home of the Golden Boy, check out the web page for more information and for tour times. https://www.gov.mb.ca/legislature/visiting/index.html

Manitoba Legislature

Upper Fort Garry Heritage Provincial Park was home to a fort established by the Hudson Bay Company. Unlike other forts in and around Winnipeg, there is no physical fort here, nor interpreters to guide you around. The only remaining physical structure is the Governor's Gate, at the north end of the park. The history of Upper Fort Garry and its buildings is relayed using interpretation, art and technology. The highlight of this park is a multi-layered, 440-foot-long steel sculpture entitled, Manitoba Liquor & Lotteries Heritage Wall. It depicts, through more than 7000 LED lights, along with sound, a 300-year timeline of important events and places of the area. This wall has been labeled "the largest piece of public art in Canada". If you do decide to spend some time here, on their website is an Upper Fort Garry App which can be downloaded. The app uses your location in the park to help explore the many symbols and stories of the fort. http://www.upperfortgarry.com

Upper Fort Garry

The Cycle Counter as you enter The Forks on Fort Gibraltar Trail is counting your passing! It keeps track of the number of cyclists that pass within a day and a cumulative total of cyclists that pass within the year. Now that's a count I'm proud to be part of!

The Splash Dash Historical River Tour is a boat tour operating from The Forks Historical Port. It is a 30-minute scenic and historical tour of the Red and Assiniboine Rivers in the vicinity of The Forks, with commentary provided by the boat captains. https://www.splashdash.ca/index.htm

Water Bus

The final point of interest, The Oodena Celebration Circle, is located at The Forks. The word Oodena is Ojibwe for "heart of the community". This natural amphitheatre was designed to pay homage to 6,000 years of Aboriginal peoples in the area. The Celebration Circle features ethereal sculptures, a sundial, interpretive signage, a naked eye observatory and a ceremonial fire pit. https://www.the forks.com/attractions/oodena-celebration-circle

Oodena Circle

Enjoy the waterbus!

Quick Notes

Distance – 30.9 km

Parking – Assiniboine Park by the Duck Pond

Options to shorten – yes

    1 – Waterbus Loop – 18.5 km

    2 – Forest Loop – 12.9 km

Bike repair station – Assiniboine Park between the Lyric Theatre and the Duck Pond

Suggested coffee stops – Tall Grass Prairie Bread Company at 859 Westminster Avenue, The Forks

Bathrooms – Assiniboine Park in the Duck Pond Shelter, The Forks

Points of Interest –

    Eve Werier Memorial Pond in Assiniboine Forest

    Back Alley Arctic in the alley between Canora and Ethelbert Street and between Wolseley and Westminster Avenue.

    Louis Riel Statue on the Manitoba Legislative grounds facing Assiniboine River

    Manitoba Legislative Building at 450 Broadway Avenue

    Upper Fort Garry Heritage Provincial Park at 130 Main Street

    Cycle Counter on Fort Gibraltar Trail as enter The Forks

    Splash Dash Historical River Tour at The Forks Historic Port

    Oodena Celebration Circle at The Forks

Trails

Assiniboine Parkway Trail – asphalt
William R. Clement Multi-use Path - asphalt
Harte Trail – crushed limestone
Aspen Trail – wood chip
Traverse Trail – wood chip
Sagimay Trail – wood chip
Oak Ridge Trail – wood chip
Preston Trail – crushed limestone
Assiniboine Park Trail – asphalt
Railway Bridge Trail – asphalt/crushed limestone
Cornish Path – dirt/crushed limestone
North Winnipeg Parkway Trail – asphalt/crushed limestone
Wellington Multi-use Path – crushed limestone

Safety Cautions

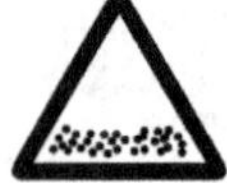  

Detailed Directions

Km Total	Km Leg	Direction	Location, notes
0	0	Start	**Assiniboine River Park Bridge, north of the duck pond.** **Assiniboine Park:** Bathrooms are located in the Duck Pond Shelter which is open from 7am to 10pm. **Bike Repair Station:** Located between the Lyric Theatre and the Duck Pond, this is a good place to pump up your tires, if needed. **Waterbus Loop:** This loop is essentially the second half of the ride. To start from this point, while facing the bridge, turn right. The trail crosses Assiniboine Park Drive and at the split, turn left. Once out of the park, the trail crosses Wellington and continues to run on the north side of the road, along the

			Assiniboine River, until exiting to Wellington after cycling under the Route 90 bridge. Cycle past Andrew Currie Park on your right and after crossing the railway tracks is Sir John Franklin Park on your left which has a trail heading up to the railway bridge. Continue, where indicated below, to return to start. Distance – 18.5 km.
0	1.49	Left	**Assiniboine Parkway Trail (asphalt);** do not go over the bridge. When facing the bridge, turn left. Follow the trail along the south side of the Assiniboine River, behind the English Gardens and the Leo Mol Sculpture Garden and then the trail runs beside Assiniboine Park Drive. When the road curves left, the trail splits, veer right. The trail curves left and right, before exiting to Vialoux Drive.
1.49	1.16	Straight	**Vialoux Drive;** cycle past Smithdale Park and continue to the end of the road and to the access path leading to Assiniboine Parkway Trail.
2.65	1.96	Straight	**William R. Clement Multi-use Path (asphalt);** because you cannot cross Roblin from the east side of William R. Clement, when the trail splits, veer right and then left to go under the bridge to the west side of William R. Clement and turn left again. Cross Roblin, and cycle through Tom Chester Park. Turn left onto the pedestrian overpass to get back to the east side of William R. Clement. Turn right and at Grant the trail curves left and ends at the lights at Grant Avenue and Haney Street.
4.61	1.58	Right	**Haney Street;** cycle past Eldridge to Ridgewood Avenue.
6.19	0.24	Right	**Ridgewood Avenue;** cycle to first exit on left, which is a turnoff leading to Marj Edey Park.
6.43	0.04	Left	**Marj Edey Park road;** immediately when turn left at this road is the Harte Trail.
6.47	1.58	Left	**Harte Trail (crushed limestone);** cycle past Elmhurst to a large prairie field which is the Assiniboine Forest.

			At the edge of the forest is the Aspen Trail. There is a sign at the entrance of the trail.
8.05	0.85	Left	**Aspen Trail - orange (wood chip);** cycle to where this trail intersects with the Traverse Trail.
8.90	0.39	Right	**Traverse Trail - yellow (wood chip);** this trail intersects with the Sagimay Trail and for a short distance, they share the path. When the trails split, after sharing the pathway, follow the Sagimay Trail.
9.29	0.50	Left	**Sagimay Trail - pink (wood chip);** follow this trail as it curves left and cycle along the edge of the Eve Werier Memorial Pond. The trail then curves right and intersects with the Oak Ridge Trail. **Eve Werier Memorial Pond:** You might like to cycle to the observation mound for a good view of the wetlands.
9.79	0.16	Right	**Oak Ridge Trail – green (wood chip);** when this trail turns left, it merges with the Preston Trail, which is a crushed limestone trail.
9.95	0.39	Left	**Preston Trail – blue (crushed limestone);** cycle the Preston Trail to exit Assiniboine Forest at Grant Avenue. Cross Grant to the Assiniboine Park Trail.
10.34	2.17	Straight	**Assiniboine Park Trail (asphalt);** as you cycle this trail, Assiniboine Park is on your left and Tuxedo Golf Club is on your right. The trail splits at Roblin. Turn right and cycle to the lights at Shaftesbury. Cross Roblin and continue straight, past the Red River cart to Pavilion Crescent. On the south side of Pavilion Crescent is the Assiniboine Parkway Trail. **Forest Loop:** When you come to Pavilion Crescent, cross Pavilion, and continue straight on the trail which runs beside the Pavilion and the Duck Pond, then across Assiniboine Park Drive and back to the start at the Assiniboine River Park Bridge. Distance – 12.9 km.
12.51	2.93	Right	**Assiniboine Parkway Trail (asphalt)/Wellington Crescent;** cycle the trail as it runs beside Pavilion

			Crescent/Assiniboine Park Drive and exits the park at Wellington Crescent. The trail crosses Wellington and continues to run on the north side of the road, along the Assiniboine River, until it exits to Wellington shortly after cycling under the Route 90 bridge. Cycle past Andrew Currie Park on your right and after crossing the railway tracks is Sir John Franklin Park on your left which has a trail heading up to the railway bridge. **Water:** There is a water bottle filling station at Andrew Currie Park.
15.44	0.61	Left	**Railway Bridge Trail (asphalt/crushed limestone);** cycle up the rail bridge and over the Assiniboine River. At the end of the bridge, the trail splits, turn right. There are several off shoots from this trail but stay on the trail closest to the river as it passes through Omand Park, over Omand's Creek and through Halter Park, before it exits to Wolseley Avenue. **Waterbus Loop continued:** Continue from this step to return to the start.
16.05	1.01	Right	**Wolseley Avenue;** cycle eleven blocks to Garfield Street. Some of the streets before Garfield are Basswood, Sprague, Greenwood and Dominion. **Note:** Wolseley Street, from Raglan Road to Maryland Street, is designated as a Sunday/Holiday Bicycle Route, from 8am to 8pm, by the city of Winnipeg. This means, on those days, motor vehicle traffic is restricted to one block.
17.06	1.05	Right	**Garfield Street/Palmerston Avenue;** cycle along Garfield and as it curves left it becomes Palmerston. Cycle on the path in front of Robert A. Steen Community Club to stay on Palmerston. The street curves back left to Wolseley Avenue. **Tall Grass Prairie Bread Company:** Who doesn't feel like a cinnamon bun and a coffee? Why not visit the original Tall Grass Prairie bakery and sit and relax with your coffee at one of the outside tables?

			To get there, once past the Community Club, the third street is Arlington. Turn left and cycle to Westminster. Turn right and the bakery is before the next block. Enjoy! Once you've had your coffee, head back to Palmerston and continue.
18.11	0.94	Right	**Wolseley Avenue;** cycle across Maryland and Sherbrook to the end of this road at Furby Street. **Back Alley Arctic:** Not to be missed! To get to this wonderful bike-able art gallery, cycle across Wolseley where Palmerston becomes Canora Street. Almost immediately to your left is the entrance into the back alley. Cycle the stretch to the other end and return to Wolseley and continue the route. Enjoy!
19.05	0.16	Left	**Furby Street;** cycle one block to Westminster Avenue.
19.21	0.24	Right	**Westminster Avenue/Young Street;** cycle to the end of Westminster and as it curves left it becomes Young Street. Cycle to the first street, Balmoral Avenue.
19.45	0.23	Right	**Balmoral Street;** cycle past Spence to Granite Way.
19.68	0.07	Right	**Granite Way;** almost immediately is Mostyn Place Park to your right and access to the Cornish Path.
19.75	0.71	Right	**Cornish Path (dirt/crushed limestone);** the trail splits at the Assiniboine River, turn left and continue as the path runs under the Osborne Street Bridge to a green space. Follow the path as it passes the Louis Riel Statue and then veers left to exit to Assiniboine Avenue. **Note:** If the Cornish Path is flooded, continue straight on Granite Way, cross Osborne, and stay on the trail as it veers right and left, passes the Louis Riel Statue and then veers left to exit to Assiniboine Avenue. **Louis Riel Statue:** This 11 ft. bronze statue by Miguel Joyal is a fitting tribute to the man known as the Father of Manitoba. **Manitoba Legislative Building:** Have you ever graced the halls of our seat of government? If not, they offer a free tour which allows a glimpse into this amazing building. To get here, just after passing under the

			Osborne Street Bridge, the path divides, turn left, cross Assiniboine Avenue and head towards the Legislature Building. Return to this trail when done.
20.46	1.01	Right	**Assiniboine Avenue;** this street has a protected bike lane. Stay on Assiniboine Avenue to its end at Main Street. Cross Main and turn right and then left at the entrance into The Forks. This street into The Forks is called Fort Gibraltar Trail. **Upper Fort Garry Heritage Provincial Park:** This park is located to the left of Assiniboine before Main Street. Take in the Heritage Wall which has been labelled "the largest piece of public art in Canada". Return to Assiniboine when done. **Cycle Counter:** As you turn into The Forks, notice the cycle counter to your left. It records the number of cyclists that pass by within each day and a cumulative total of cyclists that pass within the year. It's nice to know Winnipeg has so many people choosing to cycle!
21.47	1.02	Left	**The Forks/North Winnipeg Parkway Trail (asphalt/crushed limestone);** there are many paths to navigate through The Forks and rather than say specifically which route to take through this area, I will leave it up to you. The aim is to eventually get to the trail along the river, but not at the river's edge, and cycle under the Provencher Bridge and continue through the greenspace. Immediately after passing Shaw Park baseball stadium, look for a small path to your right leading down to the river and to The Exchange Dock river taxi stop. There should be a sign indicating the dock. **The Forks:** There are many choices of venues for a coffee break, however, if you are regretting not stopping at Tall Grass Prairie Bread Company for a cinnamon bun, they have a second location here, so there's still an opportunity! **Bathroom Stop:** There are many bathrooms throughout The Forks.

				Splash Dash Historical River Tour: Take in some history in this half hour tour of the sights off the Red and Assiniboine Rivers by The Forks. **Oodena Celebration Circle:** This amphitheatre features ethereal sculptures, a sundial, interpretive signage, a naked eye observatory and a ceremonial fire pit.
22.49	1.52	Right With River Taxi *Or* U-turn Without River Taxi		**Exchange Dock river taxi stop;** the waterbus comes by every 15 minutes. This dock is the most northern stop and you take it to the most southern stop, which is the Hugo Dock. The distance covered is 5 km. If the Waterbus is not running or you choose not to use; once you reach the Exchange Dock, turn around and backtrack through The Forks, to Assiniboine Avenue and to the Cornish Path which takes you past the Louis Riel Statue and under the Osborne Street Bridge. At Mostyn Place Park, when the trail splits, turn right and exit to Granite Way. Turn left on Granite Way, left on Balmoral, and left at Young, which becomes Westminster when it curves right. Cycle past Sherbrook to Maryland and turn left to cycle the bridge over the Assiniboine River. Turn right at the very first street, Wellington Crescent. Pick up the route below from Wellington Crescent. **Note:** Cornish Path does continue along the river past Mostyn Place Park, but I would not recommend continuing on the path as it is very rough and not bike friendly.
24.01	0.12	Straight		**Hugo Dock;** cycle straight to Wellington Crescent. **Note:** There are a few stairs leading up the riverbank to Wellington Crescent.
24.13	3.85	Right		**Wellington Crescent/Wellington Multi-use Path (crushed limestone);** cycle across Academy and after the first block, Wellington becomes divided with a centre boulevard which has a path.

			Cycle either on the street or the path. The centre boulevard stretches from Guelph to Lindsay Street.
			Pass Currie Park and look for the start of the Assiniboine Parkway Trail to your right.
			**Note:** Wellington Crescent, from Academy Road to Guelph Street, is designated as a Sunday/Holiday Bicycle Route, from 8am to 8pm, by the city of Winnipeg. This means, on those days, motor vehicle traffic is restricted to one block.
			Water: There are two stops along this stretch where you can re-fill your water bottle. There is a water fountain on the boulevard at Wellington and Guelph and at Andrew Currie Park, located on the south side of Wellington Crescent just after the centre boulevard ends.
27.98	2.87	Right	**Assiniboine Parkway Trail (asphalt/crushed limestone);** follow this trail back into Assiniboine Park. Once in the park the trail splits, turn right. Continue as path runs along the edge of the Assiniboine River and returns to the Assiniboine River Park Bridge.
30.85	0	End	**Assiniboine River Park Bridge.**

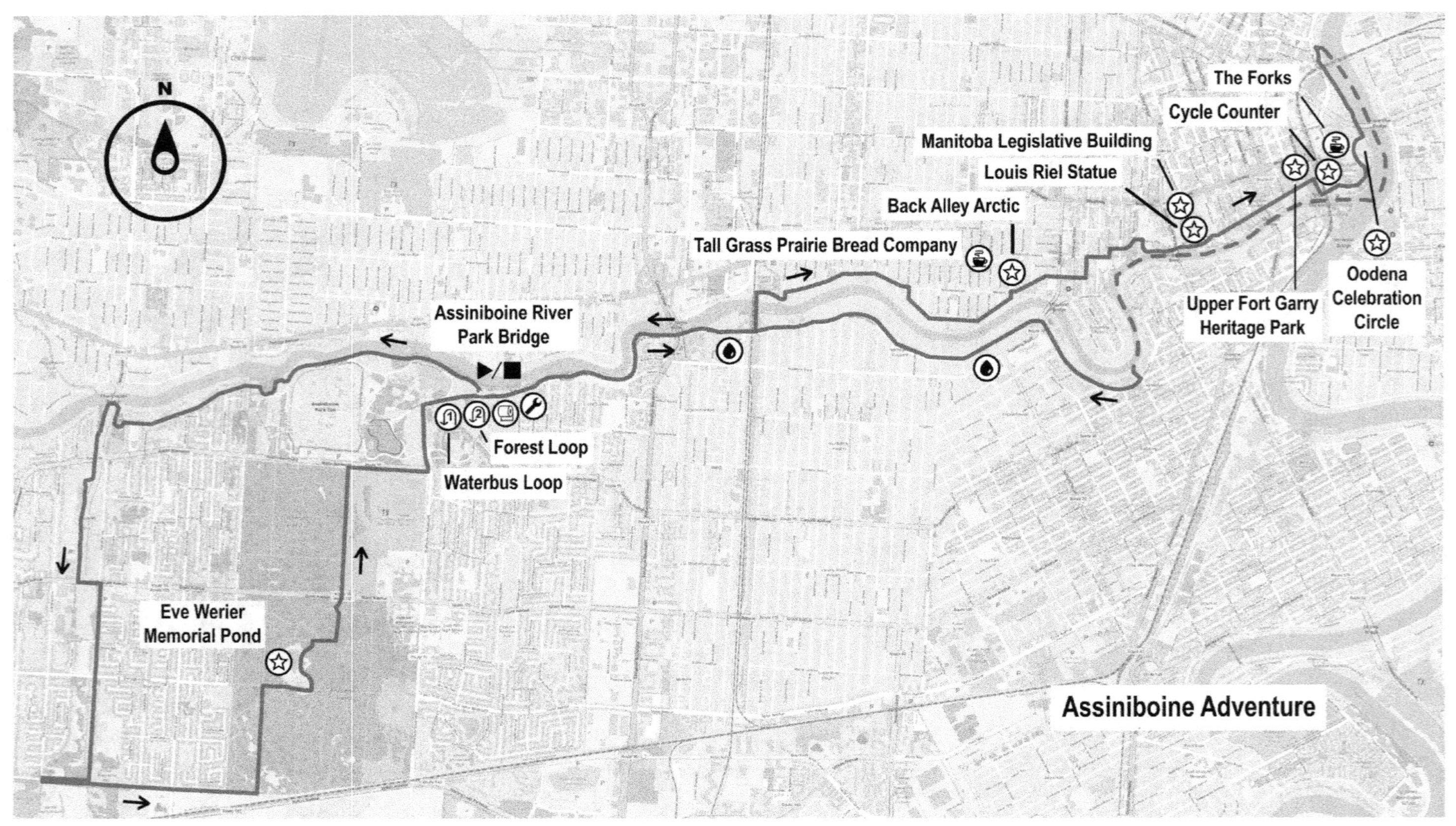

N
The Forks
Cycle Counter
Manitoba Legislative Building
Louis Riel Statue
Back Alley Arctic
Tall Grass Prairie Bread Company
Upper Fort Garry Heritage Park
Oodena Celebration Circle
Assiniboine River Park Bridge
Forest Loop
Waterbus Loop
Eve Werier Memorial Pond
Assiniboine Adventure

Westward Ho!

West Winnipeg

This route cycles through neighbourhoods in the west end of Winnipeg and goes beyond the perimeter, along the Assiniboine River, to an area called The Oaks. The street names in this area all use the oak theme, the main roads being Oak Forest Crescent and Green Oaks Lane, with the small roads off this main one called Blue Oaks, Grey Oaks, Bur Oaks, Grand Oaks, Four Oaks, Mossy Oaks, Prairie Oaks, and Hidden Oaks! Of note, Oak Forest Crescent becomes Green Oaks Lane once across Camp Manitou Road and this road is part of the east boundary between Winnipeg and Headingly. Cycling to the extreme west of Winnipeg prompted the name Westward Ho!

A short distance past The Oaks is Camp Manitou which is a summer camp and year-round outdoor recreation facility. It is located on an elbow of the Assiniboine and is therefore surrounded by water on three sides. It was founded in 1930 by a group of six service clubs – Rotary, Cosmopolitan Club, Kiwanis, Kinsmen, Optimist and YMCA. Manitou provides camping experiences to Manitoba children, youth and community groups.

This ride, being mainly in residential areas, does not pass any coffee stops directly, however, both on the way out and the way back in, the route is close to Unicity Shopping Plaza, where there are many options to stop for coffee or food.

There are a number of points of interest that may pique your interest to stop and take in:

Air Force Heritage Air Park – This is an outdoor Air Park displaying 14 Canadian military aircrafts, showing the history of military planes. Also in the park is the Garden of Memories, commemorating those who trained and served in the British Commonwealth Air Training Plan. There is no admission charge to the park and can be visited at any time.

Living Prairie Museum – This is a tall grass prairie preserve. Situated on 30 acres of land, it is one of the few remaining tracts to still exist. It is a unique landscape and very rare. At one time, prior to the arrival of settlers to Canada, tall grass prairie covered vast areas of land. Today, less than 1% of this environ remains. The purpose of Living Prairie is to preserve this landscape and promote awareness and conservation of this natural area. On site is an interpretive centre, gift shop, and two short self-guided hiking trails through the preserve. A trail booklet is available at the entrance of the museum or can be downloaded on their website. Admission is free and the trails are open year-

Living Prairie Museum

round from dawn to dusk. https://www.winnipeg.ca/publicworks/parksOpenSpace/livingprairie/

Grant's Old Mill

Grant's Old Mill – This grain mill operated between 1829 and 1832 under the direction of the Metis leader, Cuthbert Grant. It was the first water mill in Western Canada at the time. The present building on this site, is a recreation of the mill and was erected in 1974. Admission is by donation. http://www.grantsoldmill.ca

Quick Notes

Distance – 29.5 km

Parking – Park in one of the lots on Silver Avenue, just west of Ferry Road

Option to shorten – yes

 Yellow Ribbon Loop – 19.3 km

Suggested coffee stops – Tim Hortons at 3649 Portage Avenue or any other coffee/restaurant shop in Unicity Shopping Complex

Bathrooms –Public Bathroom on Sturgeon Creek Greenway Trail close to Grant's Old Mill, coffee Stop

Points of Interest –

 Air Force Heritage Air Park at 186 Air Force Way

 Living Prairie Museum at 2795 Ness Avenue

 Grant's Old Mill at 2777 Portage Avenue

Trails

Yellow Ribbon Greenway Trail – asphalt

Saskatchewan Multi-use Path – asphalt

Oak Forest Trail – crushed limestone

Sturgeon Creek Greenway Trail – asphalt

Safety Cautions

Detailed Directions

Km Total	Km Leg	Direction	Location, notes
0	0	Start	**Yellow Ribbon Greenway Trail, on the north side of Silver Avenue, at Inglewood Street.**
0	6.47	Right	**Yellow Ribbon Greenway Trail (asphalt);** cycle west passing the St. James Rods Football Club and St. James Memorial Sports Park, across Air Force Way/Sharp, Whytewold, Ladywood, and Moray, cross Sturgeon at the stop sign and then cross Silver to the Yellow Ribbon Greenway Trail on the north side of the road and continue across Hamilton and Silver. The trail curves left and then right and runs alongside Sturgeon Creek and merges into Saskatchewan Multi-use Path at Saskatchewan Avenue. **Air Force Heritage Air Park:** Turn right at Air Force Way to see the military aircraft and the Garden of Memories. **Living Prairie Museum:** To get to the museum, turn left at Moray Street and left again at Ness Avenue. You might like to take a self-guided walk on one of the trails to view some of the 150 species of grasses and wildflowers and perhaps catch a glimpse of some prairie wildlife that reside here.
6.47	1.35	Left	**Saskatchewan Multi-use Path (asphalt);** cycle past Cavalier to Buchanan Boulevard.
7.82	0.04	Left	**Buchanan Boulevard;** cycle to the first street, Rigsby Crescent.
7.86	0.18	Right	**Rigsby Crescent;** cycle past Russenholt to Isbister Street.
8.04	1.54	Left	**Isbister Street;** cycle past Lumsden, Isbister Park, Hamilton, Ness, and Fairlane, to Livinia Avenue. **Yellow Ribbon Loop:** Turn left at Hamilton and cycle to Buchanan Boulevard. Continue straight, picking up the remaining ride, where indicated below, to return to start. Distance – 19.3 km.
9.58	0.18	Left	**Livinia Avenue;** cycle past Stewart/Livinia Park to Buchanan Boulevard.

			Unicity Shopping Complex: If you need to use a bathroom take this short detour. Cycle straight across Buchanan Boulevard and Livinia ends at Unicity Shopping Plaza. Bathrooms are located in Canadian Tire, Tim Hortons or McDonald's. Return to Buchanan Boulevard to continue ride.
9.76	0.60	Right	**Buchanan Boulevard;** cross Portage Avenue and continue to the end of Buchanan to Allard Avenue.
10.36	0.22	Right	**Allard Avenue;** cycle to first road, St. Charles Street.
10.58	0.52	Left	**St. Charles Street;** cycle past Lepine and Sansome to Augier Avenue.
11.10	0.33	Right	**Augier Avenue;** cycle past Gagnon and the Downs Village Mobile Home Park to Oxbow Bend Road, the last street before the Perimeter Highway.
11.43	1.35	Left	**Oxbow Bend Road;** cycle this asphalt/gravel road as it runs along the edge of the Mobile Home Park and past green space to the Assiniboine River, then turns right under the Perimeter Highway and turns right again. Cycle to the first street, Oak Forest Crescent. There is a stop sign at this corner.
12.78	1.48	Left	**Oak Forest Crescent/Oak Forest Trail (crushed limestone);** follow this road as it curves left and cycle past Blue Oaks, and Grey Oaks. Before the next road is the beginning of the Oak Forest Trail to your right. Cycle the trail as it runs beside Oak Forest Crescent and crosses Four Oaks, Mossy Oaks, Hidden Oaks, and exits at the corner of Camp Manitou Road and Green Oaks Lane. **Note:** There are postal boxes situated across the entrance of the trail.
14.26	0.42	Straight	**Green Oaks Lane;** continue straight on the gravel road to Camp Manitou. **Note:** Camp Manitou is private property and you are not allowed to enter.
14.68	0.42	U-turn	**Green Oaks Lane;** cycle to Oak Forest Trail/Oak Forest Crescent.

15.10	1.48	Straight	**Oak Forest Trail (crushed limestone)/Oak Forest Crescent;** you can either stay on the road or access Oak Forest Trail at the corner of Camp Manitou Road and Oak Forest Crescent. Follow road and/or trail as it curves right and then left and comes to Oxbow Bend Road.
16.58	1.35	Right	**Oxbow Bend Road;** follow the gravel road as it goes to the Assiniboine River, curves left to go under the Perimeter Highway and curves left again. Cycle to Augier Avenue.
17.93	0.24	Right	**Augier Avenue;** cycle to Gagnon Street.
18.17	0.49	Left	**Gagnon Street;** cycle past Sansome and Lepine to Allard Avenue.
18.66	0.34	Right	**Allard Avenue;** cycle past St. Charles and Stewart to the end of the road at Buchanan Boulevard.
19.00	1.35	Left	**Buchanan Boulevard;** cycle across Portage Avenue, past Livinia, Fairlane, and Ness to Hamilton Avenue. **Yellow Ribbon Loop continued:** Since you are already on Hamilton, continue straight across Buchanan and continue with the following directions to return to the starting point. **Tim Hortons:** To make a stop for coffee, turn right at Livinia Avenue and the road ends at Unicity Shopping Plaza. If you don't feel like Tim's, but still want to stop, other choices include McDonald's, Burger King, KFC, Subway, and Original Joe's.
20.35	1.92	Right	**Hamilton Avenue;** cycle past John Taylor Collegiate, Chapman, Cavalier, Parkdale, Parkhill, and Vimy to Wharton Boulevard and access to Sturgeon Creek Greenway Trail.
22.27	2.13	Right	**Sturgeon Creek Greenway Trail (asphalt);** veer right onto the trail which starts at Wharton Boulevard. The trail leads down to the west edge of the creek. Follow the trail across Ness and over the bridge to the east side of the creek. Continue straight and then right, under Sturgeon Road. Stay on the path closest to the creek until you come to

			the Public Bathroom by Grant's Old Mill on the grounds of the Grace Hospital. The path splits, take the trail to the left which goes behind the bathroom and exits to a parking lot and Booth Drive.  **Grant's Old Mill:** Here's your chance to learn about the milling process and the history of this particular mill. **Public Bathroom:** Located along Sturgeon Creek Greenway Trail just north of Grant's Old Mill. It is open seasonally from 7am to 7:30pm.
24.40	0.31	Left	**Booth Drive;** cycle past Athlone to Bruce Avenue.
24.71	3.44	Right	**Bruce Avenue;** cycle past Ronald, Moray, Whytewold, Mount Royal, and Sharp to Linwood. **Note:** This is a long stretch to cycle and many streets are passed. I have just listed above all the intersecting streets with stop signs or lights.
28.15	0.75	Left	**Linwood Street;** cycle across Ness to Silver Avenue. Cross Silver to access the Yellow Ribbon Greenway Trail.
28.90	0.57	Right	**Yellow Ribbon Greenway Trail (asphalt);** cycle to Inglewood Street.
29.47	0	End	**Yellow Ribbon Greenway Trail at Inglewood Street.**

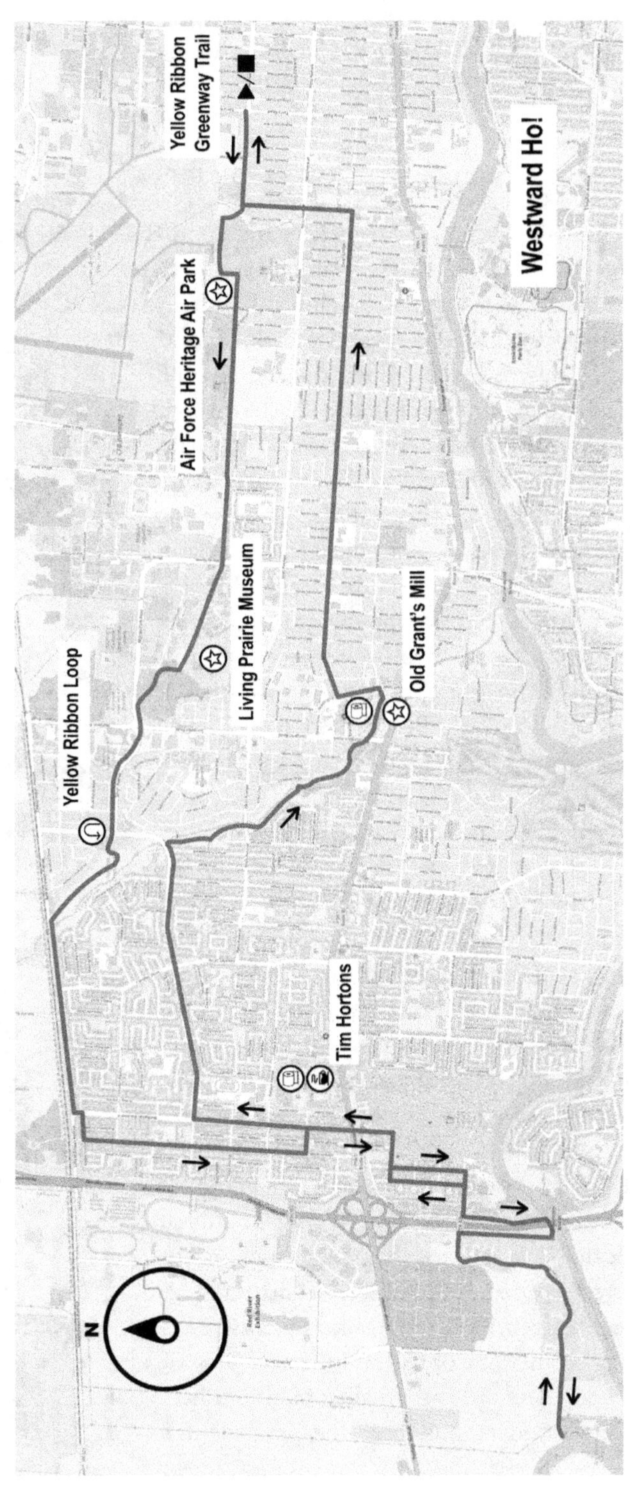
Yellow Ribbon
Greenway Trail

Westward Ho!

Air Force Heritage Air Park

Yellow Ribbon Loop

Living Prairie Museum

Old Grant's Mill

Tim Hortons

N

Beaudry Park Picnic

West of Winnipeg

This ride heads to Beaudry Provincial Park, approximately 10 km west of the city. The route out is through the Assiniboine Forest, the Harte Trail and the Headingley Grand Trunk Trail, an abandoned CN railway bed. Cycling back is via Roblin Boulevard and city streets. Beaudry Park, a point of interest for this ride, is located along the Assiniboine River and is home to a diverse forest of basswood, cottonwood and maple trees plus ferns and wild grapevines. A wide variety of wildlife calls this park home, including several songbirds, whitetail deer, fox, owls, raccoons and beavers. Beaudry is a quiet, tranquil park, the perfect place to sit with a view to the river and have a picnic while watching the river rippling by. So, if this thought appeals to you, be sure to pack a lunch. As you can probably tell, the thought appeals to me and that is why the ride is called Beaudry Park Picnic. https://www.gov.mb.ca/sd/parks/park-maps-and-locations/central/beaudry.html

Beaudry Park

If a picnic doesn't appeal to you there are other coffee stop options to consider. You can head into Headingley for lunch at either the Headingley Grill (https://theheadingleygrill.ca) or Nick's Inn (https://www.nicksinn.com). This detour is not too far and will only add a little less than 2 km return. You also have the option of waiting until you are back within Winnipeg and can stop at Roblin Grill (https://www.roblingrill.ca), or one of several restaurants close to this location.

The Headingley Grill

Besides Beaudry Provincial Park, one other point of interest worth mentioning is the Eve Werier Memorial Pond. It is located just off the Sagimay Trail in the Assiniboine Forest and requires only a short detour. This pond supplies water for wild life and waterfowl. If you're lucky, depending on the time of day and the time of year, you may come upon deer or other small animals or birds. There is an observation mound near the pond on the

Nick's Inn

Roblin Grill

Sagimay Trail and is a nice spot to stop for a few minutes before heading out on this ride.

Enjoy this route from forest to park and back again!

Quick Notes

Distance – 38.9 km

Parking – Parking lot of Assiniboine Forest at 996 Grant Avenue

Options to shorten – yes

    1 – Harte Loop – 12.9 km

    2 – Grand Trunk Loop – 24.6 km *For this loop, park at Beaudry Provincial Park. **Note:** A park permit is required to park your car. There is no service to purchase a permit on-site. Day or seasonal permits can be purchased on-line. https://www.gov.mb.ca/sd/parks/park-fees/index.html

Park Permit

Suggested coffee stops – Beaudry Provincial Park (your own home-packed lunch), Headingley Grill at 180 Bridge Road in Headingley, Nick's Inn at 5392 Portage Avenue in Headingley, Roblin Grill at 6500 Roblin Boulevard in Winnipeg

Bathrooms – Beaudry Provincial Park (non-modern), coffee stops

Point of Interest –

    Eve Werier Memorial Pond off Sagimay Trail in Assiniboine ForestBeaudry Provincial Park on MB-241

Trails

Sagimay Trail – asphalt

Aspen Trail – wood chip

Harte Trail – crushed limestone

Headingley Grand Trunk Trail – crushed limestone/dirt

South Headingley Trail – crushed limestone/asphalt

Hammond-Cullen Link Path – crushed limestone

Safety Cautions

Detailed Directions

Km Total	Km Leg	Direction	Location, notes
0	0	Start	**Assiniboine Forest parking lot;** the trailhead of the Sagimay Trail (pink) starts at the southeast corner of the lot.
0	0.56	Straight	**Sagimay Trail (asphalt);** cycle this trail as it follows along the west edge of the forest. Shortly after the trail curves left the Aspen Trail (orange) begins to your right. **Eve Werier Memorial Pond:** To get to this location requires a short detour. Do not turn off at the Aspen Trail, instead continue straight, and when the trail splits, turn left. Cycle to the observation mound for a good view of the wetlands before returning to the Aspen Trail.
0.56	1.05	Right	**Aspen Trail (wood chip);** cycle past the Traverse Trail to the exit onto Harte Trail.
1.61	5.47	Right	**Harte Trail (crushed limestone);** cycle to the end of this trail, past Elmhurst, Fairmont, Harstone, Community, Municipal, Charleswood and Dale Boulevard. The end of the trail is next to the Perimeter Hwy/Trans-Canada Hwy. Unfortunately, there is no "friendly" bike path to get across. You have to go down and up the ditch, cross the highway and down and up the ditch on the other side. The trailhead of the Headingley Grand Trunk Trail will be visible. **Portable Toilet:** There is a portable toilet located on the trail between Fairmont and Harstone. **Harte Loop:** From the Harte Trail, turn right at Dale Boulevard. Cycle past Shepton and Stonebridge to Acorn Place/Rannock Avenue. Turn right on Rannock. Cycle to the end of Rannock at Harstone Road. Continue, where indicated below, to return to start. Distance – 12.9 km.

7.08	10.60	Straight	**Headingley Grand Trunk Trail (crushed limestone/dirt);** this is a long, straight trail, with the exception of going around one field, which crosses several country roads and a train track. Shortly before exiting the trail to Beaudry Park is a Headingley Grand Trunk Trail sign and beyond is a bridge going over a creek. Cycle over the bridge and in approximately 300 m is an exit path to your right to Roblin Boulevard/MB-241 and the entrance lane into Beaudry Park.
17.68	0.76	Straight	**Beaudry Provincial Park entrance;** cycle into Beaudry Provincial Park. **Beaudry Provincial Park:** Take time to enjoy the sites, read the information boards and perhaps hike one of the trails. **Beaudry Provincial Park:** The non-modern bathrooms are located just off the parking lot. **Beaudry Provincial Park:** There are no cafés or kiosks here, but if you packed a lunch, it's a beautiful place to picnic and enjoy the views of the river. **Grand Trunk Loop:** Refer to Quick Notes for parking directions. Start from this step and continue as follows until indicated below. Distance – 24.6 km.
18.44	0.76	Turn around	**Beaudry Provincial Park entrance;** cycle to Roblin Boulevard/MB-241.
19.20	3.37	Left	**Roblin Boulevard/MB-241;** initially the highway is gravel, but as you approach South Headingley the road becomes paved. Shortly after the paved road begins, the South Headingley Trail which runs along the edge of the road, begins to your left at Thomas Drive.
22.57	3.30	Straight	**South Headingley Trail (crushed limestone/asphalt);** follow the trail on the left side of Roblin and then cross at the crosswalk to the right side of the road. The trail continues past the suburb of South Headingley before crossing the road again to the left side and following along the edge of the Assiniboine River under

			a rail bridge and under the Taylor Bridge which leads to Headingley.
			This trail then veers away from the river and runs beside Roblin.
			Exit the trail at the second time you come to Marston Drive and continue on Roblin Boulevard/MB-241.
			Headingley Grill and Nick's Inn: These two restaurants are located in Headingley. To get there, take a short detour and cycle across the Taylor Bridge over the Assiniboine River and turn left at Keough Avenue which is the first road after the bridge and right at Bridge Road. Both restaurants are close to each other. After you have enjoyed your meal, return to the South Headingley Trail and continue.
25.87	5.87	Straight	**Roblin Boulevard/MB-241;** cross Roblin to the wide asphalt shoulder on the south side of the road. Continue straight past Shelmerdine Garden Centre, Breezy Bend Country Club, A Paterson Bedding Plants, and the overpass above the Trans-Canada Hwy/Perimeter Hwy to the first street, Windmill Way.
			Grand Trunk Loop continued: Just before the turn-off to the Trans-Canada Hwy/Perimeter Hwy is Caron Road, turn right at this street.
			Cycle along Caron as it runs beside the highway. In approximately 2.3 km is the trailhead for the Headingley Grand Trunk Trail.
			Turn right onto the trail. This is a long, straight trail, with the exception of going around one field, and crosses several country roads and a train track.
			Shortly before exiting the trail to Beaudry Park is a Headingley Grand Trunk Trail sign and beyond is a bridge going over a creek. Cross the bridge and in approximately 300 m is an exit path to your right to
			Roblin Boulevard/MB-241 at the lane into Beaudry Park.
			Cycle into Beaudry Provincial Park to return to the start.
31.74	0.39	Right	**Windmill Way;** this road comes to a split, turn left, and continue to Dale Boulevard.

32.13	0.27	Right	**Dale Boulevard;** cycle past Westgrove/Brownell to Hammond Road. **Roblin Grill:** To get to this restaurant, instead of turning right on Dale, turn left. Enter the parking lot for Park West Inn, and cycle behind the Inn and use the trail at the back of the lot to go from this parking area to the next. Roblin Grill is to your right, facing Roblin Boulevard. When done, return to Dale Boulevard.
32.40	0.03	Left	**Hammond Road;** cycle to the Hammond-Cullen Link Path in the greenspace between the row of houses.
32.43	0.27	Right	**Hammond-Cullen Link Path (crushed limestone);** this trail starts at Hammond Road and ends at Cullen Drive.
32.70	0.70	Left	**Cullen Drive;** cycle past the stop signs at Betsworth, and Lismer to Rannock Avenue.
33.40	2.06	Left	**Rannock Avenue;** cycle to the end of Rannock at Harstone Road.
35.46	0.25	Left	**Harstone Road;** cycle to the first block, Eldridge Avenue. **Harte Loop continued:** Continue from this step to return to Assiniboine Forest parking lot.
35.71	2.30	Right	**Eldridge Avenue;** cycle past the stop signs at Dieppe, Buckingham, Coventry, Fairmont, Oakdale, Haney, Laxdal, and Elmhurst to Cathcart Street.
38.01	0.31	Left	**Cathcart Street;** cycle past Beauchemin to Chalfont Road.
38.32	0.62	Right	**Chalfont Road;** this road curves to the left as it runs along the edge of Assiniboine Forest. Just before Grant is the entrance to the Assiniboine Forest parking lot.
38.94	0	End	**Assiniboine Forest parking lot.**

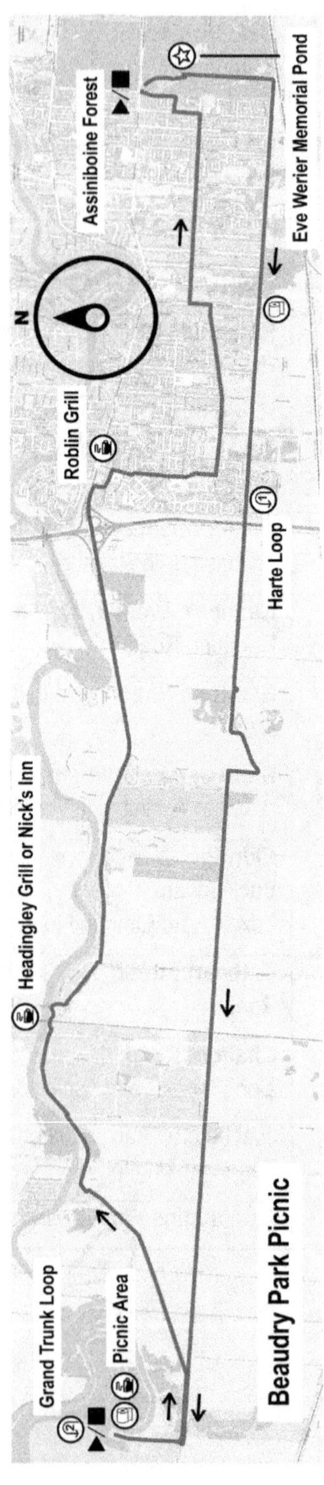
Assiniboine Forest
Eve Werier Memorial Pond
N
Roblin Grill
Harte Loop
Headingley Grill or Nick's Inn
Beaudry Park Picnic
Grand Trunk Loop
Picnic Area

Deer Run

West and southwest Winnipeg

In all my time on the bike, I have only come across deer twice; once while in Charleswood, no surprise there, and once along the Yellow Ribbon Greenway. Since this ride encompasses both those locations, I thought it would be fitting to call this ride Deer Run. Hopefully you will see deer too. Fitting in with this ride's title, there is a sculpture of three male deer on the southeast corner of Grant Avenue and William R. Clement Parkway. It's almost hidden by the shrubbery, but stop and take a look.

This bike ride links many trails together with very little time on actual roads. The first trail, Yellow Ribbon Greenway, is named in honour of the Canadian Armed Forces. It stretches 5.5 km and ends close to the Sturgeon Creek Greenway Trail. This Greenway runs along Sturgeon Creek and is one of my favourites because of how scenic it is. Of interest, Sturgeon Creek has 30 different species of fish swimming around! The Harte Trail is part of the Trans Canada Trail. This trail is on an old railway bed which used to carry the Harte Line, part of the Grand Trunk Pacific Railway, in the late 1800s. The Harte Trail leads to the Thundering Bison Trail. Don't you just love that name?! It is named to pay homage to all the bison which used to roam this land. One of the last stretches is down majestic Wellington Crescent before returning to Assiniboine Park.

I have put in a few suggestions for coffee/snack stops, one of which is IKEA for some Swedish fare, if that is what your palate is desiring. The ride also passes a Tim Hortons and a Starbucks if those are your preferences.

This particular ride is also full of worthwhile stops; *Agassiz Ice* art installation, Air Force Heritage Air Park, Living Prairie Museum, Grant's Old Mill and the Manitoba Electrical Museum. All of these attractions are on the small size. If interested, I would recommend picking one or two and exploring those attractions and then the next time you cycle the Deer Run take in the other sites. Following is just a little bit about each, but for more complete information and for times and/or entrance fees, be sure to check their websites for the most current information.

Agassiz Ice art installation – Three polished stainless-steel icebergs will grab your attention as you cross the Assiniboine River Park Bridge. The sculptures stand five metres at their tallest point, weigh 2000 kg, and are a nod to Lake Agassiz, a glacial lake which covered most of Manitoba in prehistoric times. The icebergs' changing reflection of light and landscape at different times of the day and year are the vision of the artist, Gordon Reeve, who wanted to suggest a sense of beginning and a moment of change.

Air Force Heritage Air Park – This is an outdoor Air Park displaying 14 Canadian military aircraft, showing the history of military planes. Also in the park is the Garden of Memories, commemorating those who trained and served in the British Commonwealth Air Training Plan. There is no admission charge to the park and it can be visited at any time.

Living Prairie Museum – This is a tall grass prairie preserve. Situated on 30 acres of land, it is one of the few remaining tracts to still exist. It is a unique landscape and very rare. At one time, prior to the arrival of settlers to Canada, tall grass prairie covered vast areas of land. Today, less than 1% of this environ remains. The purpose of Living Prairie is to preserve this landscape and promote awareness and conservation of this natural area. On site is an interpretive centre, gift shop, and two short self-guided hiking trails through the preserve. A trail booklet is available at the entrance of the museum or can be downloaded on their website. Admission is free and the trails are open year-round from dawn to dusk. https://www.winnipeg.ca/publicworks/parksOpenSpace/livingprairie/

Living Prairie Museum

Grant's Old Mill

Grant's Old Mill – This grain mill operated between 1829 and 1832 under the direction of the Metis leader, Cuthbert Grant. It was the first water mill in Western Canada at the time. The present building on this site, is a recreation of the mill and was erected in 1974. Admission is by donation. http://www.grantsoldmill.ca

Manitoba Electrical Museum – This museum explores the history of Manitoba's hydroelectric power from the 1870's to present and beyond through a number of exhibits. http://www.manitobaelectricalmuseum.ca

Electrical Museum

Quick Notes
Distance – 33.3 km
Parking – Assiniboine Park by the Duck Pond
Option to shorten – yes
 Assiniboine Forest Loop – 23.3 km
Bike repair station – Assiniboine Park between the Lyric Theatre and the Duck Pond
Suggested coffee stops – IKEA at 500 Sterling Lyon Parkway, Tim Hortons at 860 Waverley Street, Starbucks at 1170 Taylor Avenue
Bathrooms – Assiniboine Park in the Duck Pond Shelter, Public Bathroom on Sturgeon Creek Greenway Trail by Grant's Old Mill, coffee stops
Points of Interest –
 Agassiz Ice Assiniboine Park, north side of the Assiniboine River Park Bridge

Air Force Heritage Air Park at 186 Air Force Way
Living Prairie Museum at 2795 Ness Avenue
Grant's Old Mill at 2777 Portage Avenue
Manitoba Electrical Museum at 680 Harrow Street

Trails

Yellow Ribbon Greenway Trail – asphalt

Sturgeon Creek Greenway Trail –asphalt

Moray/William R. Clement Multi-use Path – asphalt

Harte Trail – crushed limestone

Thundering Bison Trail – asphalt

Waverley Multi-use Path - asphalt

Taylor Multi-use Path – asphalt

Wellington Multi-use Path – crushed limestone

Assiniboine Parkway Trail – asphalt

Safety Cautions

Detailed Directions

Km total	Km Leg	Direction	Location, notes
0	0	Start	**Assiniboine River Park Bridge;** this is a pedestrian bridge located north of the duck pond. **Assiniboine Park:** Bathrooms are located in the Duck Pond Shelter which is open from 7am to 10pm. **Bike Repair Station:** Located between the Lyric Theatre and the Duck Pond, this is a good place to pump up your tires, if needed.
0	0.72	Straight	**Assiniboine River Park Bridge;** cross the bridgeto the north side of Assiniboine River, then continue to cycle straight to Portage. Cross at the east set of lights to be on the correct side of the road on Overdale Street. ***Agassiz Ice* Art Installation:** Located just past the park bridge, this striking sculpture will draw your attention.

0.72	0.46	Straight	**Overdale Street;** cycle one block to Bruce Avenue.
1.18	0.19	Right	**Bruce Avenue;** cycle two blocks to Linwood Street.
1.37	0.79	Left	**Linwood Street;** cycle across Ness and Silver to the Yellow Ribbon Greenway Trail on the north side of Silver.
2.16	4.91	Left	**Yellow Ribbon Greenway Trail (asphalt);** cycle past Air Force Way/Sharp, Whytewold, Ladywood, and Moray, cross Sturgeon at the stop sign and then cross Silver to the Yellow Ribbon Greenway Trail on the north side of the road. Continue to the next street, Hamilton Avenue. **Air Force Heritage Air Park:** Turn right at Air Force Way to see the military aircraft and the Garden of Memories. **Living Prairie Museum:** To get to the museum, turn left at Moray Street and left again at Ness Avenue. You might like to take a self-guided walk on one of the trails to view some of the 150 species of grasses and wildflowers and perhaps catch a glimpse of some prairie wildlife that reside here.
7.07	0.43	Left	**Hamilton Avenue;** cycle just past the bridge across Sturgeon Creek and immediately to the right is access to Sturgeon Creek Greenway Trail.
7.50	3.08	Right	**Sturgeon Creek Greenway Trail (asphalt);** the trail curves right and goes under the Hamilton Bridge and then the Ness Bridge. When the trail splits, turn left and go over the bridge across the creek to continue under Sturgeon Road. There are several paths leading off from this path once past Sturgeon but always keep to the right. At the public bathroom, take the trail which curves right, towards Grant's Old Mill, and continue straight under Portage Avenue. Continue through Woodhaven Park, taking the trail which runs behind the RCAF jet. The trail exits at Woodhaven Boulevard.

			Turn right, cross the bridge over Sturgeon Creek and immediately to your left is a continuation of Sturgeon Creek Greenway Trail. Cycle through Woodhaven Park to the exit in a lane, continue straight to the corner of Wooddale Drive and Glendale Boulevard. **Grant's Old Mill:** Here's your chance to learn about the milling process and the history of this particular mill. **Public Bathroom:** Located along Sturgeon Creek Greenway Trail just north of Grant's Old Mill. It is open seasonally from 7am to 7:30pm.
10.58	0.23	Straight	**Glendale Boulevard;** cycle to the end of Glendale where it intersects into Assiniboine Avenue.
10.81	0.27	Left	**Assiniboine Avenue;** cycle a short distance to the continuation of the Sturgeon Creek Greenway Trail. There is a bike route sign indicating the trail.
11.08	0.17	Left	**Sturgeon Creek Greenway Trail (asphalt);** cycle the bridge over Sturgeon Creek and continue through Woodhaven Park to Assiniboine Crescent.
11.25	0.31	Right	**Assiniboine Crescent;** cycle past Thompson and Windham and just as the crescent curves left and becomes Lake Street, there is an access trail at the corner, between house #2584 and #2589, to the Moray/William R. Clement Multi-use Path, which is part of the Assiniboine Parkway.
11.56	1.81	Right	**Moray/William R. Clement Multi-use Path (asphalt);** when the trail splits, turn left and then right to go over the Assiniboine River and across Roblin. In Tom Chester Park, the trail splits in three, stay on the centre trail which goes straight ahead, past the pedestrian bridge over William R. Clement Parkway, to Grant Avenue.
13.37	0.17	Left	**Grant Avenue;** cycle to the first corner, Haney Street.
13.54	1.55	Right	**Haney Street;** cycle to the very end of the street where Haney meets Ridgewood Avenue.
15.09	0.25	Right	**Ridgewood Avenue;** cycle to the first exit on your left, which is a turnoff leading to Marj Edey Park.

15.34	0.02	Left	**Marj Edey Park road;** immediately to your left is the Harte Trail.
15.36	2.81	Left	**Harte Trail (crushed limestone);** cycle past Elmhurst, past a large prairie field which is the Assiniboine Forest, and exit to Shaftesbury Boulevard. **Assiniboine Forest Loop:** At Assiniboine Forest, just after a stand, turn left onto the Preston Trail. The trail splits, turn left. The trail then turns right, left and right again before exiting at Grant Avenue. There are other trails coming off this trail, but they are woodchip trails. Stay on the crushed limestone path and look for blue markings on the trees, the designated colour for the Preston Trail. Straight across Grant is the Assiniboine Park Trail. Cycle to Roblin Boulevard where the trail splits. Turn left and cycle to the crosswalk. Cross Roblin Boulevard and continue straight as the trail runs parallel to Commissary Road. Cross Assiniboine Park Drive and when the trail splits, turn right. Cycle behind the zoo, Leo Mol Sculpture Garden and the English Garden. Shortly after, the trail leads back to the Assiniboine River Park Bridge and the start of the ride. Distance – 23.3 km.
18.17	0.11	Right	**Shaftesbury Boulevard;** cycle over the train tracks and cross Wilkes Avenue/Sterling Lyon Parkway to Thundering Bison Trail.
18.28	4.18	Left	**Thundering Bison Trail (asphalt);** this multi-use path runs along the south side of Sterling Lyon Parkway/Wilkes Avenue. Cycle across Kenaston, Paget and Victor Lewis, and cross Waverley Street to the east side and the Waverley Multi-use Path. **IKEA or Tim Hortons:** Swedish meatballs or coffee? IKEA is just before Kenaston Boulevard and Tim's is a little further on at the corner of Wilkes and Waverley.

22.46	1.52	Left	**Waverley Multi-use Path (asphalt);** cycle to the next street, Taylor Avenue. The multi-use path is on the south side of Taylor.
23.98	1.86	Right	**Taylor Multi-use Path (asphalt);** cycle past La Grotta, Esso, Grant Park Festival and Walmart to the lights at Harrow Street. **Starbucks:** There is a Starbucks located in the Grant Park Festival at the corner of Taylor and Nathaniel Street.
25.84	2.26	Left	**Harrow Street;** cycle in the painted bike lane past Grant, Corydon, Grosvenor and Academy to Wellington Crescent. **Manitoba Electrical Museum:** To learn about Manitoba's hydroelectric power history and see some interesting displays, instead of turning left on Harrow, turn right.
28.10	2.31	Left	**Wellington Crescent/Wellington Multi-use Path (crushed limestone);** cycle either on the street or on the crushed limestone path on the centre boulevard, which stretches from Guelph to Lindsay Street. Pass Currie Park and look for the start of the Assiniboine Parkway Trail to your right. **Note:** Wellington Crescent, from Academy Road to Guelph Street, is designated as a Sunday/Holiday Bicycle Route, from 8am to 8pm, by the city of Winnipeg. This means, on those days, motor vehicle traffic is restricted to one block. **Water:** There are two stops along this stretch where you can re-fill your water bottle. There is a water fountain on the boulevard at Wellington and Guelph and at Andrew Currie Park, located on the south side of Wellington Crescent just after the centre boulevard ends.
30.41	2.87	Right	**Assiniboine Parkway Trail (asphalt);** the trail enters Assiniboine Park on the south side of Assiniboine Park Drive. Just before the first stop sign, at the cross walk, the trail divides into three, take the trail to the right.

			Cycle the trail along the Assiniboine River to return to the Assiniboine River Park Bridge.
33.28	0	End	**Assiniboine River Park Bridge.**

I don't ride a bike to add days to my life.
I ride a bike to add life to my days.

— Unknown

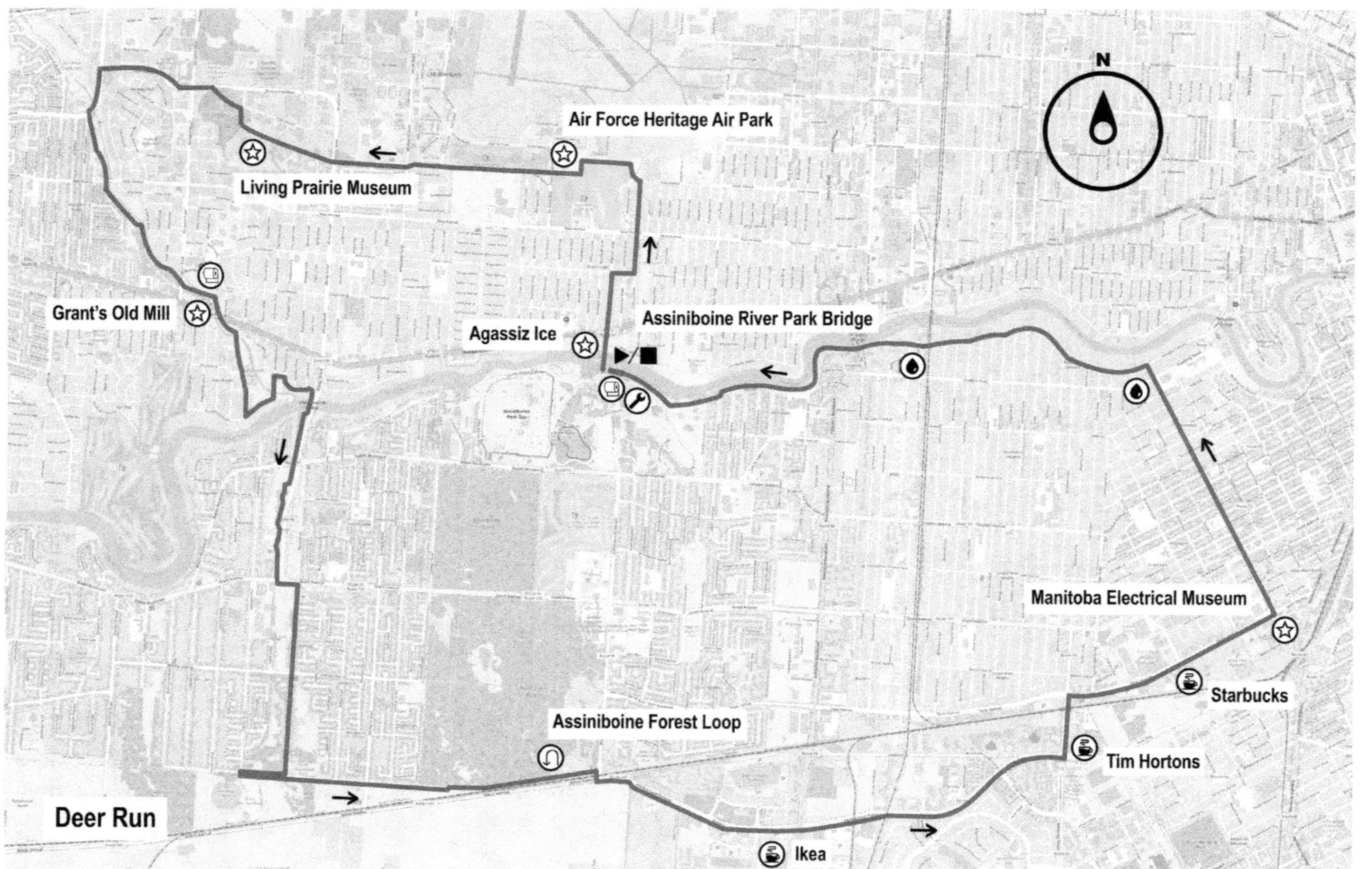
N
Air Force Heritage Air Park
Living Prairie Museum
Grant's Old Mill
Agassiz Ice
Assiniboine River Park Bridge
Manitoba Electrical Museum
Starbucks
Tim Hortons
Assiniboine Forest Loop
Ikea
Deer Run

Catfish Country

North of Winnipeg

Selkirk is a small city of about 10,000 people located 35 km north of Winnipeg. The local economy is supported by tourism, a steel mill and the Selkirk Mental Health Centre. The Mental Health Centre is the largest facility of its kind in the province and is the major employer to the inhabitants of the city. But it is the tourism angle of Selkirk from which the name of this ride comes from. Selkirk bills itself as the *Catfish Capital of the World* and attracts American anglers to come up and fish for trophy-size catfish in the Red River. *Chuck the Channel Cat*, located on Selkirk's Main Street, is the city's iconic statue representing this aspect. The fiberglass statue measures 25 feet long and is named in honour of a local sport fisherman, Chuck Norquay, who, unfortunately, drowned while fishing in the Red River. Although the route does not take you directly past this statue, you might like to take a slight detour, outlined in the detailed directions below, to visit the channel cat.

This route starts about 10 km from the north perimeter from a parking lot off Birds Hill Road. From here, we can access the Duff Roblin Parkway Trail. This trail is a 45 km trail starting at Duff Roblin Provincial Park in St. Norbert and follows the Red River Floodway ending in Lockport. Not to worry, we are only cycling the last 6.5 km of it. Then it is on to Lockport and over and then under the Lockport Bridge to get to River Road, which eventually becomes Eveline Street and takes us into Selkirk. The ride ends at the Selkirk Waterfront before heading back over the Selkirk Lift Bridge to the east side of the Red River, along PR204/Henderson Hwy back to Lockport and back to the Duff Roblin Trail and the parking lot. The route includes a fair bit of highway cycling so be sure to wear some reflective clothing so you are highly visible.

The Mighty Kiwi

As far as places to stop for coffee, I have picked two that are close to the Selkirk Waterfront. The Mighty Kiwi Juice Bar and Eatery and the Riverside Grill. The Mighty Kiwi is all about healthy eating and the Riverside Grill is a 50's style diner featuring home style cooking. To help you choose, here are the websites for each for your perusal. https://themightykiwi.ca and http://riversidegrill.ca

Riverside Grill

I recommend you get something to go and then sit and enjoy your food at the waterfront. It's a scenic spot with great views of the river and the Selkirk Lift Bridge. There is also a clock stand and the sculpture *Perilous Crossing*. This bronze sculpture depicts seven crewmen on a Hudson York Boat crossing Lake Winnipeg in late fall.

There are four points of interest on this ride. The first is Lockport Heritage Park which is located just before the Lockport Bridge on your right-hand side. From this park, you get a good view of the St. Andrews Caméré Curtain Bridge Dam, also known as the St. Andrews Lock and Dam. It's fun to stop here and sit on a bench and watch the churning water by the dam and the flocks of white pelicans who reside in the area. The park also features a short "Gifts of the Red" self-guided walk, if interested. You can also get a good view of the dam from River Road on the other side of the river.

The second point of interest is Lower Fort Garry National Historic Site located just before Selkirk. Lower Fort Garry was a Hudson's Bay Company fur trade post dating back to the 1830s. The buildings are original but the limestone walls surrounding the fort have been restored. When you step into this site, it is populated with interpreters dressed and working as people did when the fort was operating, and it is interesting to wander around the site observing the lifestyle at the time. The fort is famous for a number of "firsts". Here the first of the numbered treaties between the Crown and the area's First Nations was made, it was home to Western Canada's first prison, first asylum for the mentally ill and the first training facility for the North-West Mounted Police. If you want to stop here and step back into time, be sure to check out their website for opening times and admission prices. https://www.pc.gc.ca/en/lhn-nhs/mb/fortgarry/index?utm_source=gmb&utm_medium=fortgarry

Fort Garry

The last two points of interest are *Chuck the Channel Cat* and the bronze sculpture *Perilous Crossing*, both of which I have mentioned above.

Enjoy your ride!

<u>Quick Notes</u>

Distance – 39.5 km

Parking – Donald Road parking lot, off Birds Hill Road. From the Perimeter Highway, turn north onto PTH 59, turn left onto Birds Hill Road/MB-202N at the lights. After 8 km, the parking lot will be on your right, at the end of Donald Road.

Option to shorten – yes

Lockport-Selkirk Loop – 26.4 km *For this loop, park in the Lockport parking lot, 7 km further up Birds Hill Road/Mb-202N from the Donald Road parking lot

Suggested coffee stops – The Mighty Kiwi Juice Bar and Eatery at 201 Manitoba Avenue, Riverside Grill at 386 Eveline Street

Bathrooms – Lockport Heritage Park (non-modern) at 23022 Provincial Highway 44, coffee stop

Points of Interest –

Lockport Heritage Park at 23022 Provincial Trunk Highway 44 on the east side of the Red River

Lower Fort Garry National Historic Sites at 5925 PTH 9A

Chuck the Channel Cat at 168 Main Street, Selkirk

Perilous Crossing Art Installation at Selkirk Waterfront

Trails

Duff Roblin Parkway Trail – crushed limestone

PTH 9 Trail – asphalt

Safety Cautions

Detailed Directions

Km Total	Km Leg	Direction	Location, notes
0	0	Start	**Donald Road parking lot.**
0	6.54	Left	**Duff Roblin Parkway Trail (crushed limestone);** facing the floodway, exit the parking lot onto Duff Roblin Parkway Trail. The trail runs between the Red River Floodway on your right and Birds Hill Road/MB-202N on your left. Exit the trail at the next parking lot.
6.54	0.08	Left	**Lockport parking lot;** cycle through the lot to Birds Hill Road/Mb-202N. **Lockport-Selkirk Loop:** Refer to Quick Notes for parking directions. Start from this step and continue as follows until return to this lot. Distance – 26.4 km.
6.62	0.62	Right	**Birds Hill Road/Mb-202N;** cycle to the end of the road where intersects with Henderson Highway.

7.24	0.58	Right	**Henderson Highway/PR204;** cycle past the Half Moon Drive In to PTH 44E.
7.82	1.04	Left	**PTH 44E;** cycle over the Lockport Bridge to PR238, which is just before Skinner's. **Caution:** The corner of Henderson Highway/PR204 and PTH44E is a very busy corner, use extreme caution when crossing. **Caution:** Cycling over the Lockport Bridge can be challenging as it is not bicycle friendly. My suggestion is to cycle up the bridge on the shoulder. The shoulder gradually disappears as you near the top of the bridge. I stop, get off my bike, check there is no traffic behind me, and then climb onto the sidewalk and walk across the bridge. On the other side, I get off the sidewalk, back onto the shoulder, and continue my ride. **Lockport Heritage Park:** This park is located on your right just before the Lockport Bridge. Stop and take a look at the churning waters by St. Andrews Lock and Dam and see the many pelicans. **Lockport Heritage Park:** A non-modern bathroom is located behind the buildings on the east side of the park.
8.86	0.49	Left	**PR238;** shortly after turning onto PR238, it intersects with Stevens Ave E. Turn left. Cycle to River Road.
9.35	2.10	Left	**River Road;** this road runs along the edge of the Red River. Notice all the fisherman on the water as they try to catch a trophy-size catfish. River Road curves left and runs into PTH 9/Main Street. Just before the highway is an asphalt trail running along the east side of the road.
11.45	2.26	Right	**PTH 9 Trail (asphalt)/PTH 9/Main Street;** follow the path which merges into a street towards Lower Fort Garry National Historic Site. This small street ends in a turnaround, at the left side of the turnaround is a trail which leads to the next section of road which runs past Lower Fort Garry.

		⭐	This trail exits on River Road N. **Lower Fort Garry National Historic Site:** Step back in time when you visit this site where many "firsts" took place.
13.71	5.70	Right	**River Road N/Eveline Street;** follow the road as it runs next to the Red River. River Road N becomes Eveline Street when you enter Selkirk's City Limits. This is a long stretch. You pass stop signs at Manchester/Idell, Strathnaver, Sutherland, and Eaton Avenue/PR204. Cycle past Clandeboyne to Manitoba Avenue/Superior Avenue. ⭐ *Chuck the Channel Cat:* You'll have to take a slight detour to visit *Chuck*. Once on Eveline, look for Maple Drive which is the third street past the stop sign at Manchester. Turn left and cycle to Main Street. Turn right and *Chuck the Channel Cat* is located on your right, before you reach the next block. Be sure to take a selfie with this icon of Selkirk before returning to Eveline and continuing your ride. ⭐ *Perilous Crossing* **Art Installation:** This bronze sculpture is located at the Selkirk Waterfront and depicts crewmen crossing Lake Winnipeg on a Hudson York Boat. ☕ **The Mighty Kiwi Juice Bar and Eatery and Riverside Grill:** Both these venues are close to the Selkirk Waterfront. Get something to go and sit at the waterfront. It's a scenic spot with great views of the river and the Selkirk Lift Bridge.
19.41	0.10	Right	**Superior Avenue;** cycle to the Selkirk Waterfront.
19.51	0.10	U-turn	**Superior Avenue;** cycle to Eveline Street.
19.61	0.19	Left	**Eveline Street;** cycle to the stop sign at PR 204/Henderson Hwy.
19.80	11.89	Right	**PR204/Henderson Highway;** cycle over the Selkirk Lift Bridge and follow the highway. When you reach the turnoff for Lockport, follow the signage which takes you over the half cloverleaf and turning right.

				Cycle to the first intersection which is the continuation of PR204/Henderson Highway. **Note:** I always find this stretch long and wonder when it will be done. Something I find helpful to get a sense of how much farther I have to go is watching the house numbers go down. The addresses start around 8800 close to Selkirk and go down to 7200 close to Lockport. **Caution:** This highway has a narrow asphalt shoulder. You should wear reflective clothing to be sure you are noticeable on the roadway.
31.69	0.60	Left		**PR204/Henderson Highway;** cycle past Half Moon Drive In to MB-202S/Birds Hill Road.
32.29	0.59	Left		**Mb-202S/Birds Hill Road;** cycle to the Lockport parking lot turnoff from which you had previously exited the trail.
32.88	0.08	Left		**Lockport parking lot;** cycle through the lot to the Duff Roblin Parkway Trail.
32.96	6.54	Right		**Duff Roblin Parkway Trail (crushed limestone);** return to the Donald Road parking lot.
39.50	0	End		**Donald Road parking lot.**

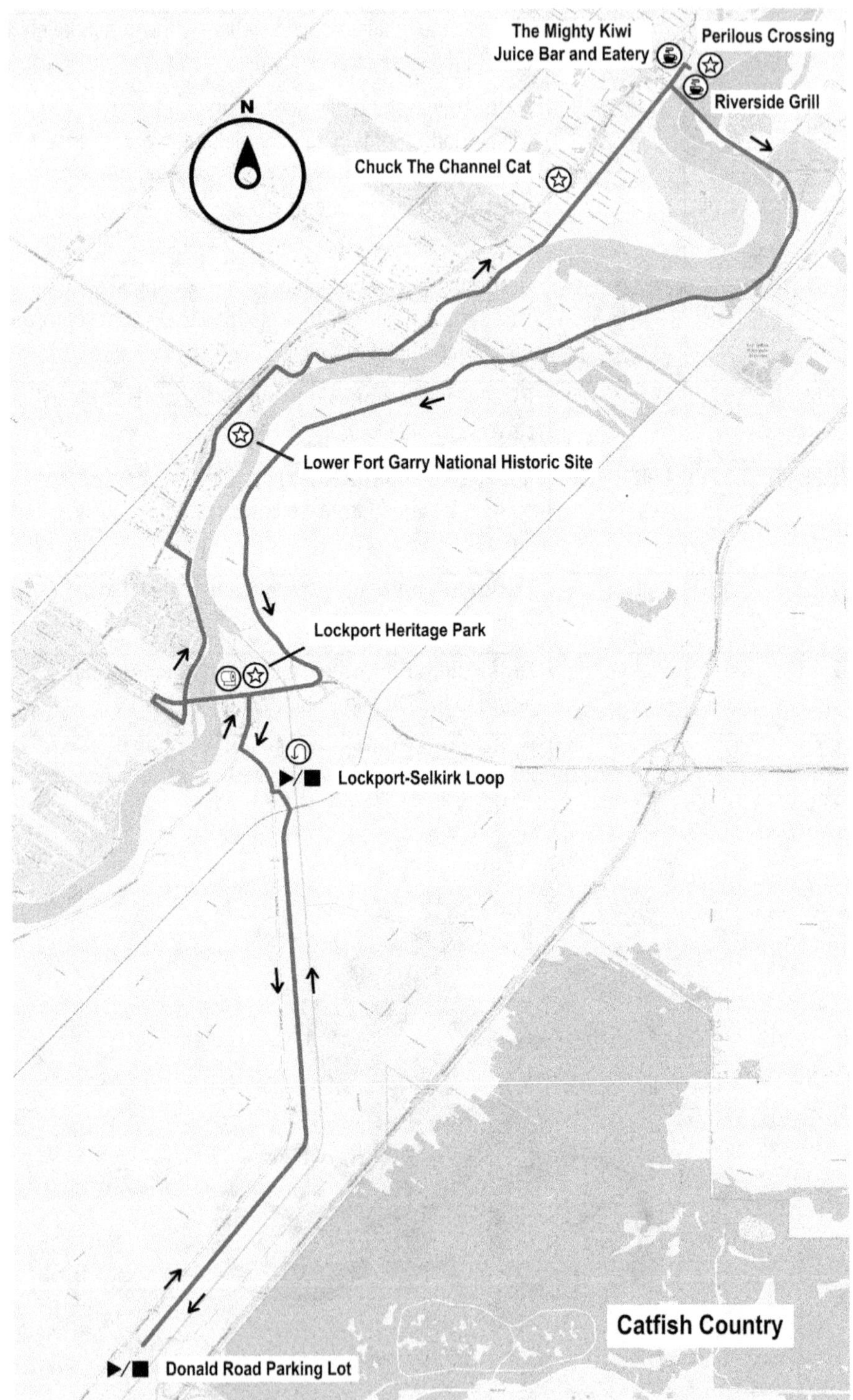
N
The Mighty Kiwi
Juice Bar and Eatery
Perilous Crossing
Riverside Grill
Chuck The Channel Cat
Lower Fort Garry National Historic Site
Lockport Heritage Park
Lockport-Selkirk Loop
Catfish Country
Donald Road Parking Lot

Hot Dog! Let's go to Lockport!

North of Winnipeg

Lockport is a small community located 27 km north of Winnipeg and is one of the oldest settlements in Canada. Archeological excavations carried out in this area in the 1980's found evidence of human activity dating back more than 3000 years. There were indications crops were being grown in the 1400's, due to the discovery of charred corn kernels, hoes made from shoulder blades of bison and underground storage pits. This discovery suggests this settlement was established by the first farmers in the northern part of the Red River valley and that they long pre-dated the arrival of European settlers.

This is a great ride, longer than the usual 30 km, but well worth it. The ride heads out on Main Street or PTH 9, with a turn off at River Road. River Road takes you away from the busy highway and the ride then becomes a leisurely spin along the west side of the Red River which is fairly peaceful and offers great views over the river. The ride back is via Henderson Highway. Because virtually this whole ride is on highways, use caution and I recommend wearing high-visibility clothing.

Apart from the historical aspects of Lockport, they are probably most famously known for their hot dogs. This is the home of the original Skinner's hot dog. Skinner's opened up in 1929, first as a small stand and then a permanent restaurant on River Road. This particular restaurant is the oldest hot dog outlet in continuous operation in Canada. Over the years, Skinner's expanded and there is another location on Highway 44, also in Lockport. https://www.skinnershwy44.ca

Skinners

Half Moon Drive In

Skinner's though, is not the only option for a hot dog in Lockport. Another long-time outlet is the Half Moon Drive In on Henderson Highway. This equally iconic hot dog establishment opened in 1938. The diner décor is steeped in the 1950s but, if you prefer, you can also sit out back at one of the picnic tables overlooking the Red River. http://halfmoondrivein.com

As you can see, hot dogs and Lockport, have a long history, hence the name Hot Dog! Let's go to Lockport!

There are three points of interest I would like to suggest for this ride; St. Andrew's-on-the-Red Anglican Church, Lockport Heritage Park and to note the remnants of pioneer land allocations along Henderson Hwy/PR 204.

St. Andrew's-on-the-Red Anglican Church and Cemetery plus the Rectory are designated national historic sites. This Church, built between 1845 and 1849, is the oldest operating church in Western Canada. The building was designed by Archdeacon William Cockran, who was instrumental in establishing the Anglican denomination in Manitoba. The cemetery located here was the final resting place of many Hudson Bay Company officers and of some of the early settlers in the area, including William Cockran.

St. Andrew's Rectory

Lastly, there is a stone arch near the church which lists the names of those killed from this area in the First World War. Across from the Church is a small museum. If you have the time, wander around the grounds, it's well worth it. http://www.standrews rectory.ca/

Lockport Heritage Park is just over the Lockport Bridge on PTH 44 on the east side of the Red River. From this park, you get a good view of the St. Andrews Caméré Curtain Bridge Dam, also known as the St. Andrews Lock and Dam. It's fun to stop here and sit on a bench and watch the churning water and the flocks of white pelicans who reside in the area. White pelicans arrive in Manitoba between early April and early June and migrate south to California and the Gulf of Mexico near the end of September. So as long as you come here between those months, you will see pelicans. There is also a short "Gifts of the Red" self-guided walk, if interested.

When you leave Lockport and turn onto Henderson Hwy/PR 204, look to the right, towards the river, and to your left. Note what appears to be narrow strips of land, separated by tree-lines, fences or field edges. These are the remnants of pioneer land allocations. At the time of settlement, each landholder was allocated a long narrow strip of land, a long lot, extending away from the river, so each could have river frontage.

So, have I sold you on heading out to Lockport?

Quick Notes
Distance – 49.9 km
Parking – Kildonan Park at 2015 Main Street, park in the lot by the Chief Peguis
     Pavilion
Option to shorten – yes
     Henderson Loop – 35.8 km *For this loop, park in the small lot off Henderson
          Highway, by the river, just past the Perimeter Highway
Suggested coffee stops – Skinner's at 608 River Road or at 100 PTH 44, Half Moon
     Drive In at 6860 Henderson Highway
Bathrooms – Kildonan Park in the Pavilion, Lockport Heritage Park, coffee stops
Points of Interest –
     St. Andrew's-on-the-Red at the corner of River Road and St. Andrew's Road

Lockport Heritage Park at 23022 Provincial Trunk Highway 44 on the east side of Red River

Land Allocation Remnants along Henderson Hwy/PR 204

Trails

Kildonan Park Trail – asphalt

Kildonan Park Golf Course Trail – crushed limestone

PTH 9 Trail – crushed limestone/asphalt

Chief Peguis Greenway Trail – asphalt

Safety Cautions

Detailed Directions

Km Total	Km Leg	Direction	Location, notes
0	0	Start	**McKay Drive;** ride starts on McKay Drive by the children's playground at the southeast corner of Kildonan Park parking lot. **Kildonan Park:** Bathrooms are in the lower level of the Chief Peguis Pavilion located just off the parking lot. They are open daily from 8am to 9pm. **Henderson Loop:** Refer to Quick Notes for parking directions. Exit the parking lot and, at lights, cross to the east side of Henderson Hwy/PR 204 and cycle on the paved shoulder to Lockport Road/PTH 44. Turn left and cycle to Lockport Heritage Park to view St. Andrews Lock and Dam. When you are ready, turn around and head back to Henderson Hwy/PR 204 and return to parking lot. Distance – 35.8 km.
0	0.29	Left	**McKay Drive/Riverview Drive;** as the road curves left, McKay Drive becomes Riverview Drive. Shortly after the curve, the road meets with the Kildonan Park Trail which runs beside the river.

0.29	1.23	Right	**Kildonan Park Trail (asphalt)/Kildonan Park Golf Course Trail (crushed limestone);** cycle the Kildonan Park Trail as it follows along the edge of the Red River. At the edge of the golf course the trail changes from asphalt to crushed limestone and becomes the Kildonan Park Golf Course Trail. At the end of the golf course, the Chief Peguis Greenway Trail begins.
1.52	0.30	Left	**Chief Peguis Greenway Trail (asphalt);** take the first right which leads under the Kildonan Settlers Bridge. Continue straight to exit on Scotia Street.
1.82	0.34	Straight	**Scotia Street;** cycle to the end of the road and then onto the crushed limestone path which links to the continuation of Scotia. Cycle to the stop sign at Rivercrest Avenue.
2.16	0.79	Right	**Ridgecrest Avenue/River Grove Drive;** stay on Ridgecrest as it curves left and becomes River Grove Drive. Cycle past many streets to the stop sign at Red River Boulevard.
2.95	0.38	Left	**Red River Boulevard;** cycle past Sandalwood and Meadowcrest to Main Street.
3.33	2.98	Right ⚠	**Main Street/PTH 9;** cycle past the Perimeter Hwy, River Trail and Nye to Grassmere Road/Evelyn Avenue, where a trail off the highway begins. **Caution:** The shoulders are asphalt and easy to cycle till just after the Perimeter overpass, but then become gravel and are quite rough. The trail in the next step starts approximately 0.5 km after the overpass. Use caution on the gravel shoulders.
6.31	6.85	Straight	**PTH 9 Trail (crushed limestone/asphalt);** this trail is a mix of crushed limestone paths and streets and runs parallel to the highway. Cycle to Hiawatha where the trail veers to the right and then left to go down a backlane to the next street, Minnehaha. Turn left and then right to get back onto the trail. Cycle across Lister Rapids, Masters and River Springs to the lights at Allenford Drive.

			Cross PTH 9 to continue on the trail on the west side of the highway.
			Cycle across Northumberland and just past Everlasting Memorials, the trail turns left, over the railroad tracks, and then right. At the next street, Willis Road, turn right and the trail begins left next to the highway.
			Cross Jackman and Miller to Parks Creek Drive. Turn left on Parks Creek and when ends, turn left again to stay on Parks Creek. This road curves right and right again and end at PTH 9. Cross to the wide asphalt shoulder on the east side of the highway.
			Note: At the time of writing this book, work was being done on PTH 9 just past the perimeter and it is possible the trail may, in the future, begin earlier than indicated here.
13.16	1.34	Left	**PTH 9;** cycle to the lights at River Road.
14.50	9.96	Right	**River Road/PR 238;** follow this quiet, winding road along the edge of the Red River. At Lockport, at the corner with Skinner's Restaurant, is Stevens Ave E/PR 238.
			St. Andrews on the Red: Stop and peer inside the oldest operating church in Western Canada.
			Skinner's Restaurant: Dog, cheese dog, cheese bacon dog, chili dog, super dog, smokie dog...is your mouth watering yet?
24.46	0.39	Left	**Stevens Ave E/PR 238;** cycle Stevens to the first road PR238N.
24.85	0.09	Right	**PR 238 N;** cycle to Lockport Road/PTH 44.
24.94	0.99	Right	**Lockport Road/PTH 44;** cycle over the Lockport Bridge, past Melody Lane, to Henderson Highway.
			Caution: The Lockport Bridge is not bike friendly. It just has two narrow lanes, with no shoulders. There is a sidewalk on the north side, with a steep curb at each end. When I crossed this bridge, I rode the shoulder to the beginning of the bridge and then crossed to the north side to the sidewalk. I crossed the bridge on the sidewalk and then went back onto the shoulder and

			crossed back to the south side to continue. Traffic can be heavy, so use caution.
			Skinner's Restaurant: If you missed the last location, it's not too late to indulge in a hot dog!
			Lockport Heritage Park: Located to your left just over the bridge, this park offers great views of the locks. Many pelicans can also be seen at the base.
			Lockport Heritage Park: A non-modern bathroom is located behind the buildings on the east side of the park.
25.93	20.47	Right	**Henderson Highway/PR 204;** stay on Henderson as you pass a number of churches: St. Nicholas Ukrainian Orthodox Church, Holy Trinity Ukrainian Catholic Church, Corpus Christi Roman Catholic Church, and St. Nicholas Orthodox Church, eventually you pass the community of East St. Paul and the Perimeter. Continue to Chief Peguis Greenway. **Note:** I find this length long to cycle. One thing I like to do, to have a sense of how far I have to go from Lockport to the Perimeter, is watch the house numbers go down. The numbers start around 6900 in Lockport and go down to around 2450 at the Perimeter. **Half Moon Drive In:** Last chance for a Hot Dog! Footlong, deluxe dog, moon dog, super dog, chili dog, turkey smoky dog, and more! **Land Allocation Remnants:** Notice the narrow strips of land, the long lots, along the Red River, a throwback to the first settlers.
46.40	2.06	Right	**Chief Peguis Greenway Trail (asphalt);** the trail starts on the north side of Chief Peguis, goes under the Kildonan Settlers Bridge to the south side, and then curves left and left again to go over the bridge. Just before Main Street the trail splits, turn left and continue to Kildonan Park Golf Course Trail.
48.46	0.83	Right	**Kildonan Park Golf Course Trail (crushed limestone)/Kildonan Park Trail (asphalt);** cycle behind the golf course and into Kildonan Park. The Kildonan Golf Course Trail is made of crushed limestone and when you pass the Golf Course, the trail

			is asphalt. This is the beginning of the Kildonan Park Trail. Take the second exit right from the trail, just after Lord Selkirk Creek, to Peguis Drive, by the Witch's Hut. **Caution:** There is a steep dip at the end of the trail as it exits to the road.
49.29	0.05	Left	**Peguis Drive;** the first street to your right is Lord Selkirk Drive.
49.34	0.41	Right	**Lord Selkirk Drive;** follow this road back to the parking lot.
49.75	0.17	Left	**Kildonan Park parking lot;** cycle through the lot to the southeast corner by the children's playground and to McKay Drive.
49.92	0	End	**McKay Drive.**

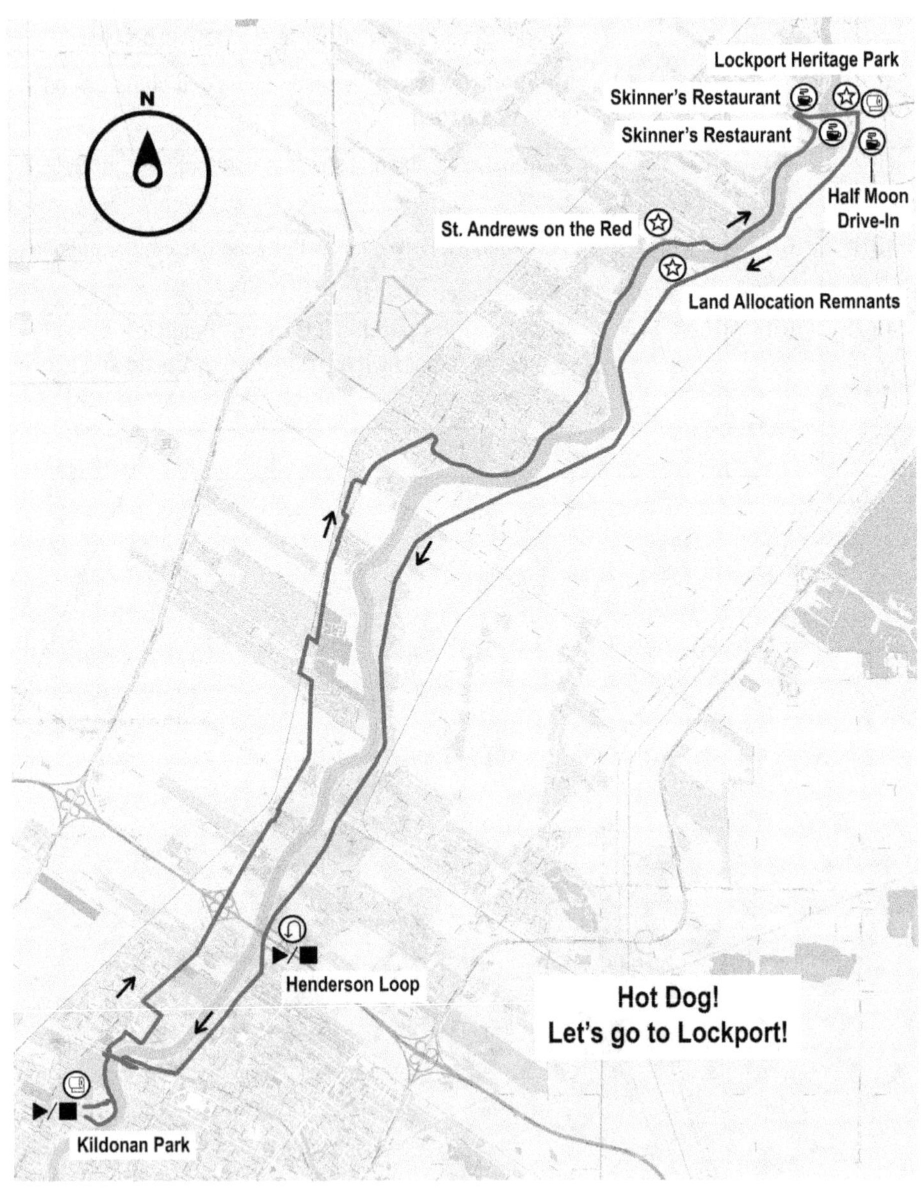
N
Lockport Heritage Park
Skinner's Restaurant
Skinner's Restaurant
Half Moon
Drive-In
St. Andrews on the Red
Land Allocation Remnants
Henderson Loop
Hot Dog!
Let's go to Lockport!
Kildonan Park

Exploring Birds Hill 1

25 km Northeast of Winnipeg

There are so many places to cycle in Birds Hill Park that I couldn't fit them all into one ride, so I've designed two rides, with very little overlap. This ride features the Lakeview and Bluestem trails, plus a short leg to Pope's Hill and the second ride features South Drive and the Duff Roblin, Aspen, and part of the Lakeview trail. There are other trails in the park, but not all allow bikes on them. Some are specific for hikers or horseback riding, so if you intend to explore beyond these rides, pay attention to the signage for the trails. I highly recommend when you enter the park you ask for a Birds Hill Interpretive Map for an overview of the park and its trails.

Birds Hill Provincial Park, opened in 1967, serves as a near-by oasis to Winnipeggers who want to escape the hustle and bustle of city life and explore the outdoors. It is a park of campgrounds, lakes and trails and provides year-round opportunities to partake in activities such as hiking, cycling, horseback riding, and cross-country skiing. It is also home to the Winnipeg Folk Festival every July, one of North America's largest folk music events. If you are a fan of the Folk Festival and come here to camp during that time, you might want to consider bringing your bike and doing the two rides in this book.

Here's a bit of trivia for you. Although there are over 200 species of birds which have been identified in this park, its name is not a nod to the birdlife. The park is actually named after James Curtis Bird, the first Speaker of the Manitoba Legislative Assembly in 1870 and an employee of the Hudson Bay Company.

The two trails featured on this ride are the Lakeview and Bluestem. The Lakeview Trail runs around Birds Hill Lake and Kingfisher Lake and winds through the woods. Birds Hill Lake is for humans to enjoy, but Kingfisher Lake is for wildlife, providing a habitat for ducks, shorebirds, frogs, and turtles, among others. The Bluestem Trail is a 14 km looped trail north of North Drive. This is a grass and dirt trail and more suited for a mountain bike, but I have a commuter bike and had no trouble riding it.

There are four points of interest on this ride. An Overlook, from which you can see the lakes and the surrounding parkland, is on the Lakeview Trail close to North Drive. Stop and take a look at the amazing surroundings that make up Birds Hill Park and read the interpretive signs which explain Manitoba's park system.

Griffiths Hill, the highest point in the park at 265 m above sea level, is on the Bluestem Trail. It's well worth the climb up the viewing tower to see the landscape and read the interpretive signs about the area and learn what an esker is, how it was formed and how it was used by the early settlers.

Pine Ridge Cemetery on Nimowin Road is used and maintained by the congregation of Immaculate Conception Church at Cook's Creek. Here, the original settlers who worked this land are now buried. There are about 350 graves but no one knows the exact number because some people could have been buried before records were properly kept. To be buried in this cemetery today, one must be a descendant of these original pioneers.

Finally, this route goes to Pope's Hill. On September 16, 1984, Pope John Paul II, the first pope to visit Canada, made his way through Birds Hill Park in the Popemobile to a waiting crowd of 200,000. On this site he conducted a large open-air multi-cultural celebration of faith, hence the name Pope's Hill. There is a short, asphalt walkway to the Papal site, with interpretive signs at the beginning of the trail.

At the end of the ride, you might like to lock up your bike and sit back and relax in the sun by the lake or buy an ice cream at the beach.

Enjoy!

Quick Notes

Distance – 23.4 km

Parking – West Beach parking lot in Birds Hill Provincial Park. **Note:** A park permit is required to park your car. Day passes can be purchased when you enter the park, seasonal passes can be purchased at the campground office or on-line. https://www.gov.mb. ca/sd/parks/park-fees/index.html

Park Permit

Options to shorten – yes

    1 – Lakeview Loop – 5.8 km

    2 – Bluestem Loop – 13.5 km *Park in the lot at the end of Stables Road, by the riding stables, and follow the detailed directions below.

Suggested coffee stops – Birds Hill Concession by the beach, close to the east parking lot, restaurant by the riding stables

Bathrooms – Public Bathrooms close to the west and east parking lots, Public Bathroom by riding stables at end of Stables Road

Points of Interest –

    Overlook on Lakeview Trail

    Griffiths Hill on Bluestem Trail

    Pine Ridge Cemetery on Nimowin Road

    Pope's Hill off Festival Drive

Trails

Lakeview Trail – asphalt

Bluestem Trail – dirt/grass

Safety Cautions

Detailed Directions

Km Total	Km Leg	Direction	Location, notes
0	0	Start	**West Beach parking lot;** this lot is split into two halves. Between the two halves is Lakeview Trail.
0	5.14	South (towards the lakes)	**Lakeview Trail (asphalt);** follow the navy Lakeview Trail markers as the trail exits the west parking lot towards Birds Hill Lake and Kingfisher Lake, which you pass on your left. The trail then skirts through some woods along the edge of the camping area before heading back towards the lakes. Pass the lakes and continue on the trail heading north as it passes through the East Beach parking lot and then curves to the left. When you reach the overlook, the trail splits, turn right and go across North Drive. This trail ends at the Bluestem Trail. **Public Bathroom:** There are two bathrooms locations just off of the Lakeview Trail, one at each end of the beach by each parking lot. To reach the one by the West Beach parking lot, the trail splits almost as soon as you leave the lot. Veer right for the bathrooms. Return to the Lakeview Trail to continue when done. To reach the bathrooms on the other side of the lake, by the East Beach parking lot, they are located on the west side of the concession stand. Return to Lakeview Trail to continue when done. **Overlook:** Stop and take a look at the amazing surroundings that make up Birds Hill Park. **Water:** There is a water tap by the Overlook.

				Lakeview Loop: Follow the direction above but when the trail splits, do not turn right. Continue straight and the trail curves left and heads back to the West Beach parking lot. Distance – 5.8 km.
5.14	12.78	Left		**Bluestem Trail (dirt/grass);** follow the asphalt path, which at this point is a shared path for the Bluestem and Aspen Trails and look for the entrance to the Bluestem Trail to your right. You are looking for a dirt trail into the bush. This trail runs counter clockwise making a loop through the parkland. It is very well marked and you needn't worry about getting lost. This trail is mostly meant for a mountain bike but I have a commuter bike and did not have any trouble riding this trail. There are other trails which share portions of this path, so always make sure you are following the Bluestem Trail markers. The trail exits into the parking lot by the riding stables. Exit the parking lot to Stables Road. **Griffiths Hill:** Climb the viewing tower and discover what an esker is. **Riding Stables Restaurant:** Need a refreshment break? There is a coffee shop close to the parking lot. **Public Bathroom:** There are public bathrooms in the same building where the restaurant is located. **Bluestem Loop:** This loop is of the Bluestem Trail only. Refer to Quick Notes for parking directions. The trailhead is located off the parking lot. Follow the Bluestem Trail markers to return to the parking lot when complete. Distance – 13.5 km.
17.92	0.27	Right		**Stables Road;** cycle to Nimowin Road.
18.19	0.40	Straight		**Nimowin Road;** cycle to North Drive. **Pine Ridge Cemetery:** Many of the original settlers who lived in this area are buried here. **Water:** There is a water tap by the cemetery.

18.59	1.05	Left	**North Drive;** stay on North Drive as it curves right and come to Festival Drive.
19.64	0.57	Left	**Festival Drive;** cycle to Pope's Hill. **Pope's Hill:** This short trail takes you to the site where Pope John Paul II conducted a large open-air multi-cultural celebration of faith.
20.21	1.50	U-turn	**Festival Drive/East Beach parking lot entrance;** follow festival drive back and cross North Drive into the East Beach parking lot. Cycle to the Lakeview Trail running through the middle of this parking lot. **Birds Hill Concession:** Now might be a good time to stop for ice cream, but you'll have to do a bit of a detour. When you reach the Lakeview Trail, instead of turning right as in the next step, turn left and just as you reach the beach area, the concession stand will be to your right. When done, return to Lakeview Trail and turn left to get back to the East Beach parking lot and continue the route.
21.71	1.69	Right	**Lakeview Trail (asphalt);** follow the trail as it curves several times and winds past the Overlook and back to West Beach parking lot.
23.40	0	End	**West Beach parking lot.**

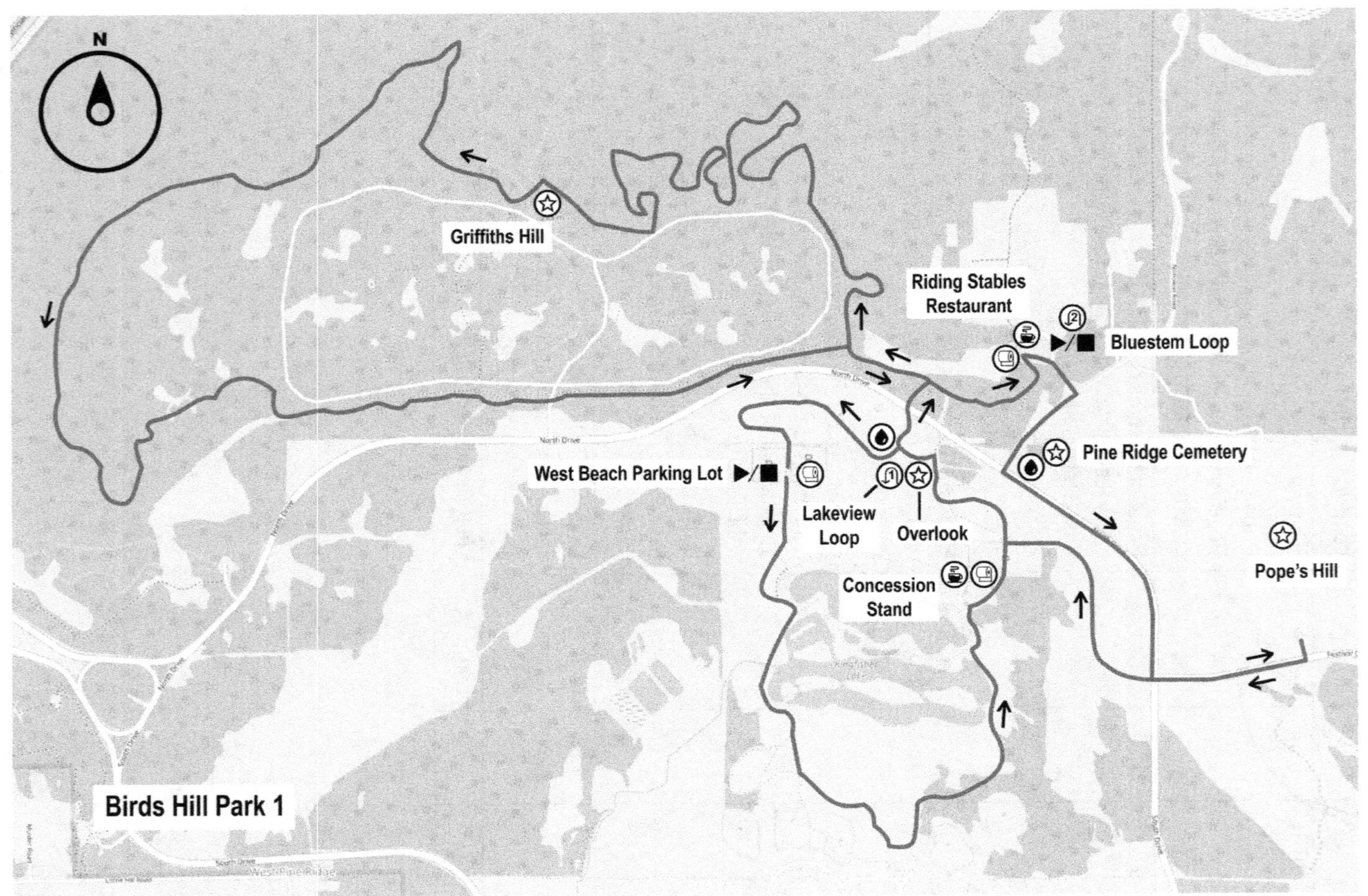
N
Griffiths Hill
Riding Stables
Restaurant
Bluestem Loop
Pine Ridge Cemetery
West Beach Parking Lot
Lakeview
Loop
Overlook
Pope's Hill
Concession
Stand
Birds Hill Park 1

Exploring Birds Hill 2

25 km Northeast of Winnipeg

There are so many trails in Birds Hill Park I couldn't fit them all into one ride, so I've made two rides, with very little overlap. This ride features South Drive and the Duff Roblin, Aspen, and Lakeview trails while the first ride featured the Lakeview and Bluestem trails, plus a short leg to Pope's Hill. There are other trails in the park, but not all allow bikes on them. Some are specific for hikers or horseback riding, so if you intend to explore beyond this ride, pay attention to the signage for the trails. I highly recommend when you enter the park you ask for a Birds Hill Interpretive Map for an overview of the park and its trails.

Birds Hill Park is a mosaic of landscapes including asker ridges, prairie land, meadows, bogs, and aspen, oak and mixed boreal forests. This land is home to an abundance of wildlife including frogs, garter snakes, hawks, squirrels, and over 200 species of birds. It is also home to a population of white-tailed deer which fluctuates in count between 250 and 450.

The three trails featured in this ride are the Duff Roblin, Aspen and Lakeview Trails. The Duff Roblin Parkway Trail, which crosses PTH 59 via an overpass, connects Birds Hill Park to the main Duff Roblin Parkway Trail which runs along the Red River floodway. The Aspen Trail is a looped trail north of North Drive. This is a grass and dirt trail and more suited for a mountain bike, but I have a commuter bike and had no troubles riding it. And finally, the Lakeview Trail runs around Birds Hill Lake and Kingfisher Lake and winds through the woods.

As a break during your ride or as a destination once your ride is complete, you can't go wrong with a stop at Pineridge Hollow, an eatery and shopping experience all in one. This restaurant serves wholesome, comforting foods using local produce. Pineridge Hollow is also a place to shop for unique clothing, jewelry, home furnishings, home décor and giftware. The building is located on beautifully landscaped grounds, a popular venue for weddings and other events, so it's worth wandering around the outside before returning to your bike or car. This restaurant can be accessed from within Birds Hill. It is located off of South Drive. The road is not marked but it is directly opposite to the Prairie Winds Trail. The road leads to a parking area and a back-gate entrance to Pineridge Hollow. https://www.pineridge hollow.com

Pineridge Hollow

There are two points of interest worth mentioning on this ride. The first is the Overlook, from which you can see the lakes and the surrounding parkland, is on the

Lakeview Trail close to North Drive. Stop and take a look at the amazing surroundings that make up Birds Hill Park and read the interpretive signs which explain Manitoba's park system.

The second is Pine Ridge Cemetery on Nimowin Road which is used and maintained by the congregation of Immaculate Conception Church at Cook's Creek. Here, the original settlers who worked this land are now buried. There are about 350 graves but no one knows the exact number because some people could have been buried before records were properly kept. To be buried in this cemetery today, one must be a descendant of these original pioneers.

This popular park attracts more than a million visitors annually; discover what all the fuss is about and enjoy!

Quick Notes

Distance – 29.1 km

Parking – West Beach parking lot in Birds Hill Provincial Park. **Note:** A park permit is required to park your car. Day permits can be purchased when you enter the park or on-line, seasonal permits can be purchased at the campground office or on-line. https://www.gov.mb.ca/sd/parks/park-fees/index.html

Options to shorten – yes

    1 – Lakeview Loop – 5.8 km

    2 – North-South Loop – 13.8 km

    3 – Aspen Loop – 6.4 km *For this loop, park in the lot at the end of Stables Road, by the riding stables

Suggested coffee stops – Pine Ridge Hollow off of South Drive, Birds Hill Concession by the beach, close to the east parking lot, restaurant by the riding stables

Bathrooms – Public Bathrooms close to the west and east parking lots, Public Bathroom by riding stables at end of Stables Road

Points of Interest –

    Overlook on Lakeview Trail

    Pine Ridge Cemetery on Nimowin Road

Trails

Lakeview Trail – asphalt

Duff Roblin Parkway Trail – asphalt

Aspen Trail – dirt/grass

Safety Cautions

Detailed Directions

Km Total	Km Leg	Direction	Location, notes
0	0	Start	**West Beach parking lot on the Lakeview Trail which runs between the two halves of the lot.**
0	1.15	Left	**Lakeview Trail (asphalt);** cycle north on the trail, heading towards North Drive. The trail curves left and then right. At the Overlook, the trail splits. Turn left to exit on North Drive. **Public Bathroom:** There are bathrooms located on Lakeview Trail, close to the picnic area, before you reach the Overlook. **Overlook:** Stop and take a look at the amazing surroundings that make up Birds Hill Park. **Water:** There is a water tap by the Overlook. **Lakeview Loop:** Do not do any of the ride below. Lakeview Trail runs through the centre of the West Beach parking lot and is a loop. Start the trail from the parking lot and you can go in either direction. It loops around Birds Hill Lake and Kingfisher Lake and runs along the edge of the campground on the southern edge and along North Drive on the northern edge of the trail. Distance – 5.8 km.
1.15	2.92	Left	**North Drive;** cycle past West Beach turnoff, Group Use Area 1 and the Chickadee Trail to the Cedar Bog/DRPT (Duff Roblin Parkway Trail) exit. **North-South Loop:** Do not exit at the Cedar Bog/DRPT turnoff. Continue straight on North Drive and when the road curves right towards the park entrance/exit, turn left, where indicated, onto South Drive.

			This road circles the camping and beach areas of Birds Hill Park. Once you cycle past Festival Drive, South Drive becomes North Drive. Cycle past Nimowin and when you reach the Overlook, turn left onto the Lakeview Trail. At the Overlook where the trail splits, turn right and follow the Lakeview Trail to return to West Beach parking lot. Distance – 13.8 km.
4.07	2.63	Right	**Duff Roblin Parkway Trail (asphalt);** follow the road to the parking lot and the entrance to the Duff Roblin Parkway Trail. Cycle the trail to the overpass over PTH59. Cycle to the middle of the overpass. **Note:** If you would continue, this trail connects to the Duff Roblin Parkway Trail which runs along the Red River floodway. This trail along the floodway starts at Duff Roblin Provincial Park in St. Norbert and ends in Lockport, a distance of 45 km!
6.70	2.63	U-turn	**Duff Roblin Parkway Trail (asphalt);** cycle back to North Drive.
9.33	8.26	Right	**North Drive/South Drive/North Drive;** continue on North Drive and when it curves right towards the park entrance/exit, look for signage to turn left onto South Drive. Cycle past Bur Oak/Oak Ridge Trails, Historic Kudlowich Homestead and Prairie Winds Trail. Continue straight past Birds Hill Campground and Pine Ridge Trail. Cycle past Festival Drive and South Drive again becomes North Drive. Cycle to Nimowin Road. **Pineridge Hollow:** Enjoy some food or shopping either now or at the end of your ride. To get here, while on South Drive, the access road to Pineridge Hollow is opposite the Prairie Winds Trail. The road leads to a

			parking area and a back entrance into the Pineridge Hollow grounds.
17.59	0.41	Right	**Nimowin Road;** cycle past the cemetery to Stables Road. **Pine Ridge Cemetery:** Many of the original settlers who lived in this area are buried here. **Water:** There is a water tap by the cemetery.
18.00	0.25	Left	**Stables Road;** when the road divides, veer left into the riding stables parking lot and to the trail head for the Bluestem and Aspen Trails. **Riding Stables Restaurant:** Need a refreshment break? There is a coffee shop close to the parking lot. **Public Bathroom:** There are public bathrooms in the same building where the restaurant is located.
18.25	5.68	Straight	**Aspen Trail (dirt/grass);** enter the trailhead for both the Aspen and Bluestem Trails. The beginning of the path is asphalt. Follow the path to the stop sign and across the road from the sign is the start of the Aspen Trail. Other trails intersect or share parts of this path, so be sure to follow the brown Aspen Trail markers. Just before you get back to the start of the trailhead, this path runs parallel to North Drive and an asphalt path crosses this path. This asphalt path is part of the Lakeview Trail. **Aspen Loop:** This loop is of the Aspen Trail only. Refer to Quick Notes for parking directions. The trailhead is located off the parking lot. Follow the Aspen Trail markers to return to the parking lot when complete. Distance – 6.4 km.
23.93	5.13	Right	**Lakeview Trail (asphalt);** cycle across North Drive and when the trail splits by the Overlook turn left. The trail enters the lakes area and you pass Birds Hill and Kingfisher lakes on your right, then through the outskirts of the campground and back towards the lakes, passing them again on your right side.

			Continue straight to return to the West Beach parking lot. **Overlook:** Stop and take a look at the amazing surroundings that make up Birds Hill Park. **Birds Hill Concession:** Now might be a good time to stop for ice cream. **Public Bathroom:** There is a public bathroom just after the East Beach parking lot. It is located on the west side of Birds Hill Concession stand. Return to Lakeview Trail when done to continue.
29.06	0	End	**West Beach parking lot.**

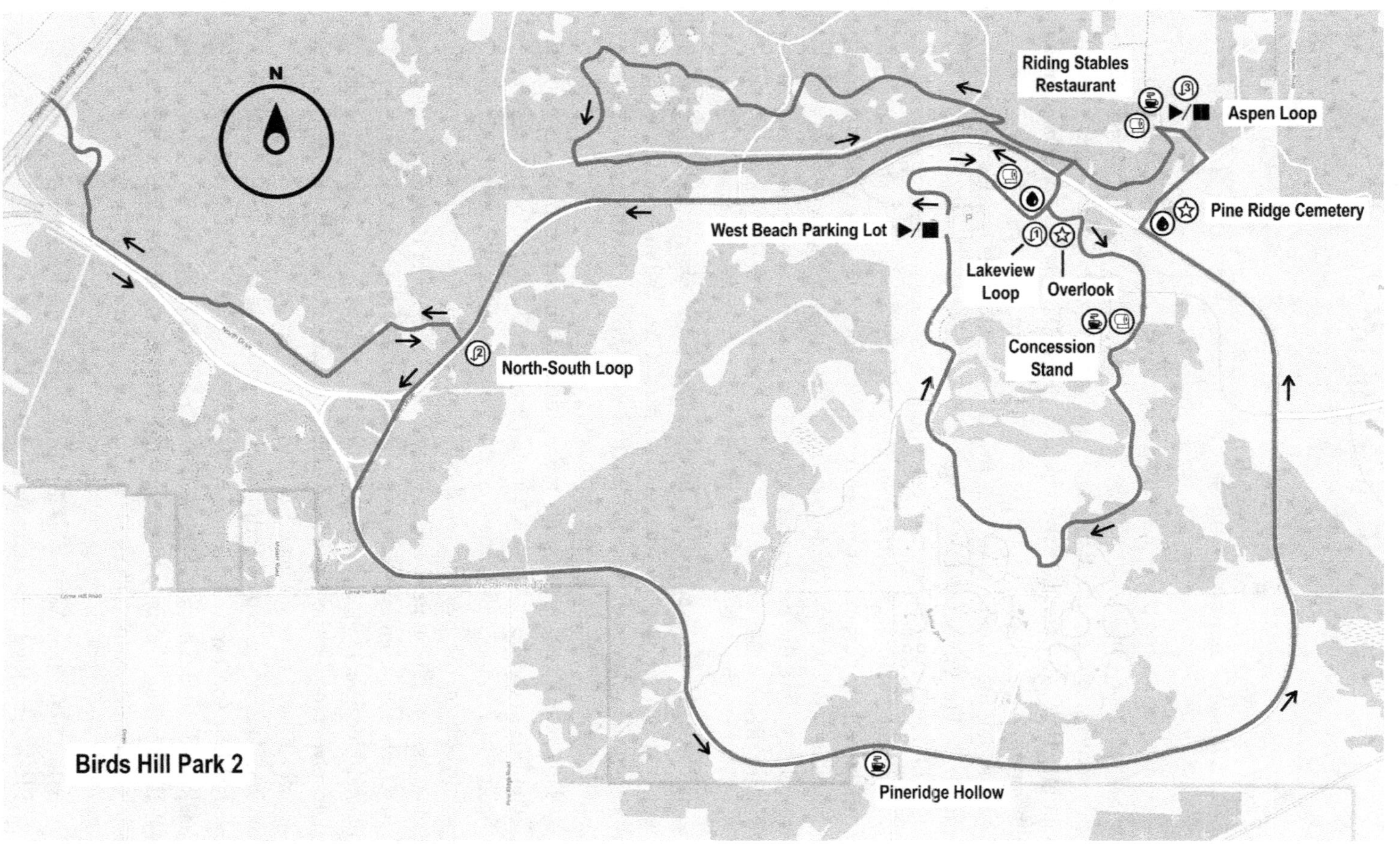
N
Riding Stables
Restaurant
Aspen Loop
Pine Ridge Cemetery
West Beach Parking Lot
Lakeview Loop
Overlook
Concession Stand
North-South Loop
Birds Hill Park 2
Pineridge Hollow

Power Circuit

110 km Northeast of Winnipeg
Level of Difficulty – easy to moderate

Pinawa came into being in 1963 when Atomic Energy of Canada Limited built homes for the employees of its newly built Whiteshell Nuclear Research Establishment, a research and development laboratory. Located on the shores of the Winnipeg River, its name is derived from the First Nations word *pinnowok*, meaning calm waters.

It should be noted the present townsite of Pinawa is actually not its original beginnings. The original townsite, now called Old Pinawa, was born in the early 1900s. In 1908, Manitoba's first year-round hydroelectric generating station was opened by the Winnipeg Electric Company in Old Pinawa. This station was needed for the increasing demand for power from Winnipeg to run its streetcars. The dam harnessed power from the Winnipeg River and diverted the flow down the Pinawa Channel. In 1951 the generating station was closed down so the full flow of the Winnipeg River could enter the Seven Sisters hydro station, and the town was abandoned.

Because the ride starts close to the dam of the old hydroelectric generating station and then follows the Channel and part of the Winnipeg River, both vital to the generating station, I have called this ride Power Circuit, to commemorate Manitoba's first hydroelectric power station.

This ride is mostly on trails more suited to mountain bikes. It is the most difficult ride in this book. I ride a commuter bike and sections of the trail were quite difficult and I had to walk. However, that being said, I still enjoyed this ride. Note there are bears in the area and you should be prepared, just in case, and you will also need bug spray. The route starts in Pinawa Dam Provincial Park on the Old Pinawa Trail which then seamlessly becomes the Alice Chambers Trail. The next trail, the Channel Heritage Trail, is the most difficult of all the trails. The beginning of this trail involves crossing the Pinawa Channel on the Suspension Bridge where there are stairs which need to be navigated at both ends. Next, the directions take you to the Ironwood Trail which is pleasantly flat and easy to cycle as it runs along the Winnipeg River. When you exit this trail, you are on a road which leads back to the Alice Chambers Trail and back to Pinawa Dam Provincial Park.

If you would like to do this ride, but don't want to do the trails, or perhaps want to do a combination of trails and road, you can substitute as follows:

MB-520 for the Old Pinawa Trail and Alice Chambers Trail
PR-211 for the Pinawa Chanel Heritage Trail

Willis Drive/Dorchester Avenue for the Ironwood Trail

There are two options for a coffee stop, both in Pinawa. One is in the Pinawa Golf Club Restaurant (https://www.pinawaclub.mb.ca/restaurant-information/) which is a sit-down indoor restaurant with a patio and the other is The Burger Boat (https://www.facebook.com/TheBurgerBoatPinawa/) which is a food stand with picnic table seating.

Pinawa Golf Club Rest.

The ride features three points of interest plus an activity you might like to try:

Pinawa Dam Provincial Park: The dam ruins, part of Manitoba's first year-round hydroelectric generating station, are a majestic site as water flows through the ruins forming rapids and waterfalls. A Dam Ruins Walk has signage explaining how electricity is generated and an Old Pinawa self-guided trail showcases landmarks of the former town. The park also has picnic tables and you can even take a swim here, something you might like to do after your ride!

The Burger Boat

Pinawa Suspension Bridge: The bridge is part of the Pinawa Channel Heritage Trail, so you will be crossing it with your bike. Completed in 1998, it is 4 metres above the water, 54 metres long and 1 metre wide. Of note, this bridge was built by volunteer labour under the direction of the Pinawa Trails Group and, because of this, is known within the community as the "Labour of Love". Information on both the Pinawa Dam Provincial Park and the Suspension Bridge can be found at: https://pinawa. com/p/attractions

Prov. Park & Bridge

Ironwood Trail: Along the Ironwood Trail which runs through Ironwood Park, are Ironwood trees, a rare find in Manitoba. The name Ironwood is used to describe woods or plants which have a reputation for hardness with a wood density of over 1000 kg/m^3 causing them to sink in water. Also along this trail, it is common to spot deer and you will see why Pinawa is called the Deer Capital of Manitoba.

Pinawa Channel Float: The Channel Float is a popular tourist activity as it offers 2 – 3 hours of relaxation as you float down the Channel taking in the scenic view along the way. The float starts at the Diversion Dam and ends at the Suspension Bridge. To get more information, check out their website as you need to book ahead. http://www.floatandpaddle.ca

Channel Float

Quick Notes

Distance – 27.8 km

Parking –Pinawa Dam Provincial Park, located off MB-
520 N. **Note:** Pinawa Dam Provincial Park is part of
Whiteshell Provincial Park and therefore a park
vehicle permit is required. There is no service to
purchase permits on site. Day or seasonal permits
can be purchased on-line. https://www.gov.mb.ca/
sd/parks/park-fees/index.html

Park Permit

Option to shorten – yes
Pinawa Loop – 11.7 km *For this loop, park in the
lot by the Pinawa Suspension Bridge

Suggested coffee stops – Pinawa Golf Club Restaurant at 1 Willis Drive, The Burger
Boat by the Pinawa Marina

Bathrooms – Pinawa Dam Provincial Park (non-modern), Suspension Bridge (non-
modern), Pinawa Beach, coffee stops

Points of Interest –
Pinawa Dam Provincial Park
Suspension Bridge at Pinawa
Ironwood Trail in Pinawa
Pinawa Channel Float

Trails

Old Pinawa Trail – dirt/rock
Alice Chambers Trail – dirt/rock
Pinawa Channel Heritage Trail – dirt/rock
Ironwood Trail – crushed limestone

Safety Cautions

Detailed Directions

Km total	Km leg	Direction	Location, notes
0	0	Start	**Pinawa Dam Provincial Park;** the Old Pinawa Trailhead is located south of the parking lot and leads into the bush. **Pinawa Dam:** The dam is located a short distance from the parking lot and worth a look either before you start your ride or on your return. **Pinawa Dam Provincial Park:** Bathrooms (non-modern) are located just north of the parking lot.
0	8.07	Straight	**Old Pinawa Trail (dirt/rock)/Alice Chambers Trail (dirt/rock);** these two trails are part of the Trans Canada Trail and run between the edge of the Pinawa Channel and MB-520. The Old Pinawa Trail runs for the first 5.5 km and then it seamlessly becomes the Alice Chambers Trail. The trail exits at the end of Dorchester Avenue by the path to the Suspension Bridge which is part of the Pinawa Channel Heritage Trail.
8.07	3.70	Left	**Suspension Bridge/Pinawa Channel Heritage Trail (dirt/rock);** follow the trail to the suspension bridge and cross its 54 m length to continue on the trail as it runs along the left side of the Pinawa Channel. There are many other trails exiting from this one, be sure to follow the blue and white arrow signs to stay on the Heritage Trail. The trail ends at the Diversion Dam and PR 211. **Suspension Bridge:** Who doesn't love a suspension bridge?! **Suspension Bridge Bathroom:** In the parking lot by the Suspension Bridge are non-modern bathrooms. **Pinawa Loop:** Refer to Quick Notes for parking directions. Start from this step and continue as follows until you return to this spot. Distance – 11.7 km.

11.77	0.74	Right	**Diversion Dam/PR 211;** cross the diversion dam to the beginning of PR 211. Cycle to the first street left, Willis Drive. **Pinawa Channel Float:** The Channel Float is a popular tourist attraction and starts from the Diversion Dam. It is a relaxing activity after the bike ride, but has to be pre-booked.
12.51	0.47	Left	**Willis Drive;** cycle along the edge of the golf course and turn left into the Pinawa Golf and Country Club parking lot. The Ironwood Trail starts at the back corner of the lot, by the beach. **Pinawa Golf Club Restaurant:** This is a sit-down restaurant where you can enjoy a meal or a drink.
12.98	5.00	Right	**Ironwood Trail (crushed limestone);** this trail runs past the Pinawa Beach and runs along the edge of the Winnipeg River. The trail exits to Willis Drive at the Pinawa Marina and once past the marina and The Burger Boat, pick up the Ironwood Trail again. As Willis Drive turns right and becomes Dorchester Avenue, so too does the trail turn right, leaving the river and travels through some bush to exit on Dorchester Avenue. **Pinawa Beach Bathroom:** Flush toilets are located just off the trail by the beach. They are only open during the summer months and located just past the Pinawa Golf and Country Club parking lot. **Ironwood Trail:** Look for ironwood trees and you should see deer along this path. **The Burger Boat:** This food trailer is a good spot for a burger, fries or ice cream.
17.98	1.76	Left	**Dorchester Avenue;** cycle across PR 211 and continue straight. Cycle past the Pinawa Cemetery and the trail to the Suspension Bridge to the start of the Alice Chambers Trail.

19.74	8.07	Right	**Alice Chambers Trail (dirt/rock)/Old Pinawa Trail (dirt/rock);** follow this trail back to Pinawa Dam Provincial Park.
27.81	0	End	**Pinawa Dam Provincial Park.**

Nothing compares to the
simple pleasure of a bike ride.

— John F. Kennedy

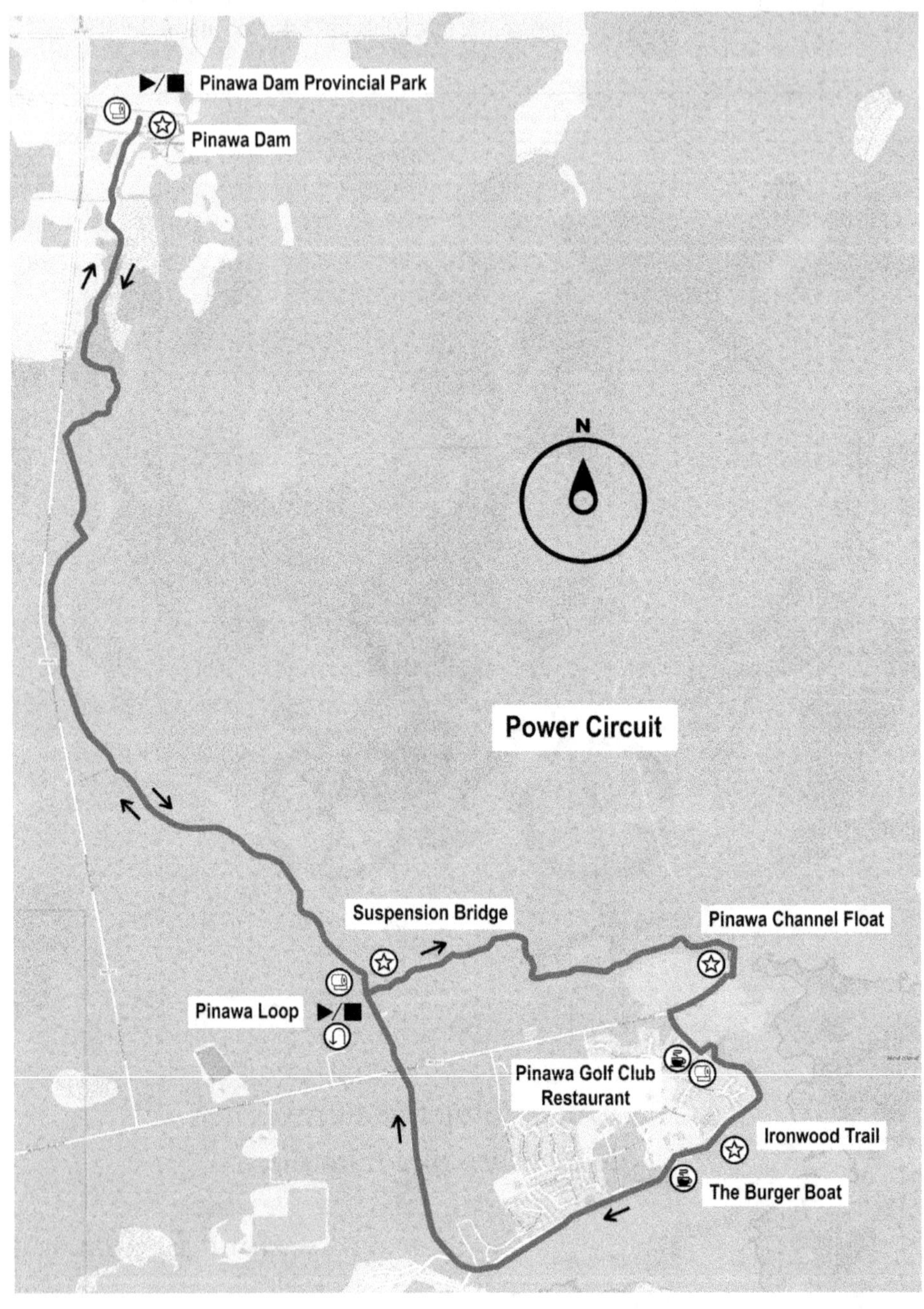
Pinawa Dam Provincial Park
Pinawa Dam
N
Power Circuit
Suspension Bridge
Pinawa Channel Float
Pinawa Loop
Pinawa Golf Club
Restaurant
Ironwood Trail
The Burger Boat

Deep South

South Winnipeg

This entire ride is beyond the Perimeter Highway to the south, hence the name, Deep South. The route starts in Duff Roblin Provincial Park and goes along the Duff Roblin Parkway Trail towards Grande Pointe, rides around the perimeter of this community and heads back to the park on roads. There are two small sections, about 4.5 km total, on the wide asphalt shoulders of PTH 59. For safety reasons, be sure to wear high visibility clothing.

Duff Roblin Provincial Park was designated a provincial park in 2008. The park is named in honour of Mr. Dufferin (Duff) Roblin, who served as premier of Manitoba from 1958 to 1967, and commemorates two of his achievements, the establishment of a provincial system of parks and the construction of a flood control system for Winnipeg. This park is located at the inlet of the Red River Floodway.

In 1960, the Manitoba Government, under Duff Roblin, passed the Provincial Parks Act to guide the creation and management of provincial parks. The purpose was to protect natural landscapes and provide recreational space. Over the years, Manitoba has preserved park spaces of varying size, scope and diversity, in order to showcase the land's natural, historical and cultural features.

In this ride, we use a portion of the Duff Roblin Parkway Trail, along the Red River Floodway, which is affectionately known as Duff's Ditch. The impetus to make this floodway, which diverts water from the Red River around Winnipeg, was the disastrous Red River Flood of 1950. The work on the floodway began in 1962 and during the six years it took to complete, 76 million cubic metres of earth were removed. As of writing this book, it is the largest excavation project in Canada and one of the largest in the world. The Floodway extends 47 km from St. Norbert to Lockport and is a width equal to the Red River. In 2008, the Floodway was recognized as one of the 16 engineering marvels in the world by the International Association of Macro Engineering Societies. It has been used twenty times since completed to control the Red River flood levels. When the floodway was constructed, it was meant to protect us from a 1-in-100-year flood event. The 1997 "flood of the century" took our ditch to the limits of its capacity. After this flood, several measures, including upgrading the floodway and its structures, were undertaken to improve our flood protection measures and it is now upgraded to withstand a 1-in-700-year flood event. The Red River Floodway was designated a National Historic site in 2000. While cycling, as a point of interest, be sure to stop and take a look at the enormity of our floodway.

It is worthwhile to spend some time in the Duff Roblin Provincial Park, either before or after the ride, to learn more about Duff Roblin the man and some of his initiatives, including, of course, more information about the floodway and other flood protection measures in Manitoba. There is a viewing station for a better look at the floodway. Note the parking area for the park is different from the parking area where the ride begins. The two parking areas are about 1 km apart and you can either cycle from one to the other or move your car from lot to lot.

There are no coffee stops along this route as it doesn't go past any eating establishments. However, halfway through the ride, you will be going by Grande Pointe Park where there are some picnic shelters, so you might want to pack a snack or lunch and stop there before heading back.

Quick Notes

Distance – 30.8 km

Parking – Duff Roblin Provincial Park, parking for access to the Duff Roblin Parkway Trail is off of St. Mary's Road just past Courchaine Road

Options to shorten – yes

1 – Grande Pointe Loop – 13.6 km *For this loop, park in the Prairie Grove parking lot at the 8 km mark of the Duff Roblin Parkway Trail. To reach this lot, drive out of the city on St. Anne's Road. At the first street past the perimeter, Prairie Grove Road, turn left. As you approach PTH 59, take the exit for PTH 59 North. Follow the cloverleaf under PTH 59 and as it turns left to go up to the highway is the entrance to the Prairie Grove parking lot.

2 – Floodway Loop – 16.7 km

Suggested coffee stop – Home-packed lunch at Grande Pointe Park at 423 Berenat Road, Grande Pointe

Bathrooms – Duff Roblin Provincial Park (non-modern) off Courchaine Road, Grande Pointe Park (non-modern) at 423 Berenat Road, Grande Pointe

Points of Interest –
Red River Floodway beside the Duff Roblin Parkway Trail
Duff Roblin Provincial Park off Courchaine Road

Trails

Duff Roblin Parkway Trail – crushed limestone

Safety Cautions

Detailed Directions

Km total	Km Leg	Direction	Location, notes
0	0	Start	**Duff Roblin Parkway Trailhead;** located just off the parking area.
			Duff Roblin Provincial Park: Worth a stop, either before or after the ride. Read the signage about Duff Roblin and his achievements, as well as learn more about the floodway. Climb the viewing tower to get a good look at the landscape. Note that the parking area for this park is different than for the beginning of the ride.
			Duff Roblin Provincial Park: The bathrooms (non-modern) are located just off the parking area.
0	7.49	Straight	**Duff Roblin Parkway Trail (crushed limestone);** follow the trail as it runs beside the Winnipeg Floodway under St. Mary's Road and under a railway bridge towards PTH 59.
			Just before the trail passes under PTH 59 is an exit to the cloverleaf.
			Red River Floodway: The Duff Roblin Parkway Trail runs beside this amazing architectural achievement.
7.49	0.61	Left	**PTH 59 Cloverleaf;** follow the cloverleaf as it curves right to the stop sign at Prairie Grove Road.
			Grande Pointe Loop: Refer to Quick Notes for parking directions. Exit the Prairie Grove parking lot to PTH 59 Cloverleaf and turn left, cycle to the stop sign at Prairie Grove Road and continue with the directions following until indicated. Distance – 13.6 km.
8.10	0.24	Right	**Prairie Grove Road;** cycle to PTH 59.
			Floodway Loop: At Prairie Grove Road, turn left instead of right. This loop eliminates the cycle around Grande Pointe. Continue, as indicated below, to return to start. Distance – 16.7 km.
8.34	1.71	Right	**PTH 59;** take the turn-off to the right for Hallama Drive in Grande Pointe.

10.05	3.21	Left	**Bernat Road/Hallama Drive;** from the turn-off, left is Bernat Road and right is Hallama Drive. These two roads form a circle around Grande Pointe. Cycle past Carriere, Bernard, Shady, Keweriga, and Grande Pointe Park to Hallama Drive/PTH 300. **Grande Pointe Park:** You'll have to bring your own coffee and/or snacks, but there is a picnic shelter located here and it is a pleasant place to stop. **Grande Pointe Park:** The bathrooms (non-modern) are located close to the picnic shelter.
13.26	6.12	Right	**Hallama Drive/PTH 300;** cycle past Berard, Louis, Hince, Keweriga, Penny, and Grande Pointe Road. Cycle over the railroad tracks and Hallama curves right and then right again and again over railroad tracks. Cycle to the access to PTH 59 previously used to enter Grande Pointe and turn left towards the highway.
19.38	2.79	Left	**PTH 59;** take the first exit to the right for Prairie Grove Road. Stay on the cloverleaf as it curves around and goes under Hwy 59 and then curves right towards the stop sign at Prairie Grove Road. **Grande Pointe Loop continued:** Exit the cloverleaf at the entrance to the Prairie Grove parking lot.
22.17	1.22	Left	**Prairie Grove Road;** cycle over the railroad tracks and continue to the end of the street at St. Anne's Road. **Floodway Loop continued:** Continue from this step to return to start.
23.39	0.31	Left	**St. Anne's Road;** cycle one block to Forbes Road.
23.70	2.83	Right	**Forbes Road;** cycle this gravel road past Two Mile Road on your right to the continuation of Two Mile Road, 0.9 km further on, to your left.
26.53	3.63	Left	**Two Mile Road/Chrypko Drive;** cycle this gravel road across Fraser where Two Mile Road becomes Chrypko Drive. The road curves right. Cycle to the stop sign at St. Mary's Road.
30.16	0.50	Left	**St. Mary's Road;** cycle past Courchaine to the parking area for Duff Roblin Parkway Trail.

30.66	0.09	Right	**Parking lot for Duff Roblin Parkway Trail;** turn into parking area.
30.75	0	End	**Duff Roblin Parkway Trailhead.**

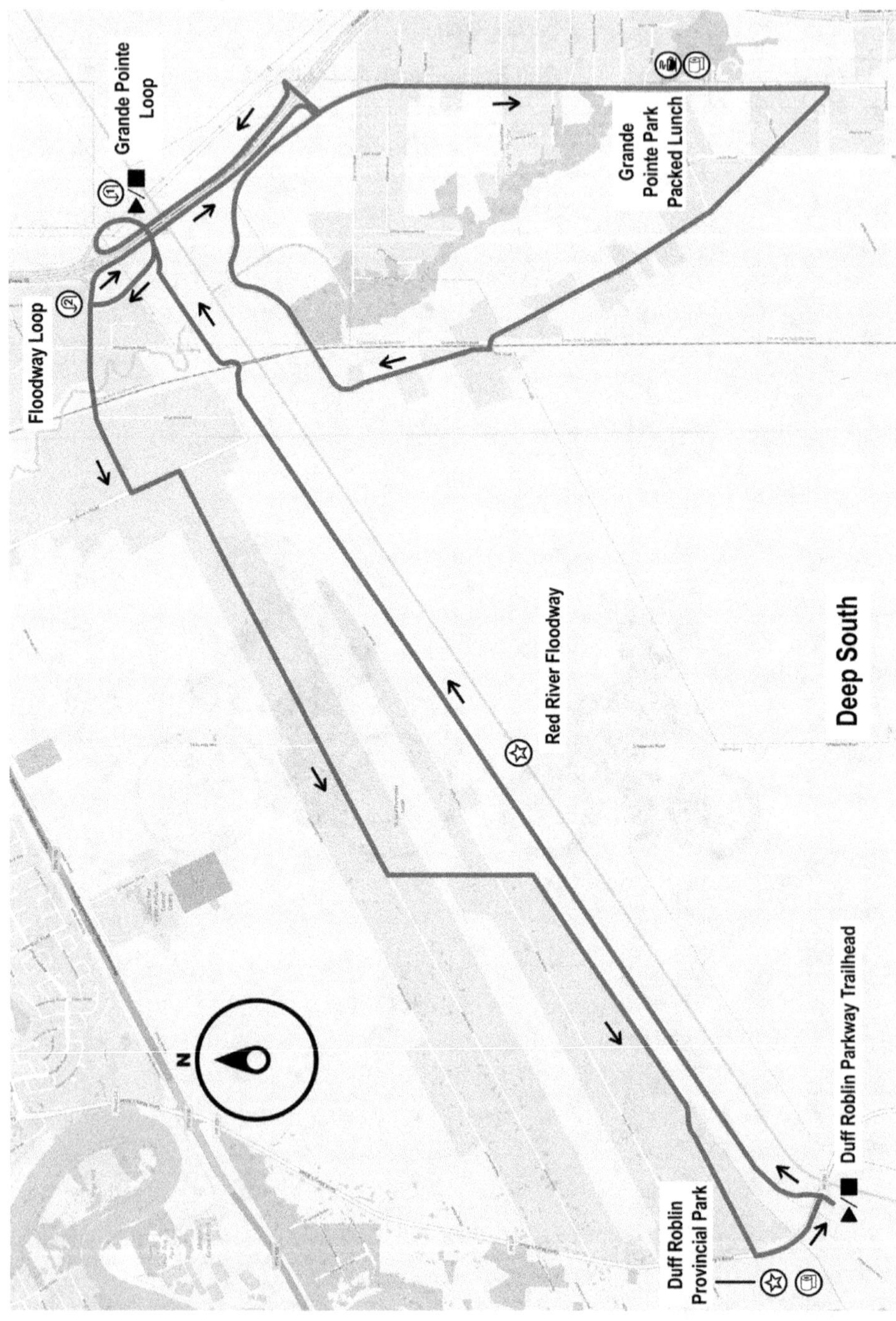

Grande Pointe Loop
Floodway Loop
Grande Pointe Park Packed Lunch
Red River Floodway
Deep South
Duff Roblin Parkway Trailhead
Duff Roblin Provincial Park
N

Birds of Prey

160 km East of Winnipeg
Level of Difficulty – easy to moderate

Whiteshell Provincial Park is located in the southeast corner of the province and contains thirteen lakes which are used for recreation in addition to many more remote lakes that are not easily accessible. This ride is between two of the recreational lakes, West Hawk Lake and Falcon Lake. Because we are going between a hawk and a falcon, I thought the name Birds of Prey was a good descriptive.

The first lake, West Hawk Lake, is the deepest lake in Manitoba at 115 meters. It is believed to have been created by a meteor impacting the granite bed rock and is listed as a World Terrestrial Impact Structure. Of note, West Hawk is a training site for scuba diving. The second lake, Falcon Lake, has several claims to fame. It inspired the name of a TV series, *Falcon Lake*, which ironically, was not filmed here but at another Manitoba lake and Neil Young wrote a song entitled *Falcon Lake* while with the band Buffalo Springfield.

The route for this ride uses the Trans Canada Trail with this section referred to as the South Whiteshell Trail. It is a popular trail for cyclists and is generally easy with a few steeper hills in the stretch between Faloma and Falcon Lake. I did this trail with my commuter bike and with the exception of walking up a few inclines, I didn't have any issues, but I believe a mountain bike would be better suited. The return trip is essentially retracing the route back to the start. If preferred, the trail runs beside PR-301 and it is possible to cycle on the road, but it tends to be a busy road and there are no shoulders, so it is quite narrow. However, it is an option, if needed. Because you are cycling through a wooded area, you might like to use some bug spray.

Be sure to stop occasionally and take in the scenery in the bush and along the shore of Falcon Lake. Also look for wild blueberries and raspberries along the edges of the trail, when in season.

There are several places you can stop for coffee. In Falcon Lake Townsite, there are two eat-in places in the shopping centre along Park Road, Falcon Lake Bakery Bistro https://www.falconlakebakery.com or The Nest Café http://falconsnestcafe.ca. Or, if you prefer, you can wait till the end of the ride and once back to West Hawk Lake, Nite Hawk Café serves up gourmet burgers, house

Falcon Lake Bakery

The Nest Café

cut fries, and ice cream desserts. http://www.nitehawk
cafe.com All the choices are good so you can't go wrong!

After your ride or in the middle, you might like to
soak up the sun and go for a swim either at West Hawk or
Falcon Lake. Summer here is so short it's nice to take
advantage of being at the beach and enjoy some leisure
time before heading back to the city.

Nite Hawk Café

Quick Notes

Distance – 26.9 km

Parking – West Hawk parking lot. To get to West Hawk
Lake, take the PTH 44 turnoff to West Hawk Lake
from the Trans-Canada Highway. Where PTH 44
makes a sharp left at the West Hawk Townsite, turn
right. There is a parking area immediately to your
right. A non-modern bathroom is located in this lot.
Note: West Hawk Lake is part of Whiteshell
Provincial Park and therefore a park vehicle permit
is required. Day or seasonal permits can be purchased
at the campground office or on-line. https://www.gov.mb.ca/sd/parks/park-
fees/ index.html

Park Permit

Option to shorten – yes
Faloma Loop – 15.0 km

Suggested coffee stops – Falcon Lake Bakery Bistro at 21A Park Boulevard, The Nest
Café at 19 Park Road, Nite Hawk Café at PTH 44 at West Hawk Lake

Bathrooms – Parking Lot at West Hawk Lake (non-modern), on the trail (non-
modern), Falcon Lake Picnic Area, coffee stop

Points of Interest –
Falcon Lake
West Hawk Lake

Trails

South Whiteshell Trail – crushed limestone

Safety Cautions

Detailed Directions

Km Total	Km Leg	Direction	Location, notes
0	0	Start	**West Hawk Trailhead of the South Whiteshell Trail;** located in the northeast corner of Nite Hawk Café's parking lot. If you park as per directed above, Nite Hawk Café is located west of this lot, across PTH 44. **West Hawk Lake:** Non-modern bathrooms are located in the parking lot.
0	7.50	Straight	**South Whiteshell Trail (crushed limestone);** this trail is part of the Trans Canada Trail and runs beside PR-301. The trail merges with the road when passing under the Trans-Canada Highway. The trail exits at Faloma Marina. Cycle past the Marina parking lot and across F7 road to the continuation of the South Whiteshell Trail. **South Whiteshell Trail:** Non-modern bathrooms are located on the trail about 3.5 km from the trailhead. **Faloma Loop:** When you reach the Faloma Marina, turn around and return to West Hawk Trailhead. Distance – 15.0 km.
7.50	5.70	Straight	**South Whiteshell Trail (crushed limestone);** continue on this trail as it runs between PR-301 and Falcon Lake. There are a few challenging hills just past the marina but the trail gets flatter as you get closer to the Falcon Lake Townsite. Cycle past several access roads to cottages, the campground and through Falcon Lake Picnic Area before exiting into a parking lot. Cycle through the parking lot to Falcon Boulevard and Park Road. **Falcon Lake Picnic Area:** Bathrooms are located in the park about 100 metres from the parking lot.
13.20	0.26	Straight	**Park Road;** cycle straight across Falcon Boulevard, past the Shell Station and Green Avenue to the Shopping Centre. **Falcon Lake Bakery Bistro or The Nest Café:** Feeling like a cinnamon bun and coffee or a bit more substantial meal? Here's your chance!

		⊛	**Falcon Lake:** If you continue on Park Road, it ends in a parking lot by the lake shore. You might like to take a break and walk along the beach and get your feet wet before returning to West Hawk Lake.
13.46	0.26	Turn around	**Park Road;** cycle past Green Avenue, the Shell Station and across Falcon Boulevard to enter the parking lot of the Falcon Lake Picnic Area. Cycle through the lot to the Falcon Trailhead of the South Whiteshell Trail.
13.72	5.70	Straight	**South Whiteshell Trail (crushed limestone);** cycle through the Falcon Lake Picnic Area, past the campground and past several access roads to cottages. The trail exits at F7 Road and the Faloma Marina. Cycle across the road and through the Marina parking lot to the continuation of the South Whiteshell Trail. **Falcon Lake Picnic Area:** Bathrooms are located in the park about 100 metres from the parking lot.
19.42	7.50	Straight	**South Whiteshell Trail (crushed limestone);** follow this trail back to the West Hawk Trailhead. **South Whiteshell Trail:** Non-modern bathrooms are located on the trail about 3.5 km from the trailhead.
26.92	0	End	**West Hawk Trailhead of the South Whiteshell Trail.** **Nite Hawk Café:** Gourmet burgers, house cut fries, ice cream desserts – need I say anything more? **West Hawk Lake:** Before heading back to the city, you might like to take a dip in the lake and lie in the sun for a bit. Enjoy!

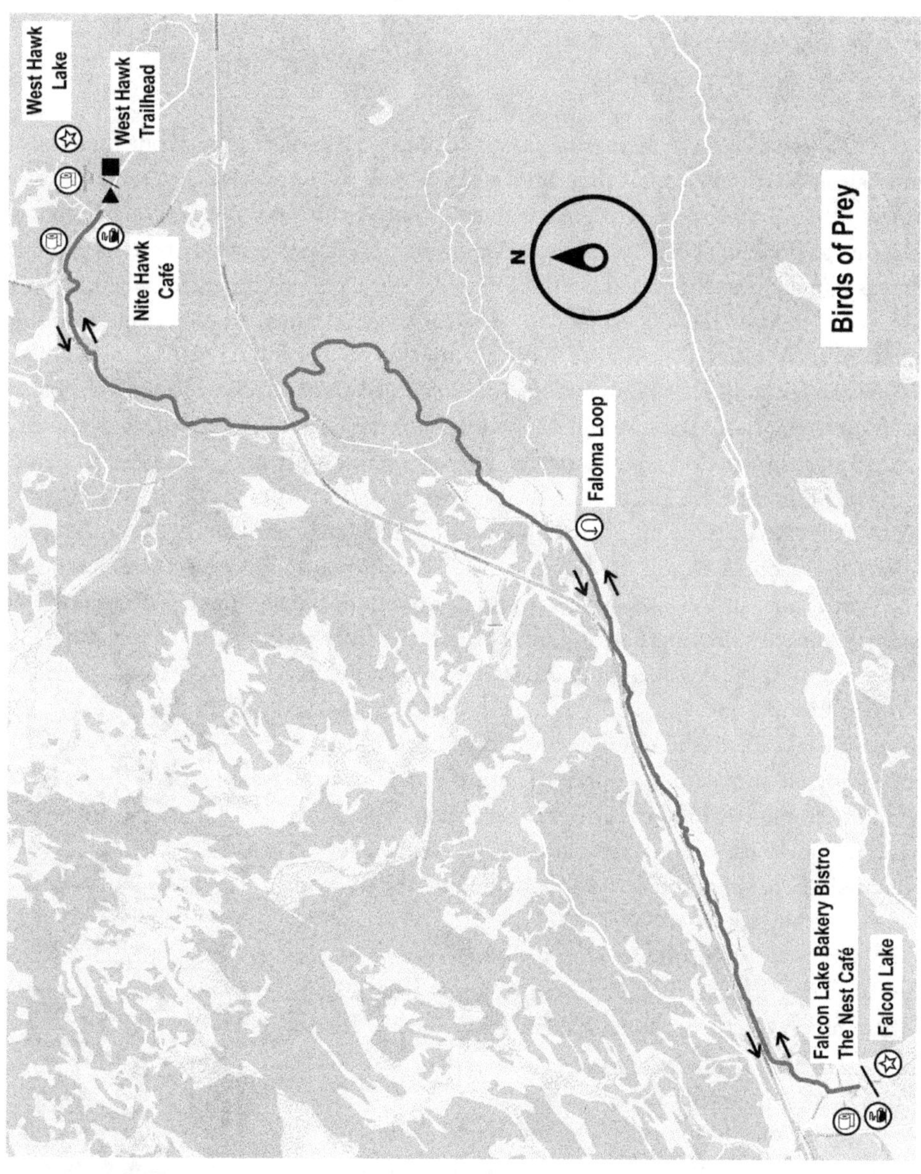
West Hawk Lake
West Hawk Trailhead
Nite Hawk Café
N
Birds of Prey
Faloma Loop
Falcon Lake Bakery Bistro
The Nest Café
Falcon Lake

Flight of the Falcon

152 km East of Winnipeg
Level of Difficulty – easy to moderate

Did you know the Peregrine falcon is not only the fastest bird, but the fastest animal on Earth? Falcons, when hunting, will soar to a great height and then dive toward their prey at speeds of greater than 320 km/hr! I was surprised when I found out that although falcons are found in Manitoba, this lake was not named after them. It was named after Pierre Falcon (b.1793 – d.1876), a Metis fur trader who was also a noted composer and singer. Falcon Lake has several claims to fame. It inspired the name of a TV series, *Falcon Lake*, which ironically was not filmed here but at another Manitoba lake and Neil Young wrote a song entitled *Falcon Lake* while with the band Buffalo Springfield. Because I liked the image of the falcons soaring through the air, and like to think of myself as soaring along the trail on my bike, I decided to name this ride, Flight of the Falcon.

This ride is made up of two bike trails. The Marsh Trail skirts along the west shore of Falcon Lake and the South Shore Trail, as you might expect, skirts around the south shore of the lake. Near the end of the South Shore Trail, it veers south for a few kilometers, leaving Falcon Lake behind and takes you to a completely different body of water, High Lake. Here the trail ends, but before turning around and essentially retracing the route back, stop and take in the tranquil views of this beautiful lake and enjoy the surrounding sounds of nature. I did this trail with my commuter bike and with the exception of walking up a few inclines, I didn't have any issues, but I believe a mountain bike would be better suited. You might want to take some bug spray with you.

Falcon Lake Bakery

The Nest Café

Once the ride is done, stop for coffee at one of the coffee shops in the shopping centre along Park Road. There are two eat-in places, Falcon Lake Bakery Bistro https://www.falconlakebakery.com or The Nest Café http://falconsnestcafe.ca.

At the end of the ride, why not spend some time at the beach soaking up the sun or going for a swim!

Quick Notes

Distance – 26.3 km

Parking – Falcon Beach parking lot. To get to Falcon Lake, take the turnoff to Falcon Lake from the Trans-Canada Highway. Once in the park, there are signs indicating which direction to go to different locations. Head towards the townsite which is on Park Road. Continue past the shopping centre and the road ends at the Falcon Beach parking lot. **Note:** Falcon Lake is part of Whiteshell Provincial Park and therefore a park vehicle permit is required. Day or seasonal permits can be purchased at the campground office or on-line. https://www. gov.mb.ca/sd/parks/park-fees/index.html

Park Permit

Option to shorten – no

Suggested coffee stops – Falcon Lake Bakery Bistro at 21A Park Road, The Nest Café at 19 Park Road

Bathrooms – Falcon Lake Change House/Bathroom located next to the Concession stand off the Boardwalk along the beach, Public Bathroom (non-modern) by the Falcon River Causeway, coffee stop

Point of Interest –
    Falcon Lake

Trails

Marsh Trail – crushed limestone
Falcon South Shore Trail – crushed limestone

Safety Cautions

Detailed Directions

Km total		Direction	Location, notes
0	0	Start	**Falcon Lake parking lot at the entrance to the Marsh Trail;** the trail starts at the northwest corner of the parking lot.
			Falcon Lake Change House/Bathroom: The bathroom is located next to the Concession Stand just off the boardwalk along the beach.

0	1.27	Left	**Marsh Trail (crushed limestone);** follow the trail along the west end of Falcon Lake. The trail exits at the Falcon Lake Marina. Once past the marina, look for the continuation of the trail at the edge of the bush. The trail exits to Ridge Road.
1.27	11.90	Left	**Ridge Road/Falcon South Shore Trail (crushed limestone);** although on Ridge Road, this section is considered part of the Falcon South Shore Trail. Cycle over the Falcon River Causeway and look for the entrance to the trail on the right of the road. There is a sign for Falcon Trails Resort at the trail entrance. Follow the trail as it goes through the bush and weaves back and forth across Ridge Road several times. Twice when the trail splits are signs indicating directions and distances. Follow the trail which leads to High Lake. **Note:** The trail is relatively easy for most of the distance. However, in the last 3 km of the trail are steeper inclines. **Public Bathroom:** Once past the Falcon River Causeway, there is a small parking area to your right with a non-modern washroom.
13.17	11.90	U-Turn	**Falcon South Shore Trail (crushed limestone)/Ridge Road;** cycle the trail back to Ridge Road and over the Falcon River Causeway to the Marsh Trail entrance. **Public Bathroom:** Just before the Falcon River Causeway, there is a small parking area to your left with a non-modern washroom.
25.07	1.27	Right	**Marsh Trail (crushed limestone);** the trail exits to Falcon Lake Marina. Cycle past the marina to the continuation of the trail. The trail exits to the Falcon Lake parking lot.
26.34	0	End	**Falcon Lake parking lot.**

			**Note:** If you would like to head to one of the coffee stop recommendations, continue along Park Road to the shopping centre.
			**Falcon Lake Bakery Bistro or The Nest Café:** Celebrate completion of your ride with a relaxing cup of coffee, a meal, or some other treat.
			**Falcon Lake:** Before heading back to the city, you might like to take a dip in the lake and lie in the sun for a bit. Enjoy!

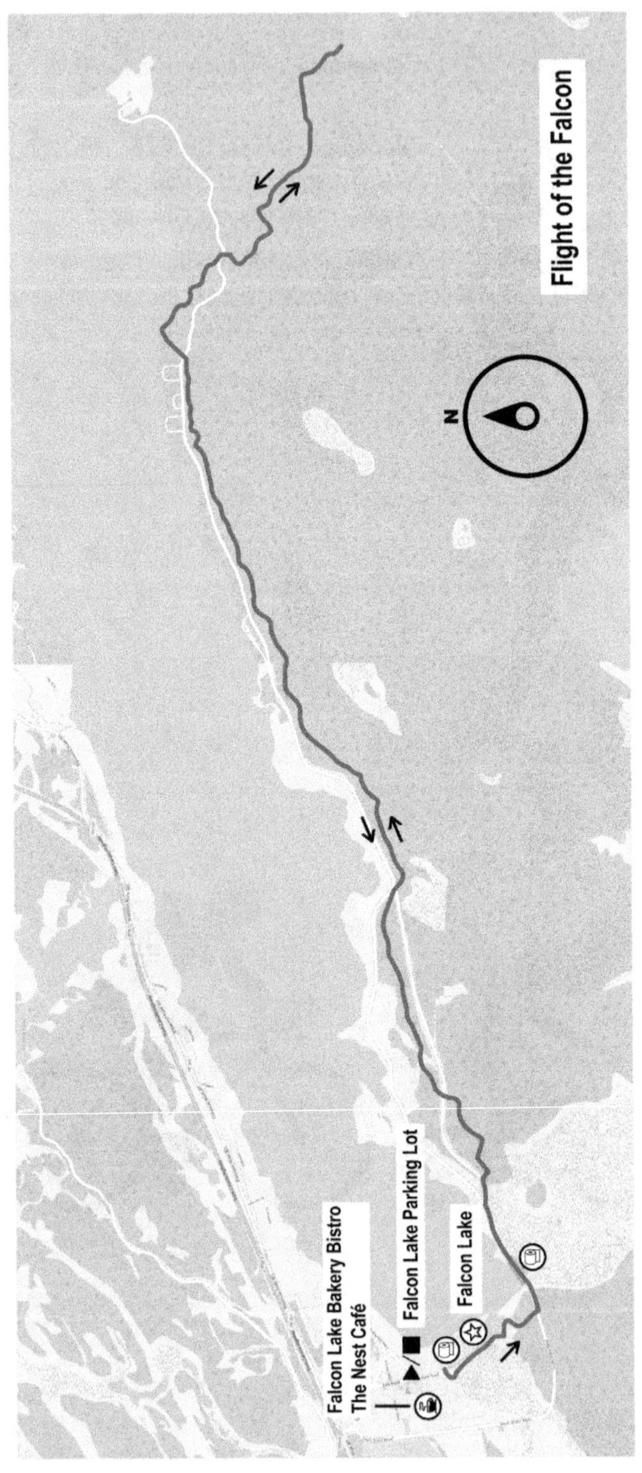

Flight of the Falcon
N
Falcon Lake Bakery Bistro
The Nest Café
Falcon Lake Parking Lot
Falcon Lake

Scenic Portage

70 km west of Winnipeg

My husband used to live in Portage la Prairie for a few years and he is an avid cyclist who has spent countless enjoyable hours cycling in and around this city. So, I have handed the reins over to him to design two rides in and around Portage. This is the first ride.

Portage la Prairie is a small city of about 14,000 people. The local economy is supported by agriculture, market gardens, potato processing, and is the administrative headquarters of the Dakota Tipi First Nations reserve. The city got its name because this was the location on the Assiniboine River from which the pioneer fur traders set off to *portage*, or carry, their canoes and cargo the 25 km or so across the prairies to Lake Manitoba, from which they could continue their journey along the water to the North-West.

Cycling in and around Portage is flat and pleasant with parks, country roads and riparian scenery. Some of this ride is on dirt tracks and gravel roads, so I wouldn't recommend going in wet weather. The ride takes in Portage's beautiful and iconic Crescent Lake and Island Park, the Portage Spillway Provincial Park, some quiet suburbs and a few trails.

As a coffee stop suggestion, I recommend Lita's Station. As you might be able to derive from its name, this restaurant has a railway theme. On display are over 1000 model trains, including two model trains running along tracks near the ceiling and another model train running under a glass topped table. The walls are painted to resemble train sections and booths are designed to look like passenger cars. There are many other additional railway touches for you to discover. Besides being a sit-down restaurant, they also sell some baked goods to take home, with butter tarts and matrimonial squares being the most popular. Be sure to check on-line for operating hours before going as they close early in the day.

There are four points of interest on this ride, three of which are shared with the second Portage route, Country Roads. The first two points of interest are art installations. Along Crescent Road, is an urban reserve belonging to the Long Plain First Nation. On the grounds of the old Portage la Prairie Indian Residential School is a striking sculpture, created by Manitoba artist Jake Goertzen, of an 85-foot tree with its branches gone and a 12-foot golden eagle sitting on top. The sculpture is a tribute to the survivors of the residential school system and as such, the eagle is looking to the east, to the sun rising on a new day and a fresh start.

Further along this same stretch, but requiring a short detour, is Canada's Largest Great Grey Owl. Jake Goertzen, who had created the Golden Eagle, also created this sculpture in collaboration with owl aficionado Bryan Mitchell. This piece stands thirteen feet tall, weighs 2140 pounds and is made up of approximately 6000 pieces of steel. It is an impressive site and worth the side trip.

The third point of interest is Portage Spillway Provincial Park. The Portage Spillway and the Portage Diversion, also known as the Assiniboine River Floodway, was built as a water control structure and is used to divert some of the flow of the Assiniboine River northward, at peak flood times, down a 29 km diversion channel emptying into Lake Manitoba near Delta Beach. This helps to prevent flooding by the Assiniboine River in the municipalities downstream from Portage to where the Assiniboine River meets the Red River in Winnipeg. Although not technically in the park, you get a magnificent view of the Spillway and its turbulent waters. You will also see flocks of pelicans gathering at the base of the spillway. This park attracts many fishermen who are hoping to catch sauger, walleye, northern pike or silver bass. The waterway is very scenic and worth a stop.

Last, the fourth point of interest is Island Park. Manitoba Tourism refers to it as Island on the Prairies, but the locals call it Island Park. This island, which is actually a peninsula, was formed by the oxbow of Crescent Lake. It is quite scenic and features several attractions including Island Park with a playground, arboretum, deer sanctuary, duck pond, tennis courts and picnic sites, Splash Island Park, an outdoor water park, Stride Place with an indoor aquatic centre, a Dutch-style windmill and a Royal Canadian Air Force CT-133 Silver Star. In addition, strawberry farms and an 18-hole golf course are also located here. The end of the route cycles through Island Park, but it is definitely worth it to stop here for a while to either explore or do some activities before heading home.

Enjoy the ride!

Quick Notes
Distance – 28.9 km
Parking – When you arrive in Portage la Prairie, the main street is called Saskatchewan Avenue. Look for Royal Road S and turn left. Royal leads to Crescent Lake and the causeway to Island Park. Park on the island as the ride starts at the causeway on the island.
Option to shorten – yes
    Spillway-Angle Loop – 21.3 km
Suggested coffee stop – Lita's Station Restaurant at 904 E Saskatchewan Avenue
Bathrooms – Island Park by the children's playground, Portage Spillway Provincial Park (non-modern), coffee stop
Points of Interest –
    Golden Eagle along Crescent Road W, between Cottonwood Drive and Yellowquill Trail
    Canada's Largest Great Grey Owl at 27 Pine Crescent

Portage Spillway Provincial Park located off Yellowquill Trail
Island Park at Crescent Lake

Trails

Crescent Lake Trail – asphalt
Portage Spillway Path – crushed limestone
Assiniboine River Dike Trail – dirt
Angle Trail – dirt
Garrioch's Creek Forest Path – dirt/crushed limestone
Island Park Trail – asphalt

Safety Cautions

Detailed Directions

Km Total	Km Leg	Direction	Location, notes
0	0	Start	**Island Park at the causeway toward Crescent Road.** **Island Park:** Bathrooms are located by the children's playground, when done, return to starting point.
0	0.26	Straight	**Island Park Causeway;** cycle over the causeway to Crescent Lake Trail.
0.26	3.29	Left	**Crescent Lake Trail (asphalt)/Crescent Road W;** cycle west with the lake on your left. The trail exits onto Crescent Road W, continues past Cottonwood and Keeshkeemaquah to Yellowquill Trail. There is a sign before the corner for Junction 1A and a stop sign at this corner. **Golden Eagle:** Notice the striking metal sculpture of an eagle sitting at the top of a tree with no branches. It stands as a tribute to the survivors of the residential school system. This sculpture is located between Cottonwood and Yellowquill Trail.

			Canada's Largest Great Grey Owl: This sculpture stands 13 feet tall, weighs 2140 pounds and is made up of approximately 6000 pieces of metal. To see it, cycle past Yellowquill Trail, at which point Crescent Road becomes Pine Crescent. The sculpture is located at 27 Pine. Once you have viewed it, head back to Yellowquill Trail and continue ride.
3.55	1.24	Right	**Yellowquill Trail;** the road veers left as you come near the Hillside Memorial Cemetery. Cycle across the Portage la Prairie Bypass/Trans-Canada Highway, past a number of homes and the City of Portage la Prairie Water Treatment Plant. Immediately after the plant, is a small gravel road which turns into a path running through the Portage Spillway Provincial Park.
4.79	0.58	Left	**Portage Spillway Path (crushed limestone);** cycle the path through the park which runs beside the spillway and exits into the parking area. Turn right to follow the access road from the parking lot to Yellowquill Trail. **Portage Spillway Provincial Park:** Stop to view the turbulent waters at the base of the spillway, the flocks of white pelicans, and the numerous fishermen on the shores. The spillway may have been near the route of the original portage, used by the early fur traders, between the Assiniboine River and Lake Manitoba. **Portage Spillway Provincial Park:** Non-modern bathrooms are located near the end of the park trail by the parking area.
5.37	0.86	Right	**Yellowquill Trail;** cycle back towards the Portage la Prairie Bypass/Trans-Canada Highway. Just before the highway is a service road.
6.23	3.43	Right	**Service Road;** cycle past the Days Inn hotel to the first right, Old Bridge Road.
9.66	1.29	Right	**Old Bridge Road;** cycle through the Portage la Prairie suburb of Southport, passing Riverside to McLenaghen Drive.

10.95	0.52	Left	**McLenaghen Drive;** this road ends on River Road/MB-240. Directly across the highway is the start of the Assiniboine River Dike Trail.
11.47	2.80	Straight	**Assiniboine River Dike Trail (dirt);** cycle the dirt trail as it follows along the edge of the Assiniboine River to your right and farm fields to your left. There are some other trails leading off of this trail, but continue by the river. At about 2.8 km is the start of Angle Road Trail/Angle Road. There are two exits to this trail very close together.
14.27	4.35	Left	**Angle Trail (dirt)/Angle Road;** follow the trail which then becomes a road. Cycle past the Prairie Abattoir, cross Portage la Prairie Bypass/Trans-Canada Highway to E Saskatchewan Avenue.
18.62	0.55	Left	**E Saskatchewan Avenue/Highway 1A;** this road used to be the main highway before the bypass was built. Cycle to 9 Street SE. There is a crosswalk at this corner. **Lita's Station:** If you feel like coffee in a cozy railway themed restaurant, complete with working model trains, be sure to check out Lita's.
19.17	0.40	Left	**9 Street SE;** cycle past Duke and Countess to Dufferin Avenue E.
19.57	0.34	Right	**Dufferin Avenue E;** cycle past 6 Street to 5 Street SE.
19.91	0.53	Left	**5 Street SE;** cycle past King, Queen, and Portage to Crescent Road and Crescent Lake Trail.
20.44	1.87	Left	**Crescent Lake Trail (asphalt);** shortly after turning onto the Crescent, there is a break in the curb to access the Crescent Lake Trail. Cycle to the end of the trail where it exits onto Armstrong Street. **Spillway-Angle Loop:** Once on the trail, turn right instead of left, and cycle to the causeway. Cross the causeway to return to start. Distance – 21.3 km.

22.31	0.05	Straight	**Armstrong Street;** cycle to the first street, Wilkinson Crescent. This area of Portage la Prairie is known as Koko Platz.
22.36	0.50	Right	**Wilkinson Crescent;** cycle past Meighen Avenue to the end of Wilkinson and the entrance to Garrioch's Creek Forest Path.
22.86	1.51	Straight	**Garrioch's Creek Forest Path (dirt/crushed limestone);** when the trail splits, turn left. The trail follows the creek and exits on Bridge Road. There are a number of exits prior, but always keep the creek to your right and do not turn off.
24.37	0.44	Left	**Bridge Road;** cycle past Meighen and Rennick to Crescent Road. Cross Crescent to access Crescent Lake Trail.
24.81	1.57	Right	**Crescent Lake Trail (asphalt);** cycle along the lakeshore to the causeway to Island Park.
26.38	0.26	Right	**Island Park Causeway;** cycle to the island, cross International Drive/Mayfair Farms Road to the Island Park path. **Island Park:** The route goes through Island Park but there are lots of other things to see and do here that you might like to explore at the end of your ride.
26.64	0.52	Left	**Island Park Trail (asphalt);** cycle past Splash Island and continue straight towards George Hill Drive. The trail curves right before the drive and curves right again as it runs past the Garden of Memory. The trail exits into the Splash Island parking lot. Turn left and cycle along the edge of the lot to pick up the Island Park Trail again. The trail enters the Island Park Arboretum. Stay on the trail which runs along the edge of the poplars. The trail exits to George Hill Drive.
27.16	0.94	Right	**George Hill Drive/Massey Crescent;** cycle past the tennis courts and across Brandon Avenue at which point George Hill Drive becomes Massey Crescent. Follow the crescent around the deer sanctuary to return to Brandon Avenue.

			Cross Brandon Avenue to access the Island Park Trail.
28.10	0.44	Straight	**Island Park Trail (asphalt);** cycle the trail through the park passing the duck pond to your left and the windmill to your right. The trail exits into a parking lot off International Drive.
28.54	0.34	Left	**International Drive;** cycle past the airplane, RCAF 277, to the stop sign at the causeway.
28.88	0	End	**Island Park at the causeway toward Crescent Drive.**

When the spirits are low, when the day appears dark, when work becomes monotonous, when hope hardly seems worth having, just mount a bicycle and go out for a spin down the road, without thought on anything but the ride you are taking.

— Sir Arthur Conan Doyle (1859 – 1930), author of *Sherlock Holmes*

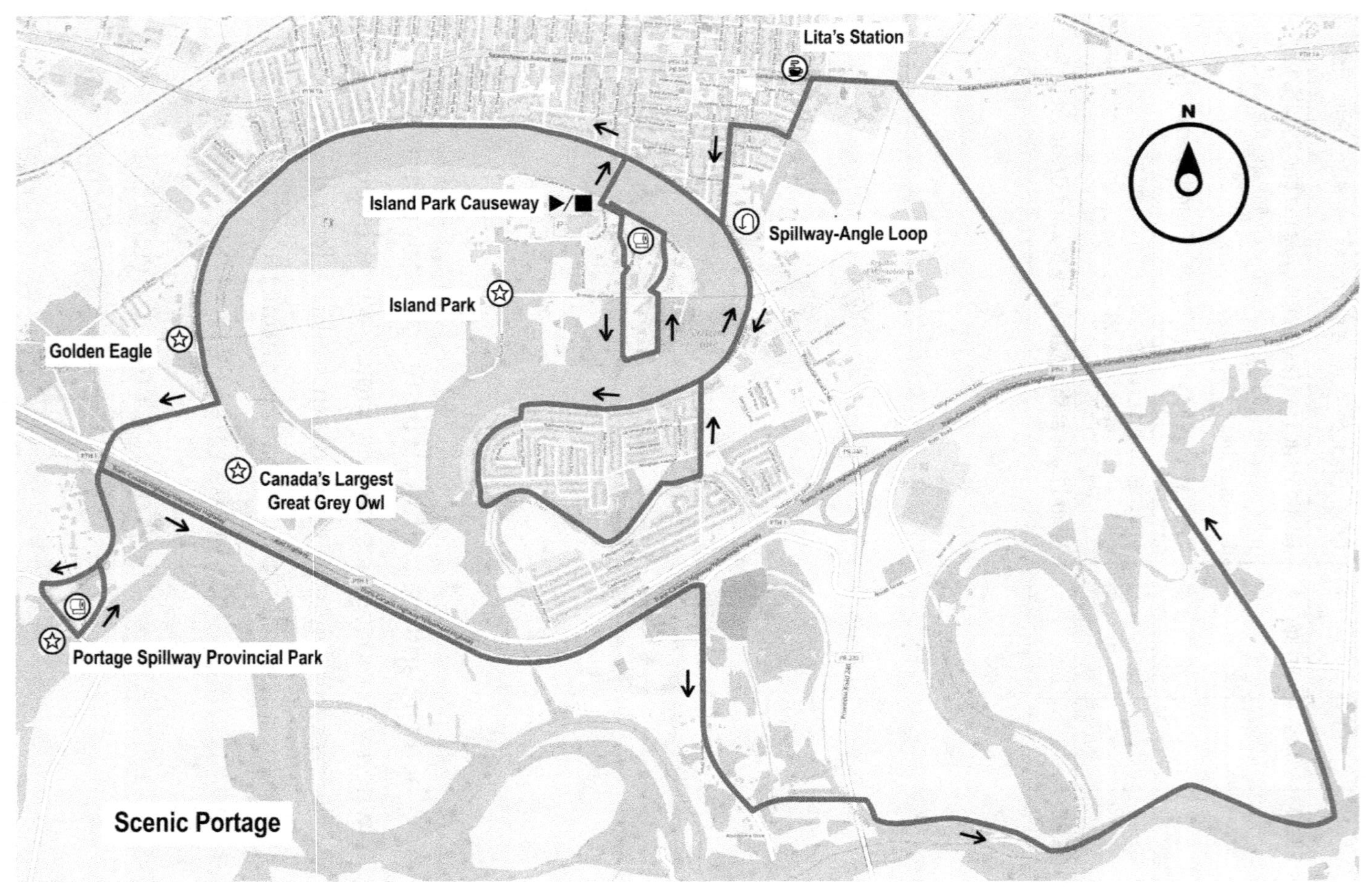
Lita's Station
Island Park Causeway
Spillway-Angle Loop
Island Park
Golden Eagle
Canada's Largest
Great Grey Owl
Portage Spillway Provincial Park
Scenic Portage
N

Country Roads

70 km west of Winnipeg

My husband used to live in Portage la Prairie for a few years and he is an avid cyclist who has spent countless enjoyable hours cycling in and around this city. So, I have handed over the reins to him to design two rides in and around Portage. This is the second ride. General information on the city can be found in the Scenic Portage chapter.

I love cycling on country roads, hence the name, and this ride follows a few. I like to see the crops develop throughout the seasons and I like the sights, smells and sounds. This route takes you past one of my favourite spots, which is indicated in the directions. It is a spot where you can stop and hear the melodious call of the Sturnella neglectus or western meadowlark. It is a great meditation spot. If you do not know their call, check out the following link. https://www.allaboutbirds.org/guide/Western_Meadowlark/sounds

Western Meadowlark

Café on Prince

A suggestion for a coffee stop is Café on Prince, a cozy coffee shop with a focus on local ingredients. They offer a variety of soups, sandwiches, salads and burgers, plus a "sips menu" of beverages. A nice place to relax before continuing the ride. https://www.206prince.com

There are five points of interest along the route, three of which are also in the Scenic Portage ride. The first two are art installations. Along Crescent Road, is an urban reserve belonging to the Long Plain First Nation. On the grounds of the old Portage la Prairie Indian Residential School is a striking sculpture, created by Manitoba artist Jake Goertzen, of an 85-foot tree with its branches gone and a 12-foot golden eagle sitting on top. The sculpture is a tribute to the survivors of the residential school system and as such, the eagle is looking to the east, to the sun rising on a new day and a fresh start.

Further along this same stretch, but requiring a short detour, is Canada's Largest Great Grey Owl. Jake Goertzen, who had created the Golden Eagle, also created this sculpture in collaboration with owl aficionado Bryan Mitchell. This piece stands thirteen feet tall, weighs 2140 pounds and is made up of approximately 6000 pieces of steel. It is an impressive site and worth the side trip.

The third point of interest is Fort La Reine Museum. This museum covers 200 years of prairie history where you can learn more about the fur trade and exploration in the region. On site are over 25 buildings, including several homes progressing from a trapper's log cabin all the way to a 1940s home. There are also several businesses which would be part of a pioneer village including a one room school house, offices of a dentist, doctor and lawyer, two churches and a general store. http://flrmuseum.com/

The fourth point of interest is the World's Largest Coca Cola Can, located near the end of the ride. It is actually an old water tower, painted up as a Coke can, a fun stop for a selfie.

Fort La Reine Museum

The final point of interest is Island Park. Manitoba Tourism refers to it as Island on the Prairies, but the locals call it Island Park. This island, which is actually a peninsula, was formed by the oxbow of Crescent Lake. It is quite scenic and features several attractions including Island Park with a playground, arboretum, deer sanctuary, duck pond, tennis courts and picnic sites, Splash Island Park, an outdoor water park, Stride Place with an indoor aquatic centre, a Dutch-style windmill and a Royal Canadian Air Force CT-133 Silver Star. In addition, strawberry farms and an 18-hole golf course are also located here. The end of the route cycles through Island Park, but it is definitely worth it to stop here for a while to either explore or to do some activities before heading home.

Enjoy the ride!

Quick Notes

Distance – 35.0 km

Parking – When you arrive in Portage la Prairie, the main street is called Saskatchewan Avenue. Look for Royal Road S and turn left. Royal leads to Crescent Lake and the causeway to Island Park. The ride starts and ends on the Crescent Lake Trail which is not on the island. Park either on the residential streets close to the start or on the island.

Option to shorten – yes

Tupper Loop – 26.0 km

Suggested coffee stop – Café on Prince at 206 Prince Avenue

Bathrooms – Island Park, by the children's playground, coffee stop

Points of Interest –

Golden Eagle Sculpture along Crescent Road W, between Cottonwood Drive and Yellowquill Trail

Canada's Largest Great Grey Owl Sculpture at 27 Pine Crescent

Fort la Reine Museum at 2652 Saskatchewan Avenue E

World's Largest Coca Cola Can at 2445 Saskatchewan Avenue W

Island Park at Crescent Lake

Trails

Crescent Lake Trail – asphalt
Fisher Trail – asphalt
Kelly K Link Path – crushed limestone

Safety Cautions

Detailed Directions

Km Total	Km Leg	Direction	Location, notes
0	0	Start	**Crescent Lake Trail, at the corner of Crescent Road W and the causeway to Island Park.** **Island Park:** Bathrooms are located across the bridge in Island Park by the children's playground. When done, return to starting point.
0	3.29	Right	**Crescent Lake Trail (asphalt)/Crescent Road W;** cycle west with the lake on your left. The trail exits onto Crescent Road W, continues past Cottonwood and Keeshkeemaquah to Yellowquill Trail. There is a sign before the corner for Junction 1A and a stop sign at this corner. **Golden Eagle:** Notice the striking metal sculpture of an eagle sitting at the top of a tree with no branches. It stands as a tribute to the survivors of the residential school system. This sculpture is located between Cottonwood and Yellowquill Trail. **Canada's Largest Great Grey Owl:** This sculpture stands 13 feet tall, weighs 2140 pounds and is made up of approximately 6000 pieces of metal. To see it, cycle past Yellowquill Trail, at which point Crescent Road becomes Pine Crescent. The sculpture is located at 27 Pine. Once you have viewed it, head back to Yellowquill Trail and continue ride.

3.29	0.63	Right	**Yellowquill Trail;** the road veers left as you come near the Hillside Memorial Cemetery. Just before the Portage la Prairie Bypass/Trans-Canada Highway is a service road, Can-Oat Drive.
3.92	2.54	Right	**Can-Oat Drive;** cycle past the cemetery and Yellowquill Wayside Park, Cobalt Industries, Portage Agri Sales, Mid-Plains Implements, Richardson Milling, and over the railroad tracks to Service Road SW.
6.46	2.06	Left	**Service Road SW (gravel);** follow the road under the Trans-Canada Highway, the road curves right, then left, as it runs along the left side of highway. Pass Paraclete Transport and Meseyton Construction just before the service road ends at Rd 40W.
8.52	1.71	Right	**Rd 40 W (gravel);** cross the Trans-Canada Highway and continue straight. Cross two sets of railroad tracks and shortly after the second set of tracks is McIntyre Road. **Caution:** Take care when crossing the highway. Take care when crossing railroad tracks. There are no warning signals in the countryside at the tracks when a train is coming; be sure to check both ways before crossing railroad tracks.
10.23	3.25	Right	**McIntyre Road (gravel);** cycle across Rd 39 W. Just before a railroad track, the road splits, veer left to go over the railroad track and to Rd 38 W.
13.48	0.84	Left	**Rd 38 W (gravel);** cycle to Richardson Boulevard.
14.32	4.87	Right	**Richardson Boulevard (gravel)/MacDonald Street (gravel/paved);** cycle past Rd 37 W and past the Portage la Prairie North Airport which is on your right. Notice a yellow "Low Flying Aircraft" sign and shortly after is a spot with a cow pasture and marsh on one side of the road and a small creek bed on the other. Pause for a moment and listen for the melodious call of the Sturnella neglectus or western meadowlark. It is one of my favourite meditation spots. Cycle past the Golden Plains Baptist Church and across PR240/Tupper Street N. Richardson Boulevard curves to the right and the name changes to MacDonald Street.

			As you near the Portage la Prairie suburb of Peony Farm, the road becomes paved. Cycle to the stop sign, this is Lincoln Avenue. **Tupper Loop:** Instead of crossing PR240/Tupper Street N, turn right. Cycle past Ayr, 7, 6, 5, and Pacific to Fisher Avenue W. Continue, where indicated below, to return to start. Distance – 26.0 km.
19.19	1.57	Left	**Lincoln Avenue;** cycle through the small Peony Farm suburb with homes to your left and the back of the McCain Foods plant to your right. Cycle past Wilson and East and the road curves right and ends on McCain Avenue.
20.76	2.82	Left	**McCain Avenue/West Naird Avenue;** cycle past Stephens and as McCain Avenue curves right, it becomes West Naird Avenue. Cycle over the railroad tracks to the stop sign at Saskatchewan Avenue E.
23.58	2.88	Right	**Saskatchewan Avenue E;** this road used to be the main highway before the bypass was built. Cycle past Fort la Reine Museum, across the railroad tracks, past 14, to 10 Street NE. Westgate Inn is at this corner. **Fort la Reine:** Explore 200 years of prairie history through exhibits of a pioneer village, and agricultural and fur trade historical exhibits.
26.46	0.42	Right	**10 Street NE;** cross Lorne and cycle another block. The road ends at Fisher Avenue E.
26.88	3.56	Left	**Fisher Avenue E/Fisher Trail (asphalt);** cycle on the road to 6 St NE and then the Fisher Trail starts to your right. Stay on the trail as it follows beside the railroad tracks. Cross 3, Tupper, 8, and shortly after, the trail curves left and crosses 18 Street NW. The trail splits, turn right on the trail that runs beside 18 Street, and then curves left to follow beside Park Drive. The trail exits onto Sissons Drive.

			Note: There is signage along the Fisher Trail remembering bits of history relevant to this stretch of land. **Café on Prince:** To try this cozy coffee shop you must take a small detour. Turn left on 2 Street NE and cycle past Victoria, Alfred and Lorne to Prince Avenue. The coffee shop is to your right. Return to the Fisher Trail when done to continue the ride. **Tupper Loop continued:** Turn right onto the Fisher Trail and continue directions to return to start.
30.44	0.64	Left	**Sissons Drive;** follow the road as it curves right, crosses Shindelman and ends at 24 Street NW.
31.08	0.69	Left	**24 Street NW;** cycle across Saskatchewan and into the parking lot for Canad Inn. Cycle around the right side of the hotel to see the World's Largest Coca Cola Can. Turn left to cycle behind the hotel and then turn left again to reach the service road. **World's Largest Coca Cola Can:** Have a bit of fun here and stop and take a selfie with the can!
31.77	0.34	Right	**Service Road;** cycle to the end of the service road and take the small path to your left leading up to Saskatchewan Avenue W.
32.11	0.24	Right	**Saskatchewan Avenue W;** cycle over the railroad tracks and enter the parking lot for the Co-op Grocery Store. Cycle across the parking lot diagonally and at the southeast corner of the lot is a crushed limestone trail leading out of the lot.
32.35	0.11	Straight	**Kelly K Link Path (crushed limestone);** the path exits onto Kelly K Street.
32.46	0.33	Straight	**Kelly K Street;** cycle past Sunset and across Crescent Road W to Crescent Lake Trail.
32.79	2.21	Left	**Crescent Lake Trail (asphalt);** follow the trail back to the starting point by the causeway to Island Park.
35.00	0	End	**Crescent Lake Trail by the causeway to Island Park.**

<table>
<tr><td></td><td></td><td></td><td>Island Park: To end your ride, you might like to spend some time on the island as there are lots of things to see and do. Have fun!</td></tr>
</table>

[On] Valentine's Day, I'll present my beloved with a shiny bauble I bought from our favorite store. Next I'll take my honey out for a sunset cruise, maybe to the spot where we first got acquainted. Later, back home, I'll give my baby a bath. Then I'll gently dry my sweetie and turn out the lights…I'm talking, of course, about my bike…I humbly submit that my bike and I make a better team than most relationships I've seen…Your bicycle invigorates you, strengthens you, relaxes you, lets you vent your frustrations without interrupting, nodding off or making judgments. Your bicycle helps you meet other people. Your bicycle always goes where you want to go. And if you buy your bicycle a box of chocolates for Valentine's Day, you get to eat them all.

— Scott Martin, roadbikerider.com

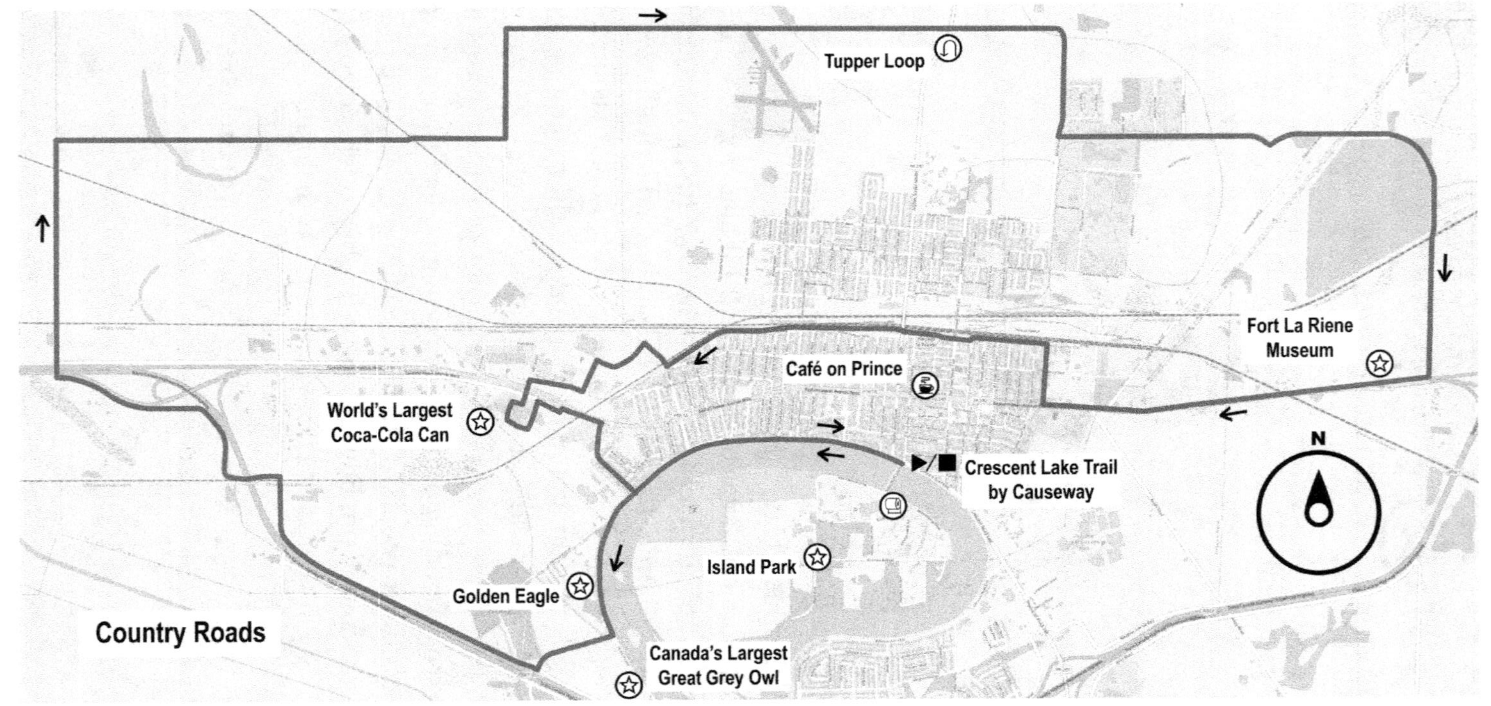
Tupper Loop
Fort La Riene Museum
Café on Prince
World's Largest Coca-Cola Can
Crescent Lake Trail by Causeway
N
Island Park
Golden Eagle
Country Roads
Canada's Largest Great Grey Owl

Acknowledgements

To Sanford Larson, my husband and soulmate, who over the years has made cycling so enjoyable and an adventure. He has been supportive of this book throughout all the stages from when it was just a thought, to my very first rough drafts, and all the way up to the final version. His comments and suggestions have been invaluable. He is the one who ensured that "right" and "left" were always correct in the directions, made up all the maps, and served as the editor on this book. My life is amazing because he is in it. Thank you.

To Erica Riedel, my friend and cycling partner. We have biked together for years and she was always game to try any route I devised. She is a master navigator, being good with directions and maps for the times when I didn't have a clue where we were. Thank you.

To Doug Gibb, my ex-brother-in-law and fellow cycling enthusiast. We had lots of great conversations about cycling routes and he introduced me to the, then new, Rapid Transit Corridor Trail. He accompanied me on some rides and told me about River Park and the bear pit which is a point of interest in the Rapid Transit route. His comment was instrumental in getting me interested in adding other points of interest throughout the book. Doug also, with his friend Bruce Wiebe, tested one of my rides and provided feedback. Thank you.

To Margo Nohlgren, who came into my life serendipitously while I was cycling in Pinawa. At the time I was testing out all my rides and my usual cycling companions, Sanford and Erica, were stuck in other parts of the world due to the COVID19 pandemic. Most of the rides I had left were on highways and out of city limits and I was not looking forward to doing them on my own. Margo was thrilled to go on the adventure and truly a gift when I needed it and is now a friend. Thank you.

To Danny and Peggy Larson, my brother-in-law and his wife, who live in Portage la Prairie and who, in Sanford's absence, helped navigate the two Portage rides and showed me new trails. I was totally impressed as they did these rides as among their first for the year. Peggy rode both rides, a total of over 60km in two days, and Danny rode one. Wow! Thank you.

To the publishing team at Prairie Heart Press, who guided me and encouraged me through the long process of producing the book you are now holding in your hands. Thank you.

Index

All index entries refer to the first page of the indicated route.

Points of Interest

Start Location

About the Author

Margaret Larson is a retired professional who fell in love with cycling later in life. She got frustrated with short rides and staying within her own neighbourhood and started developing routes throughout the city that joined many bike trails. It was an eye-opening experience as she discovered all the great art installations, historical sites, coffee shops, and charming neighbourhoods that make up Winnipeg.

Margaret splits her time between two continents. Here in North America, Winnipeg is her primary home and where her two grown children live, but she also regularly spends several months of the year in Sydney, Australia, where her husband, Sanford, resides. While in Sydney she also enjoys getting in some cycling.

Legend of Symbols

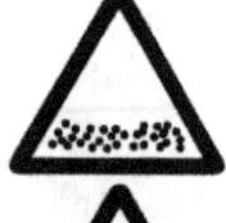 Crushed limestone trails, dirt trails, wood chip trails

 Street / highway travel

 Floating bus stops

 Flooding

 Bears

 Caution

 Bike repair station

 Option to shorten

 Bathroom

 Point of interest

 Note

 Coffee stop

 Water

 Shop